Howard Barker's Art of Theatre

MANCHESTER
1824

Manchester University Press

Howard Barker's Art of Theatre

Essays on his plays, poetry and production work

Edited by David Ian Rabey and Sarah Goldingay

Manchester University Press
Manchester and New York
distributed exclusively in the USA by Palgrave Macmillan

Published by Manchester University Press
Oxford Road, Manchester M13 9NR, UK
and Room 400, 175 Fifth Avenue, New York, NY 10010, USA
www.manchesteruniversitypress.co.uk

Distributed exclusively in the USA by
Palgrave Macmillan, 175 Fifth Avenue, New York,
NY 10010, USA

Distributed exclusively in Canada by
UBC Press, University of British Columbia, 2029 West Mall,
Vancouver, BC, Canada V6T 1Z2

British Library Cataloguing-in-Publication Data
A catalogue record for this book is available from the British Library

Library of Congress Cataloging-in-Publication Data applied for

ISBN 978 07190 8929 9 hardback

First published 2013

Typeset
by Helen Skelton, Brighton, UK
Printed in Great Britain
by TJ International Ltd, Padstow

Contents

Notes on contributors

Elisabeth Angel-Perez is a Professor of English Literature at the University of Paris-Sorbonne. She is a specialist of contemporary British theatre. Her recent publications include *Voyages au bout du possible: Les théâtres du traumatisme de Samuel Beckett à Sarah Kane* (2006), and, with Alexandra Poulain, *Endgame: Le théâtre mis en pièces* (2009). She has also published extensively on Martin Crimp, Sarah Kane, Caryl Churchill and Howard Barker. She has edited several volumes including *New British Dramaturgies, The European Journal of English Studies* vol. 7 no. 1 (2003), *Howard Barker et le Théâtre de la Catastrophe* (2006); with Nicole Boireau, *Le Théâtre anglais contemporain 1985–2005* (2007); with Alexandra Poulain, *Hunger on the Stage* (2008) and *Things on the Stage* (special issue of *Etudes Britanniques Contemporaines*, 2009). She has also translated plays and theoretical writings by Howard Barker, Caryl Churchill, Martin Crimp and David Mamet.

Mark Brown is theatre critic of the Scottish national newspaper the *Sunday Herald* and a theatre and performing arts critic for the UK newspaper the *Daily Telegraph*. He teaches in theatre studies and theatre criticism at the Royal Conservatoire of Scotland. He is a member of the executive committee of the International Association of Theatre Critics and sits on the editorial board of the IATC's webjournal *Critical Stages*. He is editor of the books *Howard Barker Interviews 1980-2010: Conversations in Catastrophe* (2011) and *Oily Cart: All Sorts of Theatre for All Sorts of Kids* (2012).

Ian Cooper is a founding member of Lurking Truth Theatre Company, which has been producing works by modern British dramatists, including Howard Barker, since 1986. His essay is adapted from a 1993 MPhil thesis on the work of Barker, Edward Bond and Howard Brenton.

Mary Karen Dahl is Professor of Theatre and Director of graduate programmes in Theatre Studies for the School of Theatre at Florida State University. She has a longstanding interest in the relationship between performance and politics and representations of violence. Her book *Political Violence in Drama: Classical Models, Contemporary Variations* was selected as a Choice Outstanding Academic Book. Essays include 'Postcolonial British Theatre: Black Voices at the Center' in *Imperialism and Drama* (ed. Gainor, 1995); 'Stage Violence as Thaumaturgic Technique' in *Violence in Drama* (ed. Redmond, 1991); and 'State Terror and Dramatic Countermeasures' in *Politics and Terror in Modern Drama* (eds Orr and Klaic, 1990). Recent work poses questions about political theory and citizenship and includes essays such as 'Sacrificial Practices: Creating the Legacy of Stephen Lawrence' in *Violence Performed: Local Roots and Global Routes of Conflict* (eds Anderson and Menon, 2008) and 'The Body *in Extremis*: Exercises in Self-Creation and Citizenship' in *Theatre of Catastrophe: New Essays on Howard Barker* (eds Gritzner and Rabey, 2006).

Jay Gipson-King holds a PhD from Florida State University and is currently an independent scholar. He has written previously on time in contemporary British theatre in his dissertation, 'History in the Age of Fracture: The Politics of Time in Recent English History Plays', as well as in presentations at the American Society for Theatre Research (ASTR) and the Association for Theatre in Higher Education (ATHE). His article on David Hare's *Stuff Happens* is published in the *Journal of Dramatic Theory and Criticism*. Jay is an active member of the theatre community in Salem, Oregon, USA.

Sarah Goldingay is a lecturer in Drama at the University of Exeter. Her most recent research has centred on the work of Howard Barker and The Wrestling School, with a chapter in *Modern British Playwriting: The 80s* and a co-edited special edition of *Studies in Theatre and Performance* with Mick Mangan (November, 2012). She has also worked as Barker's Executive Producer and is an Associate of the Wrestling School. In this capacity she has overseen the creation of the Howard Barker Archive (held at the University of Exeter), the *21 for 21* one-day festival celebrating the twenty-first birthday of Barker and The Wrestling School, and has been shortlisted for the THE Award for Excellence and Innovation in the Arts (2011). Through her collaboration with rheumatologist, Paul Dieppe, she continues to explore the relationship of performance to pain, placebo and the healing response.

George Hunka is a dramatist and theatre writer whose work has frequently appeared in a variety of publications, including *Theater* (Yale University), the *Guardian, PAJ: A Journal of Performance and Art*, and the *New York Times*. His first book is *Word Made Flesh: Philosophy, Eros, and Contemporary Tragic Drama* (2011).

Melanie Jessop is an Associate of The Wrestling School theatre company, for which she has played the roles of Gwynne in *Victory*, Dover in *Ego in Arcadia*, Nausicaa in *Blok/Eko* and the title roles in both *Judith* and *Und*. Her other stage work includes Galactia in *Scenes from an Execution* (Hackney Empire), *King Lear* and *The Seagull* (RSC), *The Duchess of Malfi* (WYP), *A Midsummer Night's Dream* (New York), *Romeo and Juliet* (Globe).

Vanasay Khamphommala is a former student of the École normale supérieure, and wrote his PhD, entitled 'Spectres of Shakespeare in Howard Barker's Work', under the supervision of Elisabeth Angel-Perez (Paris IV-Sorbonne). After teaching at Oxford (Exeter College) and the Sorbonne, he now works as an actor and director. He recently premiered his production of Barker's *Slowly* in France and directed his own play *Orphée aphone* for a staged reading at the Odéon-Théâtre de l'Europe.

Christine Kiehl is a university lecturer at Université Lumière Lyon 2. She is a specialist of contemporary British drama and more particularly of Howard Barker's plays. Her work questions the aesthetics and ethics of the body on the stage and she currently investigates pluridisciplinary artforms in drama. As Vice-President of RADAC (Research on Contemporary English Drama), she is organising a double international colloquium on the relations between theatre and cinema (Paris, March 2012 and Lyon, April 2013) with three publications. http://www.radac.fr

Charles Lamb studied literature and drama at the universities of Aberdeen, Essex and Warwick. His career was mainly as a teacher of drama in schools and colleges. Now retired, he was Head of Performing Arts at Bournemouth and Poole College and an Associate Lecturer at Winchester University. His association with Howard Barker extends back over twenty years to his production of *Fair Slaughter* at the Quay Theatre in Sudbury. Since then he has directed a number of Barker plays including the premiere performance of *Crimes in Hot Countries*. His published writing includes *The Theatre of Howard Barker* (2005). He is an Associate of Howard Barker's theatre company, The Wrestling School.

Michael Mangan (MA, PhD, Cambridge) has published books, articles and papers on a broad range of subjects including theatre and gender, theatre and social justice, Shakespeare and Renaissance theatre, the cultural history of popular performance and contemporary British theatre. He has also worked as a playwright, a director, a literary manager, a dramaturg and an actor. His monographs include *Doctor Faustus: A Critical Study* (1987), *A Preface to Shakespeare's Tragedies* (1991), *A Preface to Shakespeare's Comedies* (1996), *Staging Masculinities* (2002), *Performing (Dark) Arts: A Cultural History of Magic in Performance* (2007), *The Palgrave Companion to Theatre, Drama and Performance* (2013) and *Staging Ageing* (2013). With Sarah Goldingay he has co-edited a special issue of *Studies in Theatre and Performance* dedicated to Howard Barker's work. Michael Mangan has held Chairs in Drama at Aberystwyth, De Montfort and Exeter Universities, and is now Professor of Drama at Loughborough University.

Michel Morel is Emeritus Professor at Nancy 2. His field of research is the processes of reading activated by all kinds of text (from the press and popular writings to high literature). He is particularly interested in the affects, the original causes of our emotions, triggered at the double level of the actualisation of genre by the individual text and its concretisation by the reader. He consequently investigates generic processes, in particular narrative ones, and the critical valuations dependent on them. His approach is multidisciplinary. He has recently extended his study of forms to the axiological contents of rhetorical figures, and also to other domains of expression like poster, painting and architecture.

Eléonore Obis received her PhD in British Contemporary Drama in 2011 at the Paris Sorbonne University and has a teaching position there as a *professeur agrégé*. Her research interests focus on the representation of the body on the British contemporary stage, through the questions of staging, acting and reception. She specialises in the works of Howard Barker, Edward Bond, Martin Crimp and Sarah Kane.

David Ian Rabey is Professor of Drama and Theatre Studies at Aberystwyth University. His publications include *Howard Barker: Ecstasy and Death* (2009), *Howard Barker: Politics and Desire* (1989, 2009), *Theatre of Catastrophe: New Essays on Howard Barker* (co-edited with Karoline Gritzner, 2006), *English Drama Since 1940* (2003), *David Rudkin: Sacred Disobedience* (1997) and two volumes of plays, *The Wye Plays* (2004) and *Lovefuries* (2008). He has acted in and/or directed fourteen productions of Barker plays. He is an Associate of Howard Barker's theatre company, The Wrestling School.

James Reynolds is a Lecturer in Drama at Kingston University. His PhD research at Queen Mary, University of London, investigated performance practices in Robert Lepage's devised theatre. Published work explores Howard Barker's direction of his own plays (*Theatre of Catastrophe*, 2006); Lepage's work with objects (*Performance Research*, 2007); the cinematic adaptation of graphic novels (*Journal of Adaptation in Film and Performance*, 2009); and the relationship between addiction and performance (*Journal of Applied Arts and Health*, 2011). Forthcoming publications investigate the National Theatre's adaptations of children's literature for the stage, and Lepage's work as a director.

Elizabeth Sakellaridou is Professor of Drama and Theatre Studies at Aristotle University of Thessaloniki. Her teaching and research interests include English and comparative drama, gender and cultural studies and performance theory (especially phenomenology) – fields in which she has published extensively both independently and in international journals and collective volumes. Her latest book is *Theatre, Aesthetics, Politics: Traversing the Contemporary British Stage* (in Greek) (2012). Her most recent study on Howard Barker is 'Working at the Seams: Howard Barker's Tragic *Trauerspiel*' (in M. Middeke and C. Wald, eds, *The Literature of Melancholia: From Early Modern to Postmodern*, 2011).

Heiner Zimmermann is a retired senior lecturer from the Department of English and American Studies at Heidelberg University.

Acknowledgements

We are grateful to Barker's publishers, Oberon Books, for permission to quote from his published works.

DIR: Many, but not all, of the essays included received their first presentations at the three-day conference, 'Howard Barker's Art of Theatre', held at Aberystwyth University at the Department for Theatre, Film and Television Studies in July 2009. I am grateful for the various forms of support for that event which were provided by the institution and by many individuals, but pre-eminently grateful to Karoline Gritzner for her invaluable work alongside me in co-organising that conference. Howard Barker was in attendance throughout this event, and first presented his essay, 'The Sunless Garden of the Unconsoled' (included here), as a paper at the conference; it was subsequently published in the online journal Hyperion, and we are grateful to the editor of that journal, Rainer J. Hansche, for permission to reproduce it.

    After *Theatre of Catastrophe*, I swore I would never (co-)edit another collection of essays.

    This is it.

SG: Theatre is full of people who work more for love than for financial profit. It seems to me that this is also true of publishing. I am very fortunate to have come repeatedly into contact with those who are motivated, despite what the world continues to throw at them, by a desire to bring something meaningful into the world. Thank you.

Abbreviations and references

(All places of publication: London except where noted)

AMG *The Ascent of Monte Grappa* (John Calder, 1991)

ASIO *A Style and its Origins* (Oberon Books, 2007)

AT *Arguments for a Theatre* (third edition, Manchester, Manchester University Press, 1997)

CP3 *Collected Plays Volume Three* (John Calder, 1996)

CP4 *Collected Plays Volume Three* (John Calder, 1998)

CP5 *Collected Plays Volume Five* (Calder Publications, 2001)

DH *Dead Hands* (Oberon, 2004)

DOAT *Death, The One and The Art of Theatre* (Abingdon, Routledge, 2005)

EB *The Ecstatic Bible* (Oberon, 2004)

FTY *The Fence in its Thousandth Year* (Oberon Books, 2005)

HG *The Hang of the Gaol and Heaven* (John Calder, 1980)

LI *Lullabies for the Impatient* (John Calder, 1988)

OP1 *Plays One* (Oberon Books, 2006)

OP2 *Plays Two* (Oberon Books, 2006)

OP3 *Plays Three* (Oberon Books, 2008)

OP4 *Plays Four* (Oberon Books, 2008)

OP5 *Plays Five* (Oberon Books, 2009)

PSD *A Passion in Six Days and Downchild* (John Calder, 1985)

SD *Sheer Detachment* (Cambridge, Salt Publishing, 2009)

SN *The Swing at Night* (Calder Publications, 2001)

TD *The Tortmann Diaries* (Calder Publications, 1996)

TGBU *That Good Between Us and Credentials of a Sympathiser* (John Calder, 1990)

TM *Terrible Mouth* (Universal Edition, 1992)

Editions of Barker's plays, formerly published by John Calder and Calder Publications, are no longer available for order and purchase from this source (but may be available for consultation through library holdings). The plays formerly published by John Calder and Calder Publications are being republished by Oberon Books as part of their ongoing programme of making Barker's complete dramatic *oeuvre* available in book form.

1

Introduction: the ultimate matter of style

David Ian Rabey

Since 1969, Howard Barker has written over a hundred dramatic works (primarily for theatre, but also for radio, television and film), six published volumes of poetry, two books of philosophical and aesthetic theory (*Arguments for a Theatre*, third edition 1997; *Death, The One and The Art of Theatre*, 2005) and a third-person autobiography/reflection on practice (*A Style and its Origins*, 2007, co-credited to 'Eduardo Houth'). He is also a prolific visual artist, whose paintings and drawings have been exhibited internationally. Since the early 1990s he has directed his own writing for the stage, in a series of unforgettable productions; and he has also (under a series of aliases) extended his distinctive vision into the scenographic design (set, costume, sound) for those productions, primarily staged by The Wrestling School, a theatre company founded (in 1988) specifically to invent and refine appropriate ways to stage his texts. In France, during the season 2009–10, his drama was the subject of a major retrospective season, which comprised no less than seven theatrical productions – four of which were staged at the Odéon, the French national theatre. Barker's work has provoked shock and outrage, but also inspired passionate appreciation and unique manifestations of commitment and support. In whichever medium he works, Barker insists on the disintegrations of familiarity, in both content and methods, to yield an event which is hypnotic, and perhaps more subconscious in its intimations; where the audience member is directed back to their own compulsions to make meaning from what they experience. In the theatre, this involves a profoundly disorientating but seductive orchestration of voice, body, movement and visual design. Barker's formal experiments, distillations and transformations distinguish him as our most restless, precise and uncompromising theatrical innovator since Samuel Beckett.

This volume brings together a range of voices, including those of theatre practitioners, scholars and civilian enthusiasts from a range of nations, ages and backgrounds, to analyse Barker's astonishing range of imaginative ambitions and practical achievements. The initiative for this collection was prompted by the occurrence in 2009 of two notable manifestations of enthusiasm. In July of that year, Aberystwyth University hosted a three-day international conference on Barker's works, which drew the attendance of delegates from ten countries, and was further honoured by the constant attendance of the artist himself. Further, in October 2009, the twenty-first anniversary of the foundation of The Wrestling School was marked by a unique undertaking by Barker enthusiasts across the world: the *21 for 21* international theatre initiative of synchronised performances of Barker works on four continents, in seven languages. This volume collects some essays and testimonies provoked by those two events; but also it extends to incorporate the expression of some arguments for Barker's importance which have occurred in their wake.

An approach to Barker's Art of Theatre

Barker distinguishes his objectives from those of the conventional theatre by terming what he pursues the Art of Theatre: a felicitous term for an artist holistically engaged with so many facets of theatre artistry (writing, direction, design), and who also produces highly theatrical and interrogatory visual art. Barker compulsively speculates into the innately theatrical workings of the human consciousness: particularly at historical junctures when social catastrophe and personal crisis drive people to discover within themselves, and to express, voices (*personae*) which are new and strange, impulsive and contradictory: at odds with their usual, dominant, conventionally sensible 'selves' and rational(ised) terms of existence. The expression of such voices most often compels and provokes actions and consequences. At such moments, to borrow the words of the poet W. B. Yeats, a terrible beauty is born.

What is at stake, and what are the fundamental questions, in Barker's Art of Theatre? A first response might be: how to live, and how to die; but these terms are too general. More precisely, in Barker's own words: 'What is the style that will carry us through the times in which we live?';[1] and, to use a resonant phrase from Barker's play *Hurts Given and Received* (staged 2010), how do we 'earn our grave':[2] on what (and whose) terms do we engage with death, that of others and the prospect of our own: which is, perhaps, the ultimate matter of style. It is significant that Barker's deceptively slim autobiographical volume is titled *A Style and its Origins*: its method is to trace the development of a personal mode of being and expression (and being *through* expression), in navigation of, and negotiation with, the surprising challenges of the world, in order to arrive at a *personal* form of authority, as distinct from the political, social, institutional forms of authority which seek to inform – both set the terms for, and seek to give shape to – one's personal mode of being and expression. This further informs the ways in which characters, and people, try to gain what they want, in various situations: the dynamics of power.

Barker's writing and direction combine to create theatre events which will often (and deliberately, purposefully) create a sense of *plethora* for the audience: a sense that IT'S ALL TOO MUCH (more than we can digest, immediately or readily). This is not because Barker is incapable of disciplining his imaginings and propositions: indeed, the essays in this collection are concerned to identify and demonstrate the remarkable care with which Barker's physical, linguistic and scenographic imagery is delineated; how it subverts familiar culturally received forms and presumptions, and delves into disturbing but compelling imaginative depths which often resonate on uncomfortable emotionally instinctive levels, rather than on other more limited, immediately identifiable or entirely graspable, terms. Barker's route to the vitality of chaos, and of a philosophical anarchy, is achieved through scrupulous attention to order of detail, in order to make that sense of chaos more vivid and profound. His writing, direction and design consciously and deliberately offer more than can be analysed in the moment, or taken in on one sitting. It may provoke the reactions: THIS IS INTOLERABLE; WE CAN'T DEAL WITH IT; IT HAS NO APPARENT RELEVANCE TO ANYTHING (indeed, some details and developments may have an *evident* irrelevance, not only to the familiarities of life as we readily recognise it, but even to what the play or production have previously established). Barker:

> Rather, the work expresses a (literally) diabolical sense that life isn't enough, in the terms on offer; and because of this, the characters subject themselves to a terrible extremity; and possibly a critique of existence, not just of society, lies under this. Tragedy involves the fracturing of moral values, presenting unexpected scenes which cause disquiet. On the one hand, this sort of theatre presents itself as a laboratory in which propositions are tested out (and indeed, the walls and doors are in full operation; what you do or feel in this place, the theatre, does not, or need not, *literally* carry through directly to what you do in another [though it may inform it imaginatively]). On the other hand, this sort of theatre has an affinity with prayer: the (possibly and probably forlorn) hope that things will be made different. I actually believe that you are born knowing a great deal; however, culture conspires to obscure and conceal some of what you know, through social conditioning; hence, people sometimes recognise *and* despise what they see in the work, what the work confronts them with.[3]

When reading or rehearsing, the first encounter with a Barker text immediately throws you back onto your own resources, with questions: not least, how to BREATHE in this unfamiliar element: how to navigate and make sense of words and their arrangement on a page, how to speak them out loud. The language is purposefully defamiliarised, often taking the form of a series of incomplete utterances which are not obviously conversational. Barker:

> The punctuation is removed from my drama (as it is in the writing of Céline, the

great stylist of the twentieth-century novel) because the writing has so much internal rhythm that it will lead you into movement – only language this *contrived* will force an action upon you. It offers the gift of anxiety to the performer and the audience, offers the opportunity to live in a state of tension, where the actor's exploration of his/her own limits echo the character's.[4]

The actor and director Gerrard McArthur offers the following observations on the performance of Barker's drama, and how its layout on the page offers guidance for breathing, initiative and action:

> The vocal performance is a performance of the *sound contour* of the text, which also helps to present the *stage figure* in all its aspects: each character is a *per-sona* ('*through sound*') and the language is a plastic force you have to feel as you speak it. Being *torn* is a crucial sensation for the characters, but they don't lose focus when they speak. Their speech is clear because it is a weapon; none of the characters ever splutters (except psychologically), they are completely and artificially articulate, and *everything* is *incredibly significant* for them. Everything is manifested in the way the words are spoken: a speech may begin with the intention, 'I am going to analyze you, explain you, patrol your area'; however, each moment is a whole new level of event and response; if you stop, physically or imaginatively, you weaken the strength of your movement; the character is often feeling and expressing the question, 'What is this new HIM/HER that is happening to HIM/HER?'. In performance, you are working through this feeling and trying it out. The actor must mould the extra-linguistic elements accordingly: it may be helpful to root yourself in a speech physically through pressure against, for example, a wall or an object, and fight against that thing with a physical counter-pressure to ground the language.[5]

Barker expounds further on this sense of pressure:

> In performance, it is useful to ask yourself, 'What is the *pressure* this character is under?' The capitalised words, or bold type, often express a sense of this pressure: a painful thought, which it hurts, to some extent, to articulate. Nevertheless, the characters must HAVE their pain, LIVE WITH their pain, and EMPLOY their pain. They become energised by the scale of the problem.[6]

It may be helpful to identify some examples of such pressure(s) from Barker's drama. This is the opening speech in Barker's play *Victory* (1983):

> *A field. A man enters.*
>
> SCROPE: I know I swore. I know I promised. On the Bible. And because I can take or leave the Bible, got your child in and told me put my two hands on her cheeks and looking in her eyes say I would not disclose this place. No matter what the madness, what the torture, leave you underneath the nettles, safe. I did. I know I did.
>
> *(He points to a place. SOLDIERS enter with spades.)*   (OP1, 11)

Here, *what is done* overturns *what is said*: this establishes the keynote for a play which is, to an unusual degree, even for a Barker play, about the distance between the two, and their difference. As in a judo throw, which turns the opponent's conventional strength of body mass and weight against them as a weakness, the *unspoken* overwhelms *the spoken*. Nevertheless, Scrope needs to speak: to give himself a *mode of expression* – more so than a *means of communication*. The speech is addressed to a dead man, his former employer Mr Bradshaw. The soldiers who proceed to dig up Bradshaw's corpse ignore him, except for some subsequent taunting. Scrope's opening speech is a *sounding*: as when mariners dropped weights to determine the depth of the sea, river or lake below them. The speech sounds the depth of his loyalty to Bradshaw: it will determine the leverage involved in his betrayal of Bradshaw. He is trying to work out, through word and gesture, how he has come to where he has; to negotiate some meaning in or out of his life. It is this impulse that gives Barker's characters their philosophical dimension – not philosophical in the sense of abstract contemplation, but in the sense of trying to negotiate some meaning out of an upsurge in emotion triggered by a change in their environment, and in their selves, by crisis: the start of a new sense of time (what the protagonist of Barker's play *I Saw Myself*, staged 2008, calls 'crushed time'), which represents the end of what was formerly known, and requires decisive action, also likely to be surprising and unpredictable. It is likely to make the characters reassess and redefine what it is to be a societal being, and even to be human (as when the tapestry makers in *I Saw Myself* continue in their labours in the face of impending war).

Scrope's betrayal is expressed through a gesture. It is the speech and the gesture together that constitute the dramatic event, which starts the play: is it Scrope's fearful capitulation? His subsequent mixture of self-reproach and self-pity tries to characterise it as such. Or is it a subconscious victory, overturning former loyalties? This is the dynamic that will more fully characterise the adventures and overcomings of the play's protagonist, Susan Bradshaw.

'It is the speech and the gesture together that constitute the dramatic event' – in *this* instance. However, sometimes in Barker's work the sounding of the speech will in itself create a hinge moment, which will be further explored or expressed by an action, such as this succinct utterance and juncture from Barker's *The Ecstatic Bible*:

> I shall miss my wife profoundly. She was the greatest companion of my life and a perfect lover. Everything will be downhill from now on.
>
> *(He goes to leave, with a bitter twist of his body)*   (EB, 46)

There is a wonderful Barker work which focuses entirely on a succession of such moments, *The Forty* (written 2006). This is a compendium of forty short plays, exploring the ways that words and gestures provide a currency for negotiation: moments of extreme emotional tension which provide, through physical balance and imbalance, an excavation, and a crystallisation, of an agony. Many of these short plays show the characters trying to remake themselves, through re-presenting themselves – or else the unsuccessful attempts to fracture previous definition. These characters are caught in moments which ask of them: are they as independent, as separate, as they want to be? Are they as close to, as secure with, others as they want to be? One way or another: the dramatic event is often about an uncomfortable or surprising discovery, which speech and action combine to make manifest.

Here is a speech by Claudius from Barker's *Gertrude – The Cry* (staged 2002). Again, the actor has to chart a course through this: to make manifest a process of self-discovery:

> He made me feel turned on a wheel and dirty as if some oily rain fell on a mask a grinning thing a fairground object brass or peeling paint my life and my desires HOW I WISHED TO SAY THIS BUT I NEVER DID are REAL (*OP2*, 163)

The speech *sounds* different levels of self-awareness; it manifests how Claudius develops an idea, an image, to plumb fully, and give shape to, his predicament and feelings, which leads him to a discovery of awareness, repudiating the sensed diminishment of his self and his capacities to something reducible: it enables him to sense and say something he wished to say but never did, before now: the terms on which his life and his desires are real – although he does not explicitly identify *here* what these might be. But he expresses, and thereby discovers, a determination that they should not be reduced to images of things which can be dismissed as insubstantial. And that is his first step, in trying to repossess himself.

Gerrard McArthur writes in his essay, 'Barker, the Actor and Indeterminacy',[8] some words which I suggest you try to speak out loud:

> The actor needs to contain
> and express
> this sense …
> that as certain as he is
> of the necessity
> to speak in seeking definition,
> that very definition
> is
> fundamentally
> insecure;
> 'In Barker,
> words aren't a way of emoting,
> or a demonstration of feeling,
> they are an exposition of unsettled possibilities,
> where even the deepest of convinced feeling is
> riven with the ambiguity,
> and then

increasingly,
the expectation
that nothing is a settlement,
and that to seek settlement
is itself
false'

Here I have given McArthur's words a spatial layout which is different to their original rendering, in order to remind myself, and you, to give each detail its full weight and sounding:

So that each detail properly becomes
an additional
further
discovery

Barker's arrangements of words on the page are sometimes separated in this way to help the performer avoid generalisation. Even in the unpunctuated sections, which are driven by one specific emotional motor, it is possible to experience and express breakthroughs to new levels of awareness and contradictory feelings: Claudius's speech indicates this through the use of capitals; sometimes it is bold type instead which indicates this. Barker identifies this process in terms of the dynamics of catastrophe:

> The catastrophic moment, in history or in personal life, liberates another ego that exists within the ego. We all have a public ego, but within, there is another voice, perhaps even several other voices, speaking at the same time. When a crisis emerges in the world, this other character can appear, more beautiful, or perhaps more dreadful.[9]

No chaos, no knowledge

> History is the truth that becomes a lie, whereas myth is a lie that in the long term becomes the truth.
>
> Jean Cocteau[10]

Marina Warner has described William Blake as a 'Counter-Enlightenment' champion of the imagination; 'Counter-Enlightenment' being 'a term coined by Isaiah Berlin, adopted by E. P. Thompson and others, to characterise heterogeneous opposition from the mid-seventeenth century' onwards, to 'the cult of reason'[11] and to forms of authoritarianism which claim to be based on rational calculation. John Gray writes: 'If Euripedes is the most tragic of the Greek playwrights it is not because he deals with moral conflicts but because he understood that reason cannot be the guide of life';[12] both Warner's and Gray's terms might be extended appropriately to include Barker.

Gray notes, in his book *Straw Dogs*, how scientific promises of progress and religious promises of salvation both 'deny the experience of tragedy', the dignity of confronting tragic contingencies, or even normal unhappiness; and it is significant that Gray includes an epigraph from one of Barker's favourite philosophers, E.M. Cioran:

> The certitude that there is no salvation is a form of salvation, in fact it is salvation. Starting from here, one might organize our own life as well as construct a philosophy of history: the insoluble as solution, as the only way out.[13]

This is, indeed, the point from which many Barker characters try to determine their own lives. Compare Barker's Preface to the BBC radio production of his dramatic compendium, *The Possibilities*: 'We fail to think correctly / There is the hope / We persist in our blindness / There is the hope / We are intransigent at the wrong moment / And capitulate at the wrong moment / There is the sole chance of deliverance'.[14]

John Michael Greer notes how, according to the '*myth of progress*', 'all of human history is a grand tale of human improvement';[15] and how Christian myths of sacred history are echoed by Marxist theories which replace 'the transcendent dimension with forces immanent in ordinary history'.[16] This Utopian mythic route has since been followed by other proponents of inclusive (totalitarian) ideologies that convinced themselves that 'the world was about to be transformed into what they wanted it to be'; however, the cost of these theories, when implemented, not uncommonly 'includes a tumbled heap of human lives'.[17] Gray puts this bluntly:

> Progress and mass murder run in tandem. As the numbers killed by famine and plague have waned, so death by violence has increased. As science and technology have advanced, so has proficiency in killing. As the hope for a better world has grown, so has mass murder.[18]

This is because any fixation on a single solution will encounter 'unexpected consequences' which 'make a mockery of simplistic attempts to predict effects from causes',[19] and those 'who cling to faith in progress ... are all too likely to go looking for scapegoats when the future fails to deliver the better world they expect'.[20]

In Barker's work, we encounter various invocations and self-styled forces of 'History': dramatisations of the controlling impulse to impose a linear scheme of social progress on untidy human passions, eventually by force. The *contrary* manifestations of the insistent unruliness of individuals constitute examples of what Barker terms 'Anti-History'. He invents a different form of mythic history, diffuse, ambiguous, immanent, defiantly unresearched, defying objectivity: a 'counter-enlightenment' initiative of the imagination (Elisabeth Angel-Perez's essay in this collection develops this characterisation of Barker's work). This 'Anti-History' is presented through the frankly illusory medium of theatre and the (self-)conscious artifice of dramatic character, in ways which nevertheless work to expose the fictionality of the dominant terms of so-called 'everyday life', and momentarily suspend these terms (which are exposed as limitations, obstacles to personal knowledge; and sometimes to love). Barker:

> The liberating of pain from its social subjects, and from its so-called objective conditions, is possible only in a theatre which is essentially promiscuous in moral terms, and, far from becoming what is inevitably described as 'pessimistic', affirms the individual's right to chaos, extremity and self-description. (*AT*, 123)

As the examples which I have cited indicate, Barker's characters characteristically pursue their journeys, aspirations, desires; they demonstrate openness and frankness in their pursuit of what they believe is right, even if, at other junctures of the 'crushed' times in which they live, they have recourse to deceit (like Bradshaw in *Victory*) and demonstrate themselves to be untrammelled by conventional obligation. In Barker's *The Europeans* (written 1987), Katrin provides a particularly striking example of how Barker's protagonists frequently, and purposefully, defy appeals to guilt and duty by which Christian myths, Catholic constructs and other institutionalising forms of social inclusivity offer redemption through self-sacrifice; rather, the prime responsibility of Barker's protagonists is to their individual will, and they notably demonstrate a vital clarity of thought and emotion (it is Barker's more comic characters who do not: their confusion, and strenuous desperation in seeking simplification, become ludicrous). Barker's *Gertrude – The Cry* offers one of Barker's finest dramatisations of this: Gertrude declares and repeatedly demonstrates herself to be free of conventional moral constrictions (which supposedly make us 'human'), questioning standard notions of 'kindness' (which are shown to be fundamentally envious forms of control and coercion, through the actions of Isola and Ragusa); further, Gertrude defies the ways that forces of government (such as those set up by Hamlet) seek to subdue and neuter individual power and potential, because it wants power to be located exclusively in its own centralised forms. Gertrude, like other Barker protagonists, challenges the audience's appetites for a protagonist who is readily or consistently sympathetic, but instead offers and demonstrates a freedom and courage which may be surprisingly admirable (and, like other Barker protagonists, Gertrude exposes the province of the conventionally 'sympathetic' as that of impotence, pathos and inertia). Gertrude seeks neither consolation nor forgiveness, and therefore requires no external vindication in the hope of these things, preferring the more thoroughly inquisitive promise of the possibility of free action.[21]

From the erotic space of theatre to wild time (via the spoken body)

In Barker's drama and theatre, a principal means of resistance to institutionalised and centralised power (and its associated constructed promises of time, priorities, consolations and relief) is through eroticism, which is delineated as an imaginative process involving the appeals to the imagination made by body and word, sight and sound, together. Barker argues in a particularly fascinating and provocative recent essay, 'The Spoken Body and the Utopian Regard',[22] that our present 'Utopian society' ('a despotism which, because it is humanist, exercises its violence in the name of liberty and love') purveys the body as 'transparent, a hygienic substance ... no more than a mobile *accumulation of the facts*'. However, if 'the body has forfeited its authority on-stage and off',

> the spiritual *injury of nakedness* can be restored by one thing only – the quality of the spoken word applied to it, for a public immune now even to the most exotic manifestations of the flesh can be lent the privilege of anxiety only by an attitude to nakedness and not nakedness itself.[23]

Indeed, Barker proposes that the fully dramatic and catastrophically erotic 'restoration of nakedness – its recuperation from the withering Utopian gaze – is possible only through description, that what is *said of it* is crucially more affective than the *sight of it* alone, no matter how violated, dismembered or flayed' (adding:'We luxuriate in the paradox that the exhaustion of *visibility* implores the word to restore *perception*').[24]

I wish to make a link here with Anne Carson's analysis of erotic dynamics, and the emotional paradoxes associated with related experiences, in her book *Eros the Bittersweet*. Carson explains how the Greek word *eros* denotes a (previously unsuspected) lack, a desire for that which is missing, and how 'its activation calls for three structural components – lover, beloved and that which comes between them'; and how 'the third component plays a paradoxical role for it both connects and separates, marking that two are not one, irradiating the absence whose presence is demanded by eros'.[25] It is precisely this fraught and freighted, heat-conducting space *between* lovers, the 'ruse of heart and language'[26] manifested in the dance of desire, which Barker's theatre so often amplifies and delineates in its verbal-and-physical explorations of passion: the reach of desire 'defined in action: beautiful (in its object), foiled (in its attempt), endless (in time)'.[27] Barker's play *The Fence in its Thousandth Year* (staged 2005) is a preeminent dramatisation of the realisation that eros 'is an issue of boundaries',[28] it exists because of certain boundaries (which may invite their broaching). The entangled attractions in *The Castle* (staged 1986: for example, Stucley's homecoming speech, but also Skinner's obsession, and Ann and Krak's longings – delineated by Ian Cooper in his essay later in this collection) show how the trajectory of eros moves, in Carson's terms, 'out from the lover towards the beloved, then ricochets back to the lover himself and the hole in him, unnoticed before' ('Who is the real subject of most love poems? Not the beloved. It is that hole':[29] one of the discoveries in Barker's *Dead Hands*).

This further prompts the characters' examination of their own tactics, with a heightened awareness of the personal impoverishments of a socially valued self-control, on the edge between the apparently actual and the apparently possible. They find themselves in a 'narrative texture of sustained incongruence, emotional and cognitive',[30] where the immediately chosen words do not entirely fit their experiences (recalling McArthur's formulation, 'What is this new HIM/HER happening to HIM/HER?') as their imagination (which enlists that of the audience, differently but also similarly) reaches out from the known to what is beyond. This suspends lovers in what Roland Barthes terms 'the present, that difficult tense': 'a pure portion of anxiety',[31] an ambiguous time of vertiginous recurrence and torturous waiting, distinguished and electrified by a 'reach for something else than the facts' (to which the Utopian society would reduce the body): the reach of the erotic imagination which may carry you beyond the dominant terms and vocabulary of actions and values, 'beyond this city' and perhaps 'beyond this world'.[32]

This links with aspects of Barker's ambition for 'distinctly theatrical' medium and project:

> In order to seize back the injury of nakedness from the benign and supervisory Utopian regard, we recognize the body must be mediated through the distinctly theatrical nature of characterization. The anxiety created by the actor *naked* – in contradistinction to the bathos of the actor *undressed* – is substantially the creation of text delivered by performers with whom she shares the stage, a condition shaped by longing, contempt, the entire repertoire of erotic disorder, a condition which serves to disobjectify the flesh such that beauty or its converse is ascribable from the application of speech to the surface of the body and not discernible in the body itself.[33]

Significantly, Carson also suggests that 'Eros is the ground where *logos* takes root between two people',[34] in the moment which Socrates describes as 'a shaft sunk deep into time and emerging into timelessness'.[35] It is important to note what Barker claims is at stake here, aesthetically, culturally and politically: 'The war fought over the meaning of the body in contemporary theatre is no less desperate than the battles waged in Homer over the hero's corpse'; 'Dead or alive, the body drives us mad, and … only the word can shield our gaze from Utopia's dazzling and obliterating light'.[36] I have earlier linked this idea of erotic 'madness', a vivifying dislocation from conventional priorities, with what Alphonso Lingis calls 'catastrophic time',[37] in which ordinary time limits are transcended: what Jay Griffiths alternatively calls 'wild time', sometimes manifested in 'a resurgence of sexual energy even or especially at the point of death'.[38] This is the experience of time associated with excess, plethora, 'the resplendently unnecessary',[39] chance, flux, risk, immersion in the moment, the rawly alive, the seriously subversive play of creative energy (a 'play ethic' which Griffiths argues is far more and deeply '*ethical* than the work ethic'[40]). This helps to describe the oscillating, disruptive, mesmeric, unfocusing, refocusing, shocking, arousing, intoxicating and profoundly ethical 'wild time' – properly and profoundly questioning conventional social and individual priorities, and promises of order – to which Barker's theatre acts as a gateway.

Accumulative textures

It is only appropriate to consider what has constituted Barker's most recent trajectory of experimentation, at the time of writing. His characteristic exploration of language as a form of *expression* rather than *communication* has led Barker to explore the twin poles of 'Plethora' and 'Bare Sufficiency' (the themes of his Creative Fellowship at Exeter University, 2009–12). This consciously develops Barker's interest (discernible in earlier stage works such as *Wounds to the Face*, *Found in the Ground* and *The Forty*) in unfolding 'an assortment, rather than a sequence, of images that cascade, replacing narrative with accumulation: images that do not necessarily *connect*, although the onus on those who present them is to do so with a cogency (which might be alternately comic and disturbing)'.[41] *BLOK/EKO* (staged 2011) presented extreme events (such as the ordained systematic massacre of all representatives of the medical profession) and poetically excessive speeches of internally broken narrative and surreal imagery which were designed to test the limits of what actors could cope with, in delivery. In fact, as Barker observed, the core actors of The Wrestling School proved that this material could indeed be delivered compellingly, but the audience were offered 'language as plasticity', 'received as music and texture – rather than as history, narrative or information – because of its density'.[42] However, audiences, like most human beings (and dramatic characters), are compulsive seekers for, and makers of, meaning, though in this case (as in other Barker plays), the meanings derived are likely to vary. *BLOK/EKO* was not devoid of narrative event and process, depicting as it did intensely complex cataclysmic personal and social upheavals which were developmental and/or degenerative, comic and/or tragic, depending on one's (ever-shifting) perspectives, but Barker (as director, scenographer and dramatist) and his actors worked to minimise the possibility of any single reducible message being derived from the traditional (naturalistic) audience standpoint of analytical superiority over events presented. In compensation for the confusion associated with the refusal of immediate analysis or message, Barker aimed to offer seductive alternatives of bizarre beauty and strange elevation ('generating an aura reminiscent of the Catholic mass and the medieval church'), an impressionism 'in which the colours are not mixed by the artist but assessed individually by the audience, breathing like an anemone in the tide'.[43]

In partial contrast, Barker's *Charles V* (written 2012) incorporated not minimal language (in the style of *The Forty*) so much as language as disaggregated sound, in which a single resonant word – 'inequality' – becomes menacingly broken, 'used instrumentally' by Barker, and 'placed against a number of visual scenarios, to move the onus of meaning into the audience, without foreknowledge as to the full effect'.[44] Barker orchestrates a number of intensely grotesque scenes in which the Holy Roman Emperor (who became fascinated by automata in his secluded abdication) is surrounded by the rhythmic impulses of dead sailors and fading whores, to uneasy and curious effects: the moral authority and coercive menace of the sole word accrues increasingly surprising and interrogatory resonances when dis-integrated and replayed across various actions and tableaux. Gerrard McArthur memorably described this distinctively Barkerian form and effect as a 'framework' for introduction to the perception that 'we don't – and can't – know what we think we know'; a point of radical scepticism and uncertainty where 'words, like bones, prove brittle'.[45]

Salient indications

This collection comprises a series of complementary essays on different facets of Barker's remarkable body of artistic work, in and across different media. The actress Melanie Jessop precisely identifies the technical challenges and performative pleasures and tactics of both the Barker character and the Barker actor; and how one set of demands and initiatives can inform the other, in terms of what she identifies as 'challenges of consciousness', in 'the balancing act required when the actor and the character both "act"', in different and similar senses. From her own professional and artistic experience, Jessop analyses this profoundly self-conscious process of 'intricate tension', in which 'energy is achieved by the continued assessment of its effect on its target': a matter of anxiety, risk and choice. She deduces how both character and actor are driven to 'look into the abyss' of a continual self-fashioning in order (not to deny but) to maintain the purposeful theatricality of their situation, embracing the vulnerability and beauty experienced in this 'mirrored world', in order to enhance (rather than constrain) the sense of creative possibilities.

James Reynolds continues the exploration of the role of the actor in terms which are specific to Barker's form of tragedy: how the performer must discover effects of report and repetition, which serve to amplify meaning whilst the spectator experiences 'the power of speech to produce and replace the fictional constructions of stage reality at speed, becoming subject to a particular, vertiginous effect which may be characterised as *Barkerian*'. Reynolds notes how both report and repetition constitute structural markers, motifs which 'indicates key moments of change in the onstage reality'; and moreover how Barker's catastrophic theatre denies and subverts the Aristotelian conventions of drama, reversing 'the dominant reading-order of theatrical narrative', by designating 'suffering as a pre-condition of narrative, rather than its result'. In consequence, 'Barker's characters can follow non-traditional models of dramatic causation, as their experience of suffering frees them to create reversal and recognition for themselves'. This reversal of the Aristotelian pattern 'refuses not only its organising capacity, but also its movement towards moral consensus'; for 'repetition, while facilitating a deeper exploration of time's expressive potential, necessitates a break away from the organising capacity of chronological time'.

Elisabeth Angel-Perez also takes care to identify how Barker's work can be distinguished from the theatrically fashionable but facile dismissal of the structural principle of narrative; indeed, Barker works with a critical awareness of how narratives traditionally and importantly provide ostensibly 'all-encompassing abstract patterns, made of different myths or stories federated by one ideology and thought to be a comprehensive explanation of historical experience and knowledge'. However, 'in this rethinking of foundation myths, Barker's artistic ambition exceeds the mere will to debunk' or discard; rather, his 're-visioning' is more subversive: 'Barker revisits the small narratives that build up the grand narratives: not to buttress the enlightenment myth that their interpretations more conventionally foreground' but rather to counter the dominant claims and promises 'that reason and scientific discovery lead towards enlightenment'. Barker characteristically 'rephrases or develops themes, so that the apparent meaning of the original narratives is radically subverted'. Moreover, Angel-Perez brilliantly characterises what is at stake in the poetic reach of Barker's language: how it strives to express 'the previously unspoken', 'that place of irrationality ... which is also home for desire': the moment when, in the terms of Barker's essay, 'The Spoken Body and the Utopian Regard', '**The body makes us mad**'. Angel-Perez argues that it is this experience of enigmatic dislocation (available to all, yet defying generalisation) which continually creates the subject anew. Indeed, Angel-Perez notes how Barker's plays offer powerful stories, 'of desire and of pain, of ecstasy and agony', which testify to a faith in language and in the subject's triumphant, if painful, expression of an 'essential and sublime dislocation'.

Ian Cooper chooses to focus precisely on Barker's drama 1977–86: work neglected in a climate of theatrical cowardice, but work which nevertheless offers remarkable presages: both of the play of national and global power, and of Barker's distinctive artistry. Cooper's writing is startlingly politically incisive in tracing the forms and implications of these plays, how they show state power mobilising 'linguistic technology' and recognisably English cultural institutions (and ostensible characteristics) to annex and limit the potentially disruptive image, and iconic power, of the body – a national political process of coercive historical conditioning, no less, promoting 'an intentionally cohesive structure formed to perpetuate hierarchy and social stasis'. However, Cooper also marshals evidence of Barker's contradictory impulse to 'exhume' images which 'offer a series of delimiting constructs', chaotic events of extreme crisis, 'which provoke storms and upheavals in which characters can engage in the construction of

personal histories': events and crises which are profoundly political in their reverberations.

Cooper's essay identifies a thematic fulcrum in Barker's work: the competing
claims of state institutions, and the individual body, to iconic power. It also
provides a *salient* indication (in the military sense, of the projection of a forward
line into enemy-held territory) of directions for further meditations on Barker's
distinctive deployments of the motif of the spoken body – as a form of (self-)
expression invariably in collision with the terms of what George Hunka identifies as 'the post-capitalist culture industry'. It is not easy to contextualise Barker's
work (meaningfully rather than reductively), and even more difficult to do so in
a way which refreshes the way we might regard other artists. Hunka's essay is
properly ambitious in its succinct delineation of a post-World-War-II theatre
tradition which offers an alternative to the dominant conventions of social
realism: Hunka posits a theatre in which the condition of the speaking body
becomes the focus for dramatic exploration, 'in its status as both subject and
object, as both autonomous consciousness and as a spiritual artifact for the
spectator's meditation and contemplation'. Hunka identifies this lineage (of
contrary instinct rather than conscious influence) as beginning with Beckett's
theatrical theory and practice, which offers a 'triangulation of theatrical experience, from character to character to spectator, as the lyrical depiction of suffering,
desire, and love become, through the fracture of both social realism and collectivity, a means of poetic compassion'. Hunka notes how Beckett presents both
language and body as disconnected fragments that 'remain to be experienced and
reassembled by an individual auditor'; in his theatre, 'words become experiential,
riven by anxiety and catastrophe, fragmented and unable to contain physical
experience' (a description which significantly predicts some aspects of Barker's
Charles V). Hunka compares and contrasts the project of the American dramatist
Richard Foreman, who aims to 'reconstruct' the body through an emphasis on
'ordeal', a tension sensed and amplified between performers and spectators,
involving consciously 'difficult and uncongenial' rhythms. Barker similarly
presents and explores language which 'is no longer an avenue towards intelligibility', but does so from a consciously European perspective, in which suffering
offers 'no reconciliation or redemption', but a possible aperture of self-definition
outside the terms of the authoritarian state.

Eléonore Obis develops the formal and thematic enquiry, by focusing specifically on Barker's theatrical orchestration of nakedness in his later work: the
provocative ambiguity and instability of the naked (as opposed to 'nude') body
as a theatrical sign that creates anxiety in its artful confusion of the body of the
actor with that of the character s/he plays. Obis considers how nakedness puts
into question the oppositions between the **presentation** and the **representation** of the body, between a theatrical experience that is experiential, based
primarily on the senses, and one that is mainly intellectual. Its contradictory
bewildering power thus becomes the precisely (spatially and temporally)

deployed occasion of a 'suspension of meaning', 'which, no matter how overwritten, still has the power to be discovered **differently**'.

Our collection then appropriately pivots, to further considerations of institutional power: its claims and contentions, its premises and promises. Michael Mangan examines the underlying ideologies of systems of surveillance and punishment which would literally claim, frame, and thus contain the transgressive individual (body), and how Barker's theatre exposes the fears to which such social and political mechanisms strategically appeal. Mangan provides an explication of how 'emotion, rationality and the law' are spatially regulated by state ceremony, through further institutions and mechanisms of separation, exclusion and elimination; he further notes the persistence of 'the authoritarian edifice which dominates the psychic as well as the scenic landscapes' of Barker's plays, and how these plays are drawn to explore what Foucault termed the 'relationship between rationalisation and the excesses of political power'.

Theatre criticism may be regarded as another form of institution, or institutionalisation: the public rhetorical extending of terms and claims which locate (or separate, to elevate or dismiss) a play or dramatist. Mark Brown provides a valuable perspective, as a professional theatre critic who is prepared to analyse the presumptions and ideologies which underlie the evaluations (and therefore the power) of British newspaper theatre critics, and why their encounter with Barker's work often testifies, overtly or implicitly, to a sense of offence. As Brown points out, 'any observer of theatre trends internationally can see clearly that Barker's theatre is received with enthusiasm in many parts of the world, and faces more hostility in England than anywhere else'; importantly, Brown presents a persuasive and thoughtful analysis of why this is the case, which leads to some significant deductions about the latent terms of English culture and society. Barker may derive some wry satisfaction, at how his work is so (properly) disturbing to the general consensus of the day (the most vital way for theatre to operate, I suggest); though it is unfortunate that the institutional(ised) aesthetic (and therefore political) myopia which Brown identifies may limit a wider appreciation of Barker's work, and its distinctive qualities of imaginative courage. Brown's '21 Asides on Theatre Criticism' offers a tribute to Barker's 'Fortynine Asides for a tragic theatre' by appropriately challenging and extending the terms of theatre criticism in thoroughly Barkerian style: where wit is at the service of a purposeful seriousness.

Christine Kiehl presents a critical history of several Barker productions which have recently occurred in France, with careful consideration of their proximity to, or distance from, Barker's own sense of aesthetic style. As ever, the compulsive provocations of Barker's works throw into stark relief the assumptions (or presumptions) of those approaching them, and Kiehl pertinently asks: can his Theatre of Catastrophe be requisitioned to support such diverse dramatic and aesthetic (and therefore ethical) conceptions? Kiehl identifies what she would nominate as instructive initiatives, both misplaced and appropriate.

We then move to a series of readings of specific Barker plays, in terms which nevertheless resonate through the wider *oeuvre*. Mary Karen Dahl presents an argument (to my mind, both welcome and overdue) for establishing *I Saw Myself* (staged 2008) as a modern masterpiece, and Barker's 'most elegantly developed probe' into one of his recurrent themes, 'the ways that creative acts and actors go to work' in the world, and the associated confrontation, negotiation, self-scrutiny and sacrifice. Barker's most renowned dramatic meditation on such themes is *Scenes from an Execution*, but Dahl's reading supports the case for the superiority of this later, more complex play, not least in its analogies and oppositions, between seeing and representation, creative processes and historical narratives, existential truthfulness and readily discernible meaning. Vanasay Khamphommala carefully considers the details of the dialogic relationship between Shakespeare's *Hamlet* and Barker's *Gertrude – The Cry* (Barker's other major play of that decade) and observes how the subversion of expectation and 'the refusal of identification appears as a governing principle', in Barker's drama as in his paintings; rather, his work characteristically suggests meaning but refuses its revelation (at least in readily limited, and limitable, terms): an impulse and project of **de**limitation. Following on appropriately, Jay Gipson-King turns to *The Bite of the Night* (staged 1988, and perhaps Barker's most formally innovative and ambitious play of the 80s) to open questions of 'a politics of time', and examine how Barker manipulates time 'at multiple levels of the theatrical experience in order to upset conventional habits of viewing and attack the political-moral system embedded within linear realism', and suggests what may be at stake here: that 'unconventional depictions of time do nothing less than create a theatrical-political system that empowers its spectators'. Then Elizabeth Sakellaridou engages with Barker's recent 'chamber work' *The Dying of Today* (staged 2007, 2008) to discern notable depths in a play 'about historical narration – more precisely the recounting of world calamities'. Sakellaridou demonstrates a classicist's awareness in explaining how Barker offers 'a masterful conflation' of two stories from ancient Greece into 'a new fabula' which provocatively 'encompasses various cognitive activities in culture, including historical thinking, philosophical contemplation, psychological analysis and art theory'.

This matrix of imaginative life provides the ground from which all of Barker's works flourish, and Michel Morel opens up a full examination of what he terms Barker's 'triple excavation' – his mutually informative work in paintings, poems and plays – in a final section which aims to indicate the full range and depth of Barker's achievements across the three different media. Morel brilliantly identifies 'ambivalence' at all levels of Barker's works, 'inbuilt contradiction' effected through 'insistent return of the oxymoron': a figure of speech by which contradictory terms are used in conjunction, and term originally meaning 'an exquisiteness of thought belonging to a kind of madness', which produces the crisis of 'an unfathomable quandary between two opposite issues', and the effect of an 'agonising but knowing distance'. This is one of the distinctive achievements of Barker's 'total aesthetic', which constantly pushes 'the theatre nearer the poem and the poem (and the picture) nearer the theatre'. My essay, 'The Substrata of Experience' (coincidentally but significantly) echoes Morel's imagery of the excavation to identify both points of contact between Barker's poems and plays, and some of the distinctive divergences in the themes and styles of (the four volumes of) his poems.

Charles Lamb extends our sense of the power of the visual, and its complements and challenges to the limits of language, focusing on Barker's paintings and drawings, as forms of original visualisation which, on the one hand, inform Barker's theatre practice, and, on the other, projects its spirit into new dimensions. Heiner Zimmermann's essay provides a further expansion from this, by identifying a highly literate visual rhetoric at work in Barker's drama, consciously informed by his 'interrogation or contradiction' of European paintings, which involves the re-visioning of formative cultural myths. Zimmermann's closing deduction testifies to the constantly startling depth of discipline at work in Barker's disturbing effects: 'any hermeneutic privileging of the word over the image (and vice versa) goes against the genius of Barker's creations in pictorial and dramatic art and thus fails to promote their just appreciation'. Hence the need for as varied a consideration of Barker's work, as this multifaceted collection offers, in order to appreciate the many means and levels in Barker's initiatives, which question all answers, and offer their characteristic and uniquely *haunting* capacity: a troubling, engaging, estranging companionship.

Notes

1 Howard Barker, lecture at The Wrestling School Summer School, University of Exeter, 20–22 August 2009; notes transcribed by Rabey.
2 Howard Barker, *Hurts Given and Received* (London: Oberon, 2010), p. 31.
3 Barker, lecture at The Wrestling School Summer School.
4 *Ibid.*
5 Gerrard McArthur, at The Wrestling School Summer School; notes transcribed by Rabey.
6 Barker, lecture at The Wrestling School Summer School.
7 *The Forty* provides actors and audiences with a series of what Phillip B. Zarrilli identifies as 'active images' which (akin to Beckett's work) demand an unusual concentration on inhabitation of the moment, manifesting an 'iterative ambiguity' which is nevertheless a 'palpable experience': 'Actors cannot act ambiguity; however, they can define, embody and enact a precise set of psychophysically charged and energized actions for which there is no conclusive single referent for themselves *or* for the audience': Zarrilli, *Psychophysical Acting* (Abingdon: Routledge, 2009), pp. 126, 116.
8 Gerrard McArthur, in D.I. Rabey, *Howard Barker: Ecstasy and Death. An Expository Study of his Drama, Theory and Production Work, 1988–2008* (Basingstoke and New York: Palgrave Macmillan, 2009), pp. 258–60 (259, 258–9).
9 Howard Barker, from an interview with E. Angel-Perez and V. Khamphommala, 2 February 2009; published as 'Imagination and a Voice: On Writing Tragedy, Resisting

Political Dogmatism and Avoiding Success', in *Études Anglaises* 63/10–4 (2010), 464–72 (467).

10 Quoted in Jay Griffiths, *Pip Pip: A Sideways Look at Time* (London: Flamingo, 1999), p. 55.

11 Marina Warner, *The Inner Eye*, quoted in *Marina Warner* by Laurence Coupe (Tavistock: Northcote House, 2006), p. 115.

12 John Gray, *Straw Dogs* (London: Granta, 2003), p. 98.

13 Cioran, quoted in Gray, *Straw Dogs*, p. 117.

14 Reproduced on the dedication page of Barker's poetry collection, *Lullabies for the Impatient* (1988).

15 John Michael Greer, *The Long Descent* (Gabriola Island: New Society Publishers, 2008), p. 36.

16 *Ibid.*, p. 45.

17 *Ibid.*, pp. 46–7.

18 Gray, *Straw Dogs*, p. 96. Griffiths goes so far as to propose that 'the abstract idea of progress depends, and has always depended, on first, the rejection and then, the destruction of place'; whilst noting how devotees of progress can be 'sneeringly contemptuous of anyone who would dare speak against it', dismissing them as 'ridiculous, backwards and reactionary' (Griffiths, *Pip Pip*, p. 185).

19 Greer, *The Long Descent*, p. 53.

20 *Ibid.*, p. 68.

21 Thanks to Charmian Savill for assistance towards these paragraph's observations.

22 Howard Barker, 'The Spoken Body and the Utopian Regard', in *Gramma/Γραμμα* Volume 17, 'The Text Strikes Back: The Dynamics of Performativity' (2009), pp. 15–16.

23 *Ibid.*, p. 15.

24 *Ibid.*, p. 16.

25 Anne Carson, *Eros the Bittersweet* (Champaign: Dalkey Archive, 1998), p. 16. My thanks to Karoline Gritzner for the gift of this book.

26 *Ibid.*, p. 17.

27 *Ibid.*, p. 29.

28 *Ibid.*, p. 30.

29 *Ibid.*, p. 30.

30 *Ibid.*, p. 85.

31 Quoted in *ibid.*, p. 117.

32 *Ibid.*, p. 173.

33 Barker, 'The Spoken Body and the Utopian Regard', p. 16.

34 Carson, *Eros the Bittersweet*, p. 145. Note also Carson's disquisition on spoken words, and how consonants mark the edge of sound: 'As eros insists upon the edges of human beings and of the spaces between them, the written consonant imposes edge on the sounds of human speech' (p. 55). This links with Kristin Linklater's observations on how vowels provide the emotional inspiration, breath and "motor" of words, which consonants form and direct, in her book *Freeing Shakespeare's Voice* which I have always found valuable in teaching the speaking of Barker's texts.

35 Quoted in Carson, *ibid.*, p. 157.

36 Barker, 'The Spoken Body and the Utopian Regard', p. 16.

37 See Rabey, *Howard Barker: Ecstasy and Death*, particularly pp. 15–17.

38 Griffiths, *Pip Pip*, p. 265.

39 *Ibid.*, p. 280.

40 *Ibid.*, p. 281; especially when, as Griffiths notes, those who repeat 'time is money' never quite answer the question of '*whose* money is made from *whose* time', p. 165.

41 Howard Barker, Exeter University workshop on *Charles V*, Northcott Theatre, 26 June 2012; notes transcribed by Rabey.

42 *Ibid.*

43 *Ibid.*

44 *Ibid.* Again, Zarrilli's words on Beckett are pertinent to Barker's radical subtractions: 'In this process of reduction, Beckett appears to require the actor to overtly do less', to concentrate on simplifying and honing a specific action (such as a variant delivery of a single word), specified by the text's score for performance; 'however, what Beckett demands is that the actor does more' (Zarrilli, *Psychophysical Acting*, p. 123). Barker demands a similar precision and extreme elimination of extraneous action and behaviour.

45 Gerrard McArthur, Exeter University workshop on *Charles V*; notes transcribed by Rabey.

2

Performance within performance: Howard Barker and the acted life – some thoughts

Melanie Jessop

It is a cliché that Howard Barker's texts are rewarding for actors, who delight in the muscularity of the language, the scale of imaginative landscape and liberty from the utilitarian. Is there a Barker actor? Are the technical challenges of playing in Barker unique, or do they surface in any engagement with a poetic classical text? The definition of a Wrestling School acting style has been elusive – the company is fluid and comprises actors with a range of performance practices and processes. What is clear is that for some actors the demands of Barker's texts release an intensity of communicative ability, while for others the inevitable defeat, resulting from an attempt to pull the text towards the prosaic, is exhausting and frustrating. But behind the text there are challenges to actors which are unique in their demands. These are not technical, though they involve technique. They are not emotional, though they involve emotion. They are challenges of theatrical consciousness.

Classical text production in the late twentieth and early twenty-first century theatre has often sought to dismantle the fourth wall, the imaginary boundary between the actor and the audience which is created by the actors and supported by the audience in the collusion of suspended disbelief. This dismantling extends to the architecture of new buildings – the new Royal Shakespeare Theatre at Stratford has a stage which extends into the auditorium from its proscenium so that the audience surround it. In the pursuit of a fully shared experience, we are not alone any more, as actors or audience, having created an environment in which the audience can never forget itself as it looks across the space at itself. The politics of this aesthetic development is not for discussion here, but the loss of privacy and anonymity for the audience is significant.

A consequence of this development is that soliloquy has again become again a dialogue with an audience, as it was in the word-based theatre of the Jacobeans. This denies the audience the privilege of voyeurism – the experience of watching the character realise their internal life in an intensely self-conscious and meditative state. Instead, the audience experiences the dubious privilege of being made conscious of itself. This self-awareness means that they are also required to 'act'. Theories of acting practice derived from the 'method' school, which imply that only in the total abandonment of a consciousness of their own self does the actor truly act, do not consider the balancing act required when the actor and the character both act – when the character is consciously or unconsciously seeking to play a response in order to achieve an effect, and the actor both imaginatively inhabits that play and controls and experiences its effect as character and actor.

There is a further complexity in this interaction in relation to Barker. Howard Barker's characters are also Actors, experiencing and articulating an intense self-consciousness. A painful understanding of existential isolation is the origin of this self-consciousness, and a potent engine for the projection of self into the world, without meditation. They act out their predicaments with immense bravura and imagination. In an echo of the process undertaken by the actor in rehearsal, they engage with and review their performance of these actions. Their rhetorical skills are exceptionally varied. Their relationship to soliloquy is complex. They experiment with emotion, examining its effect on them and its achievement of effect in others. They strike poses, they make use of props. They are consummate. The actor playing in Barker is presented with the challenge of inhabiting the character's self-consciousness as they seek immersion in the forgetfulness of self that acting requires. As they rehearse their own performance, they must embody the brilliant improvisation and redesign of incident that is the character's response to existence. The intricate tension resulting from the co-existence of these states is a creative engine of immense subtlety. What follows are some thoughts on this aspect of Barker's work with particular reference to *Und* (*CP5*), a play for one woman produced by The Wrestling School in 1999, with myself as Und and Barker directing. The play was written for me, adding another layer to the complexity of the relationship between the actor's performance and that of the character. It is a useful text to examine because it is a paradigm for the taut and complex life drama of Barker's characters.

To begin by stating the obvious – Und is alone and the play is therefore ostensibly a soliloquy. It is also important to stress that the play requires a fourth wall because, as we will see, Und's relationship with an audience is not at all a relationship with *the* audience. The other two characters in the play, her visitor and her servant, never appear, though they are significant participants in the drama. However, the notion of soliloquy is entirely unhelpful in this case unless we understand that this definition applies only to those moments in the play when Und feels herself to be alone – in other words, soliloquy is the *knowledge* of isolation, experienced in the moment as a real state. The tension between soliloquy and rhetoric forms the narration by which the character's disintegration is described. Rhetoric is sometimes used as a pejorative term, as contemporary culture becomes ever more suspicious of verbal facility and praises the truth of the inarticulate response, as though its inarticulacy demonstrated its validity. We know the function of rhetoric is persuasion and seduction. For the actor its propulsive energy is achieved by the continued assessment of its effect on its target. The danger of rhetoric for the actor is the distance of its echo – that words exist for their own sake and travel aimlessly, becoming diffuse and never landing on the hard surface of response. The danger for the actor is therefore that they will act badly, whereas the danger of rhetoric for the Barker character is the experience of isolation engendered by a lack of response. They cannot act badly because that is to 'be' badly, and to experience profound existential isolation. Hence the speed with which Barker's characters pursue different rhetorical strategies, and their ability to improvise where there is not the fuel of a response, either because the character they are interacting with refuses a response or because they are not understood. In *Und*, there is no response – there is no one else there - and Und must both create the absent response imaginatively and energetically respond to it. The use of rhetoric in Barker's work therefore achieves its apotheosis in this character, whose dazzling rhetoric is spun into the hard surface of the mirror of her imagined audience (the fourth wall) as the means of persuading herself of her continued dynamic existence. The mirror is crucial – Und's audience is herself, and her relationship with her 'audience' provides the dynamic on which the drama of the piece depends. Her vitality as a character is dependent on her ability to persuade her audience (herself) and to be persuaded by its (her) continued engagement with her predicament. She is therefore acting for herself.

Und's visitor, invited to tea in a game of seduction, is unpunctual:

> He's late *(Pause)*
> He's late *(Pause)*
> Scarcely
> Scarcely
> late at all
> But late *(Pause)*
> Now is this fractional lateness merely the first instalment of considerable lateness or
> is it *(Pause)*
> Purely fractional?   (CP5, 210)

This opening beat of the piece immediately establishes the speed and fluency of cogitation with which Und will propel herself forward. The passivity of the first statement, 'He's late', is answered by a qualification which is not powerful enough to refute the statement. Greater precision is required: the lateness is 'fractional' but might become 'considerable'. Und has escaped immobility by changing her relationship to the fact of lateness by becoming its interrogator. The effect of this is to increase her confidence and commence a dance of increasingly demanding complexity with her own responses as she seeks to avoid the inevitable. She will continue this interrogation of the situation and her responses to it with hair-raising bravery throughout the play; it is after all both a means of escape from and an exposure of her aloneness. In the following, Und's interpretation of her servant's failure to respond to her commands is brilliantly elaborated to achieve a segue from the anxiety caused by her absence into a description of how well the servant knows her (and loves her) that asserts both the servant's existence and the potential vitality of her relationship with her imagined audience:

> I shout these orders no one comes it is as if she can detect so subtly is her character attuned to mine it is only chagrin that is indicated pique and all that's infantile in her beloved mistress and much is much is infantile in me I confess I would not wish it otherwise have you met the adult have you spent time with the thoroughly mature
> Oh
> Oh
> Their oceanic wisdom suffocates your soul   (*CP5*, 213)

The quality of anxiety in Barker's work is peculiarly delicate, producing a fineness of perception that separates it from more conventional experiences of that state. It is not an anxiety which clouds the mind but one which creates acute lucidity. It is not an anxiety of situation, though that of course exists in the world of the play. It is an anxiety which comes from the perpetual hypothesis of the Self. Infinite (and infinitely subtle) possibilities of experience and response can be imagined – and the resulting anxiety can only be managed by a decisive choice. The element of risk entailed in this perpetuates the anxiety in an endless energising cycle. This is very different from the performance anxiety experienced by the actor (who if well-rehearsed and technically skilled will feel a level of anxiety proportionate to those conditions) but is an anxiety of being in which the constant motion of improvisation is both exhausting and invigorating – an obvious contradiction brilliantly utilised by Barker. For the actor, this creates particular technical difficulties. A state of physical relaxation is necessary for the actor to perform – tension and stress are sensory inhibitors and will disable the dexterity required for a fully realised performance. The difficulty for the actor who is playing in Barker is that Barker's Actors are giving once in a lifetime performances (in their fictional lives). Their lives are happening to them, in real time and for them issues of survival and destruction are just that. The anxiety attendant on that state is very great and the actor must inhabit that state with sophistication and technical precision. The consequence of relinquishing that state for the actor is a lack of focus. For Und it is literally death. 'And, and, and' says Und until she can no longer hold up the weight of infinite anxiety …

> (*A pause. Her finger, dirty from the earth, is held unconsciously. She discovers it. She examines it as if it were not her own. As she does so a frame containing a painting by Ruysdael drops down beside the mirror … Pause*)

Solomon
Jacob
Solomon
Solomon
(She observes the painting. Her finger remains erect. A terrible hammering ensues. The
hammering acquires a certain rhythm, a pulse, a music. Und *does not move. It stops)*
We
(It begins again, and continues. Und *does not move. At last it stops)*
We
(And again)
We
(A new sound of dragging and friction)
Distinguished by our aristocracy
Oh the
Delicacy of our forms
O
O
I died on seeing
On seeing died
Let him in
On
Seeing
Died
(It rains, steadily, heavily)   (*CP5*, 238)

Und's fluency is ended. She no longer has the life energy required to continue
her rhetorical dance. The text begins to fracture into small pieces and this
complete exhaustion of language is the final moment of the play.

If rhetoric is the life force in *Und*, then soliloquy is the acceptance of death.
Those moments in the play where we can say that Und is soliloquising are very
few and relate directly to the understanding she has of the inevitable outcome of
her situation. Each time, she visits this state for a moment only; for example here:

Remove the tea tray
(Pause)
I am not not not furious
Why should I be
The World's peculiar not me
The World is this demeaning spectacle not me
Don't remove it *(Pause)*
Removing it endows the whole occasion with significance as if I could not bear the
sight of it before me no let it gather dust someone will collect it at some point
perhaps tomorrow or the cat will knock it off oh dear I'll say sugar oh dear milk on
all the furniture how long has that tray been there abandoned like a tennis court in
winter the occasion having been the pretext having been erased from memory
(Pause)

> He gathers Jews *(Pause)*
> The dress oh that the dress yes possibly of all the gowns it is the most extravagant I
> don't conceal it from myself I chose this to
> *(Pause)*
> **Overwhelm** *(Pause)*   (*CP5*, 211)

The apparently simple observation, 'He gathers Jews', comes at the end of a piece of scintillating rhetorical theatre which begins with a wonderfully comic contradiction – 'I am not not not furious' (Und here demonstrating the classic Barkerian insistence that the word is all that is the case), and the implication must be that it is in this state of momentary exhaustion that Und is unable to move fast enough to avoid this momentary contact with an inner knowledge.

The section that you have just read comes early in the play, and at this point Und is able to regain mobility immediately by the stimulus of an external object – the dress she is wearing. Her return to rhetoric is therefore enabled by a redirection of focus – an actor's tool par excellence. Later in the piece, as the tension between rhetoric (life) and soliloquy (death) becomes intolerable, she is less able to separate the two:

> **One must look into the abyss**
> **One must**
> **One spoils of something if**
> *(Pause)*
> One's gaze forever is averted
> *(Pause)*   (*CP5*, 231)

The first three lines are written in bold type, the fourth, placed between two 'Pauses' is not. Barker's intuitive precision here is of course characteristic and is a painfully economical expression of Und's failing powers.

Rhetoric and soliloquy are only two of the actors' tools employed by Und. She is also a hugely deft and skilled mimic of dramatic styles and employs a glittering variety of mood and tone to maintain the theatricality of her situation. It is this that defines her as an Actress. It also demands that we (the play's real audience) understand the reality of her experience is enhanced, and not lessened, by its theatricality. Howard Barker imbues this character with his intuitive dramatic expertise and sense of creative possibility. She embraces her artificiality and expresses complex truths as a result – an apparent contradiction which lies at the heart of the actor's life. In playing Und, I found that her abilities as an actress challenged mine in ways that were a revelation of the actor as a deceiver, conjuror – and 'perfect liar' (as Barker describes the character of Placida in his 1988 play, *Ursula*).

Actors try to tell the truth of the character's experience and this involves escaping from an awareness of self that will get in the way of a total imaginative commitment to that experience. Looking into a mirror on stage therefore is a peculiar and discomforting experience. The face that is reflected is mine – me – I confront the reality of myself and the success of my disguise is momentarily threatened. I experience a moment of shame at my failure to escape myself. In approaching the play, I understood that there must be a fourth wall, as any contact with the real audience would negate the fundamental isolation of the character. But who is Und talking to? She is talking to a hypothetical audience and objectifying herself. The fourth wall is a mirror, and in exposing myself to its constant imagined scrutiny, I clarified the relationship that exists between Barker's characters and the world they seek to effect. Barker's characters are mirrors, playing off their reflections in an endless transaction of forensic self-regard. When Barker is acted badly the rhetorical becomes posture, the mobility of thought mere display and self-regard is reduced to a debased form of complacency. It is only in embracing the vulnerability experienced in this mirrored world, and its beauty, that the actor can expose its reality for the character and then the shimmering play of these mirrors dazzles our minds.

3

Unearthly powers of invention: speech, report and repetition in recent Wrestling School productions

James Reynolds

Report and repetition

Repetition is a feature of Howard Barker's writing, constituting a principle in his plays, which Alan Thomas recognises in his argument that they are often 'governed by recurring complication of treatment and not by the working out of a complete, self-sufficient plot'. These 'linear structures', Thomas writes, 'are repetitions, with variation, of an idea or situation which becomes amplified in meaning'.[1] David Ian Rabey outlines the genealogy of this principle in an interview with Barker, when he observes that the 'aesthetic drive and rhythm' of Barker's exordia extend 'into the scenographic propositions and drive' of works such as *Found in the Ground*.[2] Barker's reply confirms that the repetitive, 'musical nature of the exordium' establishes a principle of repetition, one which also functions as an essential indication to spectators that 'they will not be seeing or hearing according to the conventional rules of social-realist theatre, comedy or what is routinely on offer'.[3]

Report of news from offstage is another feature of Barker's writing, one which serves to amplify meaning. Barker believes that 'Tragedy places the actor at the centre of its undertaking, demanding powers of an unearthly kind from him or her of articulation and invention'.[4] For it is the performer who must discover this power of amplification, escorting meaning forward, with each repetition or report building a complex multilayered performance. Immersed in an experience of continuous movement between perceptions of the fiction, the spectator experiences the power of speech to produce and replace the fictional constructions of stage reality at speed, becoming subject to a particular, vertiginous effect which may be characterised as *Barkerian*.

The role of the actor in Barker's own form of tragedy is my ultimate concern here; in particular, the 'unearthly' powers of invention in speech that renews, amplifies and makes real the onstage reality. From its inception, Barker's company,

The Wrestling School, has faced the challenge of how to act Barker. Part of the mission statement issued by founder members Kenny Ireland, Hugh Fraser and Barker states that 'It is intended to develop an acting method which permits the most coherent expression of text … the method for playing [Barker's texts] has not yet been properly realised'.[5] It may never be realised; indeed, Barker's continual evolution as a writer seems contrary to the establishment of a fixed method. Nevertheless, while a method may or may not be necessary for the 'coherent expression of text', it is legitimate to identify and analyse the challenges these texts presents. I begin by focusing on the devices of report and repetition and their role, before identifying their challenges, and outlining possible directions in meeting them.

First, an account of repetition and report in Barker's work is needed. As already noted, Rabey demonstrates that the 'aesthetic drive and rhythm of the exordium' extends from dramaturgy into the 'drive of the entire play';[6] and, for Barker, 'The routine of the exordium has to be repetitive', partly because of limitations of time, but also because of a need to disrupt conventional spectatorship.[7] Dramatic and thematic foci are repeated in works such as *13 Objects* (2006) (*CP2*) and *Wounds to the Face* (2012) (*CP5*), which use repetition as a structural device similar to that of musical theme and variation. Repetition is also apparent in the language of many opening speeches in Barker's recently performed and published plays – but report is also present in the following examples. Bad news, a bad journey and a late lover – each constitute an offstage stimulation for the repetitions which report them in their absence. Dneister begins *The Dying of Today* (2008) with a rhetorical interrogation:

> Do you like bad news I do I'll give you
> bad news if you want it why do you prefer bad news I ask
> myself do you like grief do you like chaos not at all only I
> think men are more beautiful flung down than standing up
> say if you want my news   (*OP4*, 87)

Eff establishes a principle of repetition in the opening of *Dead Hands* (2004):

> What a journey
> *(He sits.)*
> What a journey oh
> *(Pause)*
> What a journey let us begin with things of little or no
> consequence the weather for example   (*DH*, 7)

The repetitions of *Und*'s (2001) opening demonstrate the principle further:

> He's late *(Pause)*
> He's late *(Pause)*
> Scarcely

> Scarcely late at all
> But late *(Pause)*
> Now is this fractional lateness merely the first instalment of
> considerable lateness or is it *(Pause)*
> Purely fractional? *(Pause)*
> Fractional lateness which will lose any significance the moment
> he *(Pause)*
> Still fractional *(Pause)*
> Not so fractional now *(Pause)*   (*CP5*, 210)

Most importantly, repetition constitutes a structural marker, as it indicates key moments of change in the onstage reality. Sopron's nakedness and Eff's refrain in *Dead Hands*, the deaths in *The Seduction of Almighty God* (2006), the mirrored door in *I Saw Myself* (2009) opening to reveal a naked man – these reoccurrences, and others, are moments of realisation, of amplified meaning, marked by the reincorporation of prior speech and action. Each of these repetitions marks a significant change in the onstage reality.

Report also changes the onstage reality: in speeches, such as Isola's account of Cascan's murder by Hamlet in *Gertrude – The Cry* (2002); in the report of individual lines, such as the ever-nearer war in *I Saw Myself*; and, in *The Dying of Today*, where the report of 'bad news' is not only the play's content, but also its form. As noted, Barker's texts also combine with repetition the offstage information which often constitutes report, notably in *I Saw Myself* – where the repeated report of the nearing war was eventually overtaken by its presence – and in *Und*, where repetition and report merged in the offstage sound effects of doorbells and breaking glass. These, combined with a sequence of objects and letters which entered on a swinging tray, created an environment which reported to Und the collapse of her world through the repetitions of scenography. *The Dying of Today* explored report to the extent of inversion, with Dneister's message of bad news gradually being delivered by his chosen receiver of it.

The presence of these techniques in Barker's texts creates particular challenges for the performer. Report emphasises the narrative over the dramatic, description over mimetic representation, challenging the performer to speak the offstage world into being. Repetition structures material differently to the logic of the through line of action, doing so on the basis of reoccurrence as well as progression. Barker's most recent fictive worlds are both narrative, and landscape. The actor must navigate both elements of the text, and needs to approach their role on terms that reflect this. In order to discover such terms, it is to tradition that attention firstly turns.

Playing against the frame

Barkerian performance is positioned within a complex frame of encultured understanding of acted representation, by the text, in relation to Barker's aesthetics, and by the conceptions of the audience which meet text and aesthetics in the moment of performance. This last places a particular demand upon the performer. Elinor Fuchs argues that the Aristotelian pattern of narrative affects audience responses, even in its absence, as it gives 'shape and meaning' to dramatic narratives – albeit in the negative.[8] The actor is the focus point of a meeting between the Barker text and a cultural frame, still conditioned, Fuchs argues, by an Aristotelian theatrical syntax. The Aristotelian pattern can be summarised (simplistically, for the sake of brevity) as 'reversal-recognition-suffering'.[9] Fuchs discusses Beckett's *Waiting for Godot*, and its frustration of the expectations and conceptions which the Aristotelian pattern has produced. *Godot* frustrates the Aristotelian plot model, because of 'the absence of the reversal of which the messenger is the classic harbinger'; therefore, Fuchs argues, 'the classic plot is scooped out of [*Godot*]', reappearing as a 'super-text', which, in its denial of audiences' conceptions and expectations, gives the piece its particular values.[10]

Barker's catastrophes deny the Aristotelian pattern as Fuchs suggests Beckett does; but Barker works outside contemporary convention by reversing the pattern. The pattern of Barker's catastrophic narratives is suffering-reversal-recognition, a reconfiguration of the Aristotelian tragic pattern which reverses the dominant reading-order of theatrical narrative. Suffering is not the final phase of catastrophe; it is its pre-condition, it has already occurred, and continues as environment. As Charles Lamb argues, 'most of Barker's plays are set in catastrophic circumstances either immediately before or immediately after fairly massive social breakdowns'.[11] With suffering as a pre-condition of narrative, rather than its result, Barker's characters can follow non-traditional models of dramatic causation, as their experience of suffering frees them to create reversal and recognition for themselves. '[R]eversal', as Lamb argues, 'comprises an essential energy source' in Barkerian performance.[12]

Unlimited in this way, Barker's characters explore self in a way that exceeds a naturalistic conception of character. Knowing where a Barker character is going to is of more use to the actor than knowing where that character is coming from. Moments of reversal and recognition in Barker's work are moments where characters define their identity through choice and decision, by taking a particular direction. Report and repetition are two of the dramatic techniques Barker uses to demonstrate his characters' explorations. But such techniques mean that the actor can no longer rely on what Fuchs calls the 'crisp organising power' provided by the build-up of tension and 'formal clarity' of the Aristotelian pattern.[13] Barker creates works that unfold according to a structure of realisations, and, consequently, characters who unfold according to the direction set by those realisations. Both character and narrative therefore deny the reassertion of 'rationality and morality' that Heiner Zimmermann argues accompanies catharsis.[14] Barker's reversal of the Aristotelian pattern, therefore, not only refuses its organising capacity, but also its movement towards moral consensus.

Consequently, the actor must follow Barker's injunction to 'draw the audience into a relationship with the stage which eradicates sympathy at the outset as a prime condition'.[15] Barker's reversal of tragic form is divisive, and does not seek to draw the audience together in pity; as Christine Kiehl argues, 'No comfort is allowed in the … dislocated structure which thwarts expectation'.[16] This is, as Gunter Klotz says, 'an art that cannot be domesticated', for Barker 'cuts the umbilical cord to the aesthetic womb that has given consistency and meaning to the drama throughout the centuries of modernity'.[17] But the actor, also, is cut off from supporting frameworks of performance. This severance begins with a reversal of Aristotelian form, and continues to a rejection of naturalism's method-ologies, forms and performance style. Thus the actor faces the application of an artistic and a moral frame that still inheres from the Aristotelian model, repre-senting a pre-determined resistance to their performance which they must overcome. Barker acknowledges this challenge in his insistence on the exordium as a method of supporting the actor dramaturgically, by disrupting the 'conven-tional rules of … what is routinely on offer'.[18] Although the amplification of meaning, organisational demand, and reification of the offstage space that report and repetition offer are intrinsically challenging, exploring them can be produc-tive for the actor.

Approaches

Conventional approaches to acting cannot meet these challenges, because they are not coherent with Barker's reversal of tragic form. Character, too, must be facing in a different direction to the rest of the world. Two potential drivers of characterisation are unavailable here; as noted, these characters do not 'come from' a place that can be defined as either social or psychological. This leads Liz Tomlin to argue that due to a 'lack of secondary information', the only 'reliable dimension available' regarding these characters is constituted in what they 'say and do publicly'; that Barker's characters have 'an immediacy which denies them the possibility of a conceivable past or future'; and therefore, that they 'are denied the psychological continuity which is integral to the conventional concept of characterisation'.[19] Further to this, Tomlin cites Ian McDiarmid's observation that:

> With Howard's work it is almost like dealing with subtext as text. Everything is there for you, and it's essential for the actor to think and feel in the moment. His text has an absolute immediacy which would render any kind of naturalistic baggage inhibiting.[20]

Charles Lamb similarly argues that, in Barker, 'there is no subtext' as 'everything is articulated'.[21] The surface is everything and the grounding concept of inner life is seemingly abandoned. A rejection of contextual frames also seems apparent. Lamb argues that Barker 'presents a decentred, purely relational world which

goes beyond the quiescent fantasies of realism without the support of any autho-
rising discourses', noting that the dehumanising effect of this detachment from
recognisable contexts and discourses has to be 'overcome through the actors'.[22]
Furthermore, Roger Owen observes that 'the plays pose [deep problems] in
terms of their challenge to contextualisation',[23] and Mary Karen Dahl argues that
Barker's 'technique unmoors us from the known'; this lack of a known framework not only creates 'disturbances at the deepest, most individual and private
levels' for spectators, it challenges performers with a similar disruption of 'institutionalised power relations'.[24] What then are the grounds, if any, for acted
performance in these circumstances?

There may be no grounds for such characterisation other than the text itself,
leading Lamb to present Baudrillard's 'processes of seduction' as a grounding for
Barker's characters,[25] an alternative foundation necessary because recourse to the
'jargon of authenticity' [in] 'truth-based' discourses of acting is unavailable in
Barker's reversal of tragic form. Seduction 'extracts meaning from discourse and
detracts it from its truth'.[26] Seduction grounds character in the speech actions of
Barker's texts; the actor and their speech is their only authentication, and
whatever being they have is shared with the actor's in utterance. Yet a sense of
identity, of character – albeit relational – still seems useful. Barker's figures are
rarely so abstract that there is no sense of a 'who' that is speaking. These are
figures who realise: who are constructed by their realising; and who make reality
anew in response to their realisation. But on what terms?

Grounding performance

David Barnett describes Barker 'as a Nietzschean dramatist on a variety of
counts', arguing that characters like Starhemberg 'clearly' have the identity of the
'*Ubermensch*'.[27] Lamb, however, writes that 'Baudrillard characterises the action of
seduction as a kind of flickering', and shows that in their turbulent speech, the
'sense of identity' of Barker's characters is 'constantly dissolving itself then re-
emerging elsewhere'.[28] Both approaches can provide grounds for a sense of who
is speaking in Barker's work; yet the deliberateness of the will to power, and instability of seductive speech, seem to contradict each other.

However, the Nietzschean hypothesis of 'The subject as multiplicity' accom-
modates the will to power seeking self-creation, as well as the relational figure
exploring self-definition. It therefore provides a better model of identity for
Barker's characters than the *ubermensch*. Leslie Paul Thiele cites Nietzsche's
summary of this view of the self, from 1885: 'The assumption of one single
subject is perhaps unnecessary; perhaps it is just as permissible to assume a multiplicity of subjects, whose interaction and struggle is the basis of our thought
and our consciousness in general?'[29] The identity conceived on such grounds
is necessarily complex. But the notion of plurality in selfhood nevertheless
provides a basis for the continuous shifting and re-creation of identity in Barker's

works, a plurality of self that is entailed by the exploration of reversal and recognition.

The rapidity with which the shifts in identity can occur in such a fictional reality defies the naturalistic mode of representation, demanding skills of abrupt transformation from the actor that are more commonly found elsewhere. Barker's admiration of the marionette in meeting such challenges is worth noting here. In a response to a question at Aberystwyth, Barker stated that 'a good actor has a lot of the attributes of the puppet', citing in particular their 'emotional charge'.[30] The apparent depth of realisation (not to mention emotion) which the marionette 'experiences' provides a model of interiority for the Barker actor, as well as an important recognition of the power inherent in moments of realisation. These moments of psychic change might also reveal internal dynamics of the text, or constitute markers around which the actor can organise her performance.

For repetition, while facilitating a deeper exploration of time's expressive potential, necessitates a break away from the organising capacity of chronological time. Barker's characters 'know what they want, even though what they may want may change from one moment to the next … in an important sense, they talk reality into existence'.[31] This ontological power of language to rapidly change on-stage reality also requires a use of time at odds with the psychological continuity of naturalistic theatre. The actor must address time in relation to their role where repetition is structural, because it is a compositional device that makes time more visible through reoccurrence, often compressing and accelerating it. Thus the actor needs to perform both representational and dramaturgical functions, when they meet in the locus that repetition creates. The actor must excavate the moment of realisation as the character, but also accept the authorial function that the composition of the text demands of them. Perhaps the uncanniness of the puppet, its capacity for adaptation, and ability to create new realities from even a single word, represents a paradigm for Barkerian performance that is founded in objective, as well as subjective, being. Like the puppet, the Barker actor may need to be both conduit and creator.

Such duality must be qualified, however, as it highlights a difference between what might be thought of as the character's authorship, and the actor's. Liz Tomlin notes 'the authorship sought by [Barker's] tragic protagonist[s]'[32] as a control over their reality, reflected in Lamb's description of their 'insistent movement towards completeness and self-possession'.[33] Whereas the protagonist's authorship is sought within the frame of catastrophe, the actor's authorship is sought within the frame of performance. Although dual, the parallel between actor and character is reaffirmed with each realisation.

Negotiating language

In addressing this parallel, Andrew Renton's analysis of Samuel Beckett's way of writing is useful. Renton argues that Beckett's writing programmes his work to be a 'system', working itself 'through to its conclusion' in performance.[34] Barker's work can be thought of as programmed in a similar way, for in his work also, 'The *process* of composition becomes the trope within the composition'.[35] In Barker, this trope is characterised by a negotiation with language to render meaning, rather than a delivery of finished language, and encapsulated meanings. The struggle for as yet unknown words leaves behind traces of the writing process. Barker states that 'frequently I do not know what I am writing',[36] and, as Thomas argues, 'There is a touch of *automatisme* about Barker's writing which he acknowledges'.[37] Claire Price, who created the role of Ursula, recalls her encounter with this deliberate unknowing:

> I remember saying [to Barker], 'What does this mean?' And he said, 'I don't know, you tell me', and I said, 'Well you wrote it', and he said, 'Yes, but I may not necessarily know what it means'. It's almost like something comes to him and he's a conduit, and he writes it, and often things will go on the page that he couldn't possibly intellectualise or explain to anybody else.[38]

Most importantly, this not-knowing in Barker's writing process ties writer, actor, character and spectator together in the moment of performance, where a quadrupled struggle to render and possess language is manifested. It should be noted, however, that an authorial function such as this would be limiting for the actor, if it enclosed the performance in an interpretation of authorial intention. But both Barker's acceptance of automatisme in his writing, and his use of report and repetition function to deny intention, as they undermine any attempt to extend an authorial capacity into an authorial discourse in the text. Meaning cannot be controlled here; as Thomas argues – the 'insistent pressure on the ideas' in Barker's language causes words to 'fracture into a multiplicity of meanings'.[39]

This quadruple struggle of pressured ideas enhances the live quality of Barker's work for the spectator, both through its indeterminacy of meaning, and the intimacy with creative processes that it generates. The role of report and repetition is crucial, for their interruptive powers of reversal and recognition can rupture or structure the character's struggle for possession of language. Through such ruptures the actor can discover the offstage space, harness its uncanny powers to express realisation, and find bases for the character's inner life, context and direction. These ruptures open inner-texts for characters, constituting a space for interiority more than a subtext, but nevertheless the beginnings of an inner life grounded in the offstage space. Report, or message, frequently refers to the reality offstage; it signifies the presence of that which is not present. And this, rather than revealing psychological subtexts, or material contexts, reveals inner-texts that can be used as material for exploration and the creation of affect by the actor.

But report and repetition can structure, as well as rupture. These are dramatic devices and moments in which reversal and recognition emerge, and they facilitate the unfolding of a structure of realisations powerful enough to overcome potential resistance to the Barker text. The actor cannot overcome resistance through the representation of suffering; their arsenal is the excavation of moments of recognition, the energy of reversal released in reordering perception – and the accumulated effects of these amplified moments. This reveals the alternative organisational capacity of the structure of realisations. Repetition and report invite the actor to structure a role directionally as a sequence of moments and markers of amplified meanings, breaking any emerging through line by continuously changing the reality on stage, and compelling an acceptance of an authorial function in performance.

These devices, and their capacity to change reality on stage, might usefully be compressed into the term 'realisation' – realisation in the sense of both coming to know something new by creating it, and also of a making real of that which is unseen. Realisation as a concept theorises an alternative driver of representation for the Barker actor, one with an appropriate organisational capacity emerging from the text. As Barker's characters, actors, audience and text develop in directions marked by the ruptures and structures of language, they pass through 'stations' of realisation. In this sense, to read the Barker text is to immediately begin to perform it. Such a constructive (as opposed to revelatory) realisation is different from the contemporary 'passion for disclosure' that Barker believes shackles dramatic form to 'the already known';[40] it is a driver of performance with a passion for discovery of that which is unknown, and for creation – for the making that can occur in the singular moment of performance alone.

Notes

1 A. Thomas, 'Howard Barker: Modern Allegorist', *Modern Drama* 35/3 (1992), 433–43 (435).
2 H. Barker, K. Gritzner and D.I. Rabey, 'Howard Barker in Conversation', in K. Gritzner and D.I. Rabey (eds), *Theatre of Catastrophe: New Essays on Howard Barker* (London: Oberon, 2006), pp. 30–7 (30).
3 *Ibid.*, pp. 30–1.
4 H. Barker, 'On Naturalism and Its Pretensions', *Studies in Theatre and Performance* 27/3 (2007), 289–93 (293).
5 H. Barker, press release titled *Some Notes Towards a Change of Method in Performance and Text*, dated 18 December 1986.
6 Rabey, in Gritzner and Rabey, *Theatre of Catastrophe*, p. 30.
7 Barker, in Gritzner and Rabey, *Theatre of Catastrophe*, p. 30.
8 E. Fuchs, 'Waiting for Recognition: An Aristotle for non-Aristotelian Drama', *Modern Drama* 50/4 (2007), 532–44 (536).

9 *Ibid.*

10 *Ibid.*, p. 540.

11 C. Lamb, *Howard Barker's Theatre of Seduction* (London: Routledge, 1997), p. 43.

12 *Ibid.*, p. 42.

13 Fuchs, *Modern Drama*, p. 535.

14 H. Zimmerman, 'Images of Death in Howard Barker's Theatre', in Gritzner and Rabey, *Theatre of Catastrophe*, pp. 211–30 (211).

15 Barker, in Gritzner and Rabey, *Theatre of Catastrophe*, p. 33.

16 C. Kiehl, 'The Body Turned Inside Out', in Gritzner and Rabey, *Theatre of Catastrophe*, pp. 198–210 (209).

17 G. Klotz, 'Howard Barker: Paradigm of Postmodernism', *New Theatre Quarterly* 7/25 (1991), 20–6 (22, 23).

18 Barker, in Gritzner and Rabey, *Theatre of Catastrophe*, p. 30.

19 L. Tomlin, 'Building a Barker Character: A Methodology from *The Last Supper*', *Studies in Theatre Production* 12 (1995), 47–53 (47, 48).

20 McDiarmid, quoted in *ibid.*, p. 48.

21 Lamb, *Howard Barker's Theatre of Seduction*, p. 49.

22 *Ibid.*, p. 33.

23 R. Owen, 'Demolition Needs a Drawing, Too …', in Gritzner and Rabey, *Theatre of Catastrophe*, pp. 184–97 (196).

24 M.K. Dahl, 'The Body in Extremis', in Gritzner and Rabey, *Theatre of Catastrophe*, pp. 95–108 (95).

25 Lamb, *Howard Barker's Theatre of Seduction*, p. 40.

26 *Ibid.*, p. 35.

27 D. Barnett, 'Howard Barker: Polemic Theory and Dramatic Practice: Nietzsche, Metatheatre, and the play *The Europeans*', *Modern Drama* 44/4 (2001), 458–75 (463, 465).

28 Lamb, *Howard Barker's Theatre of Seduction*, p. 57.

29 L.P. Thiele, *Friedrich Nietzsche and the Politics of The Soul: A Study Of Heroic Individualism* (Princeton: Princeton University Press, 1990), p. 31.

30 H. Barker in dialogue with David Ian Rabey, Aberystwyth University, 26 January 2007.

31 John O'Brien, quoted in D.I. Rabey, *Howard Barker: Politics and Desire An Expository Study of his Drama and Poetry*, second edition (London: Macmillan [1989] 2009), p. 3.

32 L. Tomlin, 'A New Tremendous Aristocracy', in Gritzner and Rabey, *Theatre of Catastrophe*, pp. 109–23 (121).

33 Lamb, *Howard Barker's Theatre of Seduction*, p. 59.

34 A. Renton, 'Texts for Performance/Performing Texts', *Performance* 60 (Spring 1990), 13–29 (16).

35 *Ibid.*

36 J. Reynolds, 'Barker Directing Barker' in Gritzner and Rabey, *Theatre of Catastrophe*, pp. 56–69 (64).

37 Thomas, 'Howard Barker: Modern Allegorist', p. 434.

38 Price, quoted in Reynolds, 'Barker Directing Barker', p. 64.

39 Thomas, 'Howard Barker: Modern Allegorist', p. 437.

40 Barker, 'On Naturalism', p. 292.

4

Reinventing 'grand narratives': Barker's challenge to postmodernism

Elisabeth Angel-Perez

I define postmodernism as incredulity towards metanarratives.

Jean-François Lyotard[1]

Howard Barker's art of theatre has been rightly described as resolutely postmodern (by Lamb, Rabey, Morel, Sakellaridou and Zimmermann). Barker's obsessional need to revisit the grand narratives that are at the basis of our epistemology reads as a deliberate intention to deconstruct them and to help the spectator out of the ready-made programmes of thought sedimented by culture over the years or centuries. These grand narratives encompass: the humanist narrative (*Women Beware Women* (1986), *(Uncle)Vanya* (2010), the Judaeo-Christian narrative (*The Last Supper* (1988), *The Ecstatic Bible* (2005)), the Marxist narrative (*Claw* (1977); and variations such as the technè-oriented (*13 Objects* (2006)), nation-oriented (*The Love of a Good Man* (1980), *Hated Nightfall* (1994), *The Castle* (1985)), Freudian (*Isonzo* (2001), *Gertrude* (2002), *Und* (2001)) narratives, concerning what would be all-encompassing abstract patterns, made of different myths or stories federated by one ideology and thought to be a comprehensive explanation of historical experience and knowledge.

However, in this rethinking of foundation myths, Barker's artistic ambition exceeds the mere will to debunk. His re-visioning is more than a dismissal of something antiquated. Those myths (Homeric, Biblical, Shakespearean, fairy tales) that are instrumental in the constitution of the grand narratives may still have things to tell us. Yet, what they have to tell, in Barker's hands, may differ considerably from what their hypotexts originally proposed. Barker revisits the small narratives that build up the grand narratives, not to buttress the enlightenment myth that their interpretations more conventionally foreground: rather, in Barker's plays, the humanist metadiscourse, which claims that reason and scientific discovery lead towards enlightenment, is countered. This may suffice to term Barker a postmodern. Yet, it is striking that unlike other postmodern dramatists

(Bond, Berkoff, Kane, Crimp) who compulsively revisit classical texts or myths, Barker does not dismiss the structural concept of grand narrative. Postmodernists attempt to deconstruct grand narratives by focusing on specific local contexts as well as on the diversity of human experience. They argue for the existence of a multiplicity of theoretical standpoints rather than grand, all-encompassing theories. As opposed to this, Barker's deconstructionist treatment of the myths does not conclude on the irremediably fragmental nature of all human activities; on the contrary, he recomposes such narratives within a new catastrophist teleology that takes the tragic subject towards a continuously greater discovery of its sublime, because tragically complex, selfhood.

What Barker does therefore is both to summon and reject the atomisation of the grand narratives into the *'petits récits'* (local narratives) described by Lyotard.[2] I suggest Barker develops a language of tragedy that precisely federates and resemanticises the dead-ends of postmodernism; he converts the stylistic markers of postmodernism – markers of impotence or failure (fragmentation, aposiopeses, anacolutha) – into a re-empowered style that claims its victory over the aporias of the age.

Postmodern Barker: defeating grand narratives

Barker's postmodern qualities as a writer have been argued since the outset of Barker studies. Gunther Klotz contends that 'Barker's whole theatrical stance can be read as a paradigm of post-modernism';[3] Charles Lamb, in his latest book on Barker, dedicates a whole chapter to postmodernism and the theatre;[4] David Ian Rabey synthesises Barker's position on the subject in his introduction to *Theatre of Catastrophe*: 'Thus Barker opposes history – the imposition of moral and ideological narrative form – with Anti-history – the disruptive fragmentation of this form by the testimony and performance of individual pain …'.[5] Heiner Zimmermann identifies Barker's 'anti-humanist theatre, which deconstructs the discourse of rationality', and describes it as 'a genuine offspring of postmodernism'; he shows that Barker's theatre is characterised by an 'action [which] is fragmented and establishes no linear sequence of time', that shuns the mimesis of reality, so that its characters may seem to lack identity beyond the self-reflexive; however, Zimmermann concludes by noting how this impression is 'contradicted by the dramatist's characterization of his texts as avant-garde theatre and elitist, by his condemnation of popular mass-culture as shallow and obfuscatory – an attitude incompatible with the postmodern integration of "high" and "popular" culture'.[6] This breach in the reading of Barker as a postmodern artist deserves further exploration, which I will attempt in a Barkerian, therefore oxymoronic, style, by trying to show that Barker revives what has been stigmatised by postmodernists, at the heart of his own, nonetheless postmodernist, practice.

Barker's well-known postmodern stance can be synthesised along two different axes: structural and poetic. At the structural level, Barker dramatises pluralising impulses – he subverts the linearity of the narrative by splitting it into micronarratives, defying and denying the teleological progress assumed by humanist stories and grand narratives alike. The parables interspersed in *The Last Supper* resist the possibility of a linear progressive reading or status of the text. The compendia, *The Possibilities* (1988), *Wounds to the Face* (1997) and the aphoristic *The Forty* (2011), read as a succession of tableaux or question plays that foreground the spectator's solitary position and experience of pain, in which 'the audience is disunited' and its members 'suffer alone' (*AT*, 19). Barker here comes quite close to the *petits récits* (localised narratives) as defined by Lyotard in parallel with Wittgenstein's language games. Discontinuity is the rule. Linear progression (the stylistic expression of faith in humanist progress) is therefore denied in favour of circular or iterative motifs. Even the plays that do follow some linear narrative development and/or rewrite well-known linear stories, rephrase or develop their themes, so that the apparent meaning of the original narratives is radically subverted. All the summoned 'metanarratives' (Freudian, rational, biblical, Marxist) are subverted in their own conclusions. In Barker's stories, there is no assertion of progress ('These are not after all, stories of the Humanist era': Barker, *AT*, 175), nor is there a Marxist presentation of history that would lead to revolution, not to mention the absence of redemption in Barkerland. The grand narratives are submitted to catastrophe.

The second axis is poetic: Barker's most Barthes-like text, *13 Objects*, his *Mythologies* so to speak,[7] opens on the image of a spade digging the ground to bury whatever it is that so far constituted our familiar epistemological landscape: structure, morality and, last but not least, the steadiness of language (so do *Animals in Paradise* (2006) and *The Love of a Good Man*). The metaphor of language that Barker develops in *13 Objects* through the paradigm of objects gives a perfect account of the necessity to make do (or not) with a language already heavy with meaning. Like language, objects have a past: the camera (which is also the name of the blind daughter in *The Fence* (2005)), a kind of Eliotian objective correlative to language, dictates its meaning to its user and therefore becomes an instrument of terror.

> YOUTH: (…) I dread to contemplate the banal subject matter it has been focused on if one could wash a camera I would wash it yes or fumigate it holidays babies in prams unreturning soldiers football teams some pitiful pornography the uncleanliness of it appalls me if he was buying me a camera why not a new one…
>
> (*OP2*, 284)

Language, just like the camera, is only able to vehicle absence: 'Take my absence to him please', the Youth orders the camera. Hence, in *13 Objects*, the Idealist throws the camera away, the Billionaire ends up burning the painting, since words, as Ionesco suggests, no longer speak. Language has to be reinvented:

> A QUEEN: How silly speech is

How silly when all it really means is

(SHE WAITS. SHE RATTLES VIOLENTLY. AGAIN THE STAGE ERUPTS IN RUNNING FIGURES. SHE LAUGHS, STACCATO. SILENCE RETURNS) (*OP2*, 280)

The Poet must confront his tragic lot which is to 'struggle with the language that we possess', that is 'employ the inadequate knowing full well its inadequacy' (*OP2*, 259). But Barker, like the Poet and the Idealist (and Galactia in *Scenes from an Execution* (1990), the Carpet-Weaver in *The Possibilities*, or Sleev in *I Saw Myself*) is compelled to use a new form: to invent a new language enables the expression of the previously unspoken.

THE OFFICER: This death
   Far from being the extinction of perception
   Is itself perception
   (HE STANDS UP SWIFTLY)
   Oh
   It is so hard to say
   It is so hard to enter the territory of this
   It calls for a new language
   It calls for poetry (*OP2*, 259)

Half way between the obstetrician of *Animals in Paradise* and the embalmer-coroner of *He Stumbled*, Barker anatomises the corpse of language to exhibit its wounded flesh. On the poetic or *poietic* side therefore, what comes out of the defunct bowels of language is another language that (not unlike Céline's although in a radically different manner) elaborates a style in strict opposition to the 'done-and-dusted' 'logico-positivist rationality'.[8] Barker's tragic language, which outrageously challenges institutionalised language, goes beyond the rationality of the unified subject: its rhetoric expresses the Kristevian 'abject subject' – that is, the subject driven to the extreme verge of itself (*le sujet limite*), a subject that no longer narrates itself but cries itself out (or decries itself) with maximal stylistic intensity: language of violence, obscenity, or a rhetoric that makes the text similar to poetry'.[9] Barker's opposition to all forms of moral rationality and to the belief in the progressive emancipation of humanity finds a rhetorical translation in a number of stylistic devices, some of them splendidly analysed by Michel Morel:[10] oxymorons, aposiopeses (to which we could add anacolutha, parataxis), which defeat any attempt at delineating some kind of progression towards some possible enlightenment. Barker's style builds a subject through deeply paradoxical and dislocating combinations of roles: a character is simultaneously a mother and a murderer (*The Possibilities*), a loving wife and a traitor ('Kiss My Hands', *The Possibililities*), a nurse and a madwoman (frantically baring her breasts to all passing trains in *The Last Supper*), a thinker and a sleeper (Lvov in *The Last Supper*), Snow White and a temptress ('Dear Daddy, come and see my garden'[11]).

Yet, for all these postmodern traits, Barker despises postmodernism as chaos and distances himself from it both in his theoretical writings and in his plays: he has stories to tell.

Catastrophising postmodernism

The beginning of Barker's essay *Love in the Museum* gives us a derogatory definition of postmodernism:

> For all its apparent chaos, dislocation, fracture and repudiation of critical discipline – all that represents itself as the phenomenon of postmodernism – all contemporary culture is nevertheless driven by a number of restless imperatives – sleepless nights of intolerance – which affect it in its many seemingly diverse functions. The most frantic of these – now near to an authentic neurosis – is its loathing of the secret.
>
> (*AT*, 171)

It is precisely this loathing of the secret that Barker's theatre continuously challenges by exploring man's organic and intrinsically secret-prone subjectivity as the organising (directional) form of seemingly chaotic postmodernism. The celebration of obscurity and secret is what gives all Barker's theatre and theoretical essays a federating 'direction', therefore allowing it to resemanticise the aesthetics of fragmentation proper to postmodernism. Let us consider how Barker proceeds.

Barker engages in a subversion of the grand narratives he summons. Much more than other postmodern writers, Barker very often summons the narratives or stories that are instrumental in the constitution of the grand or meta- or master-narratives. Like other postmodern writers (Heiner Müller, for instance, with *Medea Material* or *Hamletmachine*), Barker deconstructs these stories (for example, in *Seven Lears*). Even when he does stick to the structure of the hypotext, he undermines its logic: hence Barker writes *Scenes from an Execution* in the margins of a humanist story, *Claw* as a political anti-morality play subverting the Marxist grand narrative; he dismisses the grand narrative of the nation through tales of the nation in *Victory, The Love of a Good Man, Hated Nightfall, The Castle* or the grand narrative of Christianity through parodical rewritings of the Bible in *The Last Supper, The Ecstatic Bible*; twists the Freudian metadiscourse in his staging of stories of desire and death (*Gertrude, Isonzo, He Stumbled, Dead Hands, The Fence*). These are postmodern initiatives. Yet, in these plays Barker – and this is specific to him – reinscribes a grand narrative at the heart of this deconstruction. The deconstruction of the myth shelters a reconstruction – the grand narrative of a debased yet collected subject: Gertrude and not Hamlet, The Queen and not Snow White. Unlike Müller, for instance, Barker's rewritings do not leave us with the bits and pieces of a deconstructed myth. They enable us to engrave a different story, a different linearity, so to speak, at the heart of a stammering process. Thus, in Barker's theatre, there is no such thing as a radical questioning of the concept of story-telling (such as we find in Crimp's *Attempts on her Life* or *Face to the Wall*, for instance, or in Caryl Churchill's stammering *Blue Heart*, plays in which the suspense revolves around the birth or non-birth of the story).

Even in those of Barker's plays that are most radically and structurally divorced from the aesthetics of linear story-telling (*The Possibilities*, *Wounds to the Face*), Barker's very way of writing and of characterising rests on an allegorical[12] process which makes it clear that the narrative is there, looming large, as a reference backdrop. In *The Forty*, the woman who keeps repeating 'I do not want to be hurt again', and the son bound for the army (repeating 'If I go I shant come back'),[13] send the audience back to a complete story that they all have in their imagination. The unique sentence the characters utter condenses a complete narrative (allegory) staging allegorical characters.

The constant resort to stories seems to foreground Barker's unwillingness to replace grand narratives by small, localised narratives that would tend to prove that our postmodern world is made of the cohabitation or juxtaposition of different entities, each establishing its own rules and none of them serving or supporting a grand all-encompassing theory: even when he opts for imagined and radically different circumstances, as in the various episodes of *13 Objects* for instance, Barker federates his micronarratives into a typically Barkerian grand narrative.

Barker's grand narrative: creating a system

All of Barker's creatures share a number of features and aim at getting closer to that obscure 'place of irrationality [in them] which is also home for desire' (*AT*, 173): maybe the Lacanian 'Thing' (*la Chose/das Ding*).[14] As a result, Barker's characters are essentially paradigmatic: Gertrude is kin to the Queen of *Knowledge and a Girl*, or to Judith or to Algeria, Und to Ursula. Photo is yet another Hamlet; Kidney, Cascan and the Servant are made of the same stuff. In *Gertrude* and *Knowledge and a Girl*, for instance, Barker stages two queens that appear as two exacerbated paragons or allegories of Woman. The two myths that are being revisited here (Hamlet and Snow White) enable Barker to explore the permanence of a feature: the tragic status of a character who comes to terms with her so-called monstrosity and who, because of this tension between monstrosity and transcendence, becomes sublime. In both plays, the technique used by Barker is incredibly successful: catastrophic disorientation proceeds by moving the margins into the centre, and conversely the centre out to the margins, in order to promote the tragic where one does not expect it. Snow White is supplanted by the Queen, Hamlet by Gertrude. Both plays articulate the same preoccupations and weave a network of echoes between the characters: a queen is confronted with a jealous daughter-in-law or step-daughter (Ragusa/Snow

White) and a young and incestuous wooer (Hamlet and his reflection the Duke of Mecklenburg/ Young Askew) and asserts her power through an uncontrolled fertility.

Algeria, in *The Fence*, can also be associated with this paradigm. These Queens or Duchesses are all promises of life and of death – staged allegories of Bataille's definition of eroticism as the approbation of life into death.[15] In all three plays, through an enticing mixture, the same metaphors are at work hingeing around the trope of the woman–landscape that one visits, conquers, relishes, fertilises and/or devastates. In all three plays such images of the cartography of the body delineate a sort of anti-*carte de tendre*,[16] some sort of outrageous and outraged topography: Algeria speaks of her 'flooded fields', of her 'drowned ditches' (*FTY*, 9) while Gertrude evokes 'the rivers boiling through' her kidneys, her belly or her womb (*OP2*, 160).

Therefore, it appears that Barker's plays do focus on different imaginative circumstances (revisioning Hamlet in *Gertrude – The Cry*, Snow White in *Knowledge and a Girl*, rewriting the myth of Jocasta and Oedipus in *The Fence*) which all construct the same project: showing the intrinsic secret of selfhood. The Fence (in the play of that name) that girdles Photo's secret is a paragon of the Barkerian grand narrative. Barker's plays therefore from one play to the next, keep imaginatively exploring the same motif, and remain in 'infinite conversation' with one another, to use Blanchot's words,[17] whilst generating and developing different stage images.

Consequently, the very recycling of previous literary or mythical material – hence the concept of intertextuality (either endo- or exogenous) – cannot be read in Barker's plays as the sign of some sterile circularity or stammering and as the postmodern aporetic tell-tale sign of an impossible progress. Neither is intertextuality an adjuvant to the splitting of the subject, of its atomisation (in T.S. Eliot's sense of the subject). On the contrary, Barker's use of intertextuality plants the dislocated subject into a retrieved community that shares a number of features. The subject suffers alone, yet in terms analogous to others. Intertextuality is not a confession of vain and compulsive repetition but an iterative and at times self-correcting or epanorthotic approach of the acknowledged secret.

If there be a progress in Barker's philo-poetry for the stage, its is not a humanistic evolution towards Enlightenment ('If the ideology of transparency is one of instant communication, the great narratives of antiquity – almost entirely tragic in character – possess moral ambiguitites which cannot be incorporated into the project of absolute enlightenment', *AT*, 173) – but an an 'involution' towards acknowledging obscurity, towards acknowledging that man is governed by his sense of utter mystery, the mystery of death being the terminal epitome of this mystery.[18] What Barker proposes is to bring us, through his fantastic vision of tragedy, to the almost carnal knowledge of obscurity and of secret: knowledge, here, in its biblical sense, knowledge, to put it in Henri Meschonnic's words, as 'a something in between the ecstasy of the body and the joy of knowing: the labour to get to know the unknown'.[19] Barker is not content with subverting the meaning of the myths or works of art he convokes, he rewrites them so as to turn them into the opposite of a contribution to the humanist ideal of enlightened progress and derives from them another grand narrative – his own grand narrative – which succeeds in showing, in a variety of contexts, what is immovable in man: his irrational dislocated nature whose unfathomable obscurity creates desire which in turn creates the subject. The essence of the subject is its dark, enigmatic dislocation. Dislocation is not the result of our postmodern times. Judith is not a humanist (reason-driven) subject who has become dislocated because of our postmodern eras; she is a permanent symbol of essential subjective dislocation; and so is Barker's Lear, and Gertrude and Vanya. Hence the pertinence of Barker's corrections brought to the classics he rewrites.

Barker, if a deconstructionist by method, is also a reconstructionist by credo, and most notably a reconstructionist of the one element that tragedy cannot dispense with: the subject.

Poetics of an essentialist subject

In her seminal article, '(Post)Modern Subjectivity and the New Expressionism: Howard Barker, Sarah Kane, and Forced Entertainment', Karoline Gritzner shows that far from considering 'the category of the self (as) redundant', Barker reassesses the indispensability of the subject and of 'selfhood': 'Barker locates the possibility of authentic individual experience in the realm of the tragic, which he considers to be sufficently enigmatic and powerful enough to act as a counterforce against the dominant liberal-humanist ideology of mass-culture'.[20] Gritzner shows that Barker's subject is far from being 'an empty signifier for a series of roles or socially constructed positions'.[21] I would like to continue Gritzner's brilliant analysis by showing that Barker not only distances his 'Art of Theatre' from the postmodern stance, by inventing extreme situations where the subject literally bursts into being, but also by creating a language that instrumentalises the poetic and stylistic aporias of postmodernism so as to make them triumphant expressions of idiosyncratic selfhood.

In Kristeva's words, 'the political function of poetic language is to prevent the institutionalization of the unconscious'.[22] Let's take an example of Barker's stylistic disintitutionalisation of the unconscious: Gertrude, in the graveyard:

> I met your eyes
> I said I would not and then I met your eyes
> Up came the laughter
> In a wave

> I knew it would engulf me so I turned
> My shoulders heaved as if hoisted by ropes
> I stuffed the handkerchief into my mouth and
> Marched
> Tears
> Marched
> How well I march
> No one dares run after me
> SHE HAS TO BE ALONE HER GRIEF COMPELS HER
> Admire my skirt
> OR SHAME SOME MUTTERED
> My skirt says everything to those who can read skirts
> SOME MUTTERED EVEN SHE KNOWS SHAME   (OP2, 92)

In a place of institutionalised and composed grief, Gertrude is overwhelmed by instinct and her language reflects the intertwinings of the id and of the superego. She comes to terms with what normality would call her monstrosity. This is what makes her sublime.[23]

The construction of the subject is achieved by postmodern techniques (fragmentation, anacolutha, aposiopesis, the defeat of reason); yet these tools do not construct a ruined dislocated postmodern (or post-Eliotian) subject: a subject in ruins (with 'fragments shored against my ruins', in Eliot's *The Waste Land*), such as we find in Martin Crimp or Sarah Kane's plays. On the contrary, these tools build the essential organicity of the dislocated tragic subject: a subject who accepts and revels in dislocation. Let us go deeper into this: the postmodern subject that one can find in Martin Crimp's *Attempts on her Life* (1997), for instance, corroborates an anti-essentialist reifying vision of the nomadic subject which relies on the ideal of a culturally hybrid, deterritorialised, multi-identitied, postnational subject, circulating freely across the geographical areas: a subject that claims not the right to be different, but the right to belong to several diasporas[24] according to affinities (emotional, intellectual, economic); a subject that is somehow always in exile. The tragedy of this postmodern subject is that it cannot find a form to express itself. From a *poietic* point of view, Martin Crimp and Sarah Kane are perhaps the two playwrights who most immediately come to mind when it comes to staging postmodernist subjects. In Crimp's plays, the stage becomes a laboratory to experience globalisation: in *Attempts on her Life*, the central character – or 'absence of character' as he calls it[25] – is called Ann, Annie, Anya; she never says 'I'; she never even appears, and yet she is ubiquitous ('she's off round the world. One minute it's Africa, the next it's South America or Europe ...'[26]). Parallel to this ubiquity, the unstableness of Anne's being is insistently dramatised: is Anne a woman, a car, a TV set? 'She's a terrorist threat / She's a mother of three / She's a cheap cigarette / She is Ecstasy'.[27] She is an atomised, ubiquitous postmodern subject that Crimp's seventeen scenarios (similar to an *'exercice de style'* in the terms of Raymond Queneau and the OuLiPo) precisely, yet vainly, try to encompass: the total deconstruction of the subject that no longer allows tragedy.[28]

As opposed to this, Barker reasserts contradiction or dislocation as essential in the subject: dislocation is not the symptom of a loss, but on the contrary, the symptom of wholeness: the subject's verbal blanks are not to be interpreted as a mark of the alienation of the subject from itself, but on the contrary as a proof of its being one with itself (in its contradictions) and one with the others (all tragic subjects are marked by the same aphasias and aporias). Barker's language of ruptures weaves a homogeneous fabric – made of holes and discontinuities – for its characters: for example, Algeria's utterance in *The Fence*:

> Thank you for coming
>
> *(A fractional pause.)*
>
> I must stop saying thank you many have detected in my politeness a stratagem an evasion even a hypocrisy they cannot reconcile politeness with a woman who bares her arse in public let alone sleeps with a boy I see no contradiction please do not abandon me you see I say please I say please and thank you please please people are looking at me oh dear oh dear can we go somewhere … (FTY, 40)

Barker's language of tragedy precisely resemanticises the aporias of postmodernism: the markers of postmodernism are turned into markers of tragedy. There is no such thing, in Barker's plays, as doubt concerning language. As Heiner Zimmermann puts it:

> Barker has unlimited trust in the power of language and linguistic expression … His characters ignore the ideological prison of language, which precedes the individual. They count on metaphor and poetic language and try to liberate the unconscious through vehement rhetorical outbursts and ecstatic declamations. They are not afraid of thus subjecting the hidden self, the inarticulate area that is not yet charted by the power of rationality and social norms.[29]

Aposiopesis is seldom the sign of incomprehension expressing a failure but rather the sign of incomprehension expressing a victory, a stupendous revelation, a revelation that precisely hinges around the necessity of secrecy. Michel Morel, in his analysis of this figure of rhetoric, defines Barker's rhetoric in terms of one that constantly reactivates 'black (or negative) epiphanies' and draws a convincing parallel with Keats's negative capability.[30] Barker's asemic silences and linguistic apnoeas never embody defeat: they represent 'Writing Degree Zero', for the signifier but not for the signified. As Giorgio Agamben puts it, silence is not the 'other' of language but its very fabric.[31]

The same resemanticisation affects the mode of fragmentation. Based on parataxis or anacolutha, the process of fragmentation demonstrates Barker's continuous dismissal of the idea of a hegemonic collegial truth, and conversion of this into as many local truths as there are subjects, in a distinctive piece of mimetic writing (rather than the confession of impotence): it is also to be read as the hallmark of man's intrinsic and universal compartmented solitude. The structural fragmentation – which partakes of an aesthetics of rhapsody (in the etymological meaning of the word: *rhapsein*: to sew together) – seems to merge into a symphonic demonstration of the self at the end. The poetics of fragmentation (aposiopesis, anacolutha, non-sequiturs) is heard as a powerful and beautiful piece of mimetic writing to express the discontinuous obscure subject that speaks (of) its secrecy: the subject finds a shape in an attempt to recapture something of the romantic ideal of adequacy between the signifier and the signified.

If anything, Barker's latest plays are stories: love stories, stories of desire and of pain, of ecstasy and agony. This is the language of tragedy invented by Barker, a language that, far from the dessicating barrenness of distanciated postmodernism, far from the bankruptcy of a language threatened (with engulfment) by silence, places the subject right in the middle of its affects and triumphantly, if painfully, expresses its essential and sublime dislocation.

Postmodernism – inasmuchas it foregrounds a dislocated and obscure subject – reads as Barker's grand narrative. Barker reverses, carnivalises, catastrophises postmodernism itself and turns it into a grand narrative, the tragic grand narrative. Not unlike Habermas, Barker catches Lyotard in his own nets, calling postmodernism another grand narrative, thus refuting Lyotard's thesis as self-destructing and showing the possibility of transcending it. Yet his position is at the extreme opposite of the Habermasian position – Barker's aim is not to defend the supremacy of reason or moral rationalism (Kant), nor to reconcile technical progress and moral rationality. The grand narrative he invents rests on the divorce of reason and morals (Barker's language is without ethical limits) and on the universality of the dislocated subject. 'How to emerge from postmodernity?'[32] or 'To think after the postmodernists'?[33] (As Meschonnic and Petit put it in their respective titles.) A whole part of today's critical literature is busy trying to solve the debate between Lyotard's postmodern stance and Habermas's attachment to the enlightened reason and to a vision of humanity resting on the idea of progress. Barker may well be showing us that this debate is the place of a conceptual stagnation. Meschonnic asks: 'And what if art, unobtrusively, was immobile? Or rather, anchored not in a dimension but in something different. Neither in time, nor in space, but in the subject?'[34] Barker opens a dimension which is neither temporal nor geographic, the dimension of the subject, and there he invents a language of tragedy that, like music, never lies.

Notes

1 J.-F. Lyotard, *The Postmodern Condition: A Report on Knowledge* (Manchester: Manchester University Press, 1989), p. xxiv.
2 *Ibid.*

3　G. Klotz, 'Howard Barker: Paradigm of Postmodernism', *New Theatre Quarterly* 7/25 (1991), 20–6.

4　C. Lamb, *The Theatre of Howard Barker* (Oxford: Routledge, 2005).

5　K. Gritzner and D. I. Rabey (eds), *Theatre of Catastrophe: New Essays on Howard Barker* (London: Oberon, 2006), p. 18.

6　H. Zimmermann, 'Howard Barker in the 90s', in *British Drama in the 1990s: Anglistik and Englishchunterrcht* 64 (Heidelberg, 2002), 181–201 (189, 181–201).

7　With Barker, no 'Bifteck and French Fries' (see R. Barthes, *Mythologies* (Paris: Seuil, 1957), pp. 77–9), but a few highly metaphorical toys or tools, often detached from their traditional function in Baudrillard's fashion (see J. Baudrillard, *Le Système des objets* (Paris: Gallimard, 1968)) and ready to express the meaning of Barker's characters' Catastrophic world. See E. Angel-Perez, 'Les Mythologies de Howard Barker' (en collaboration avec Robin Holmes): Preface to *13 objets* et *Animaux en paradis*, de Howard Barker, trad. by J.-M. Déprats and Marie-Lorna Vaconsin (Paris: Éditions Théâtrales, 2004).

8　J. Kristeva, *Pouvoirs de l'Horreur: Essai sur l'abjection* (Paris: Seuil, 1980), p. 47: my translation.

9　*Ibid.*, p.166.

10　M. Morel, 'Rhétorique du non sens', in Elisabeth Angel-Perez (ed.), *Howard Barker et le théâtre de la Catastrophe* (Montreuil: Éditions Théâtrales, 2006), pp. 173–89.

11　H. Barker, *Knowledge and a Girl*, in *Gertrude – The Cry and Knowledge and a Girl* (London: John Calder, 2002), p. 99.

12　The allegory is used by Barker in its two meanings: as condensed narrative or as paradigmatic character. See Morel, *Howard Barker et le théâtre de la Catastrophe*.

13　H. Barker, *The Forty* (unpublished).

14　See in particular Jacques Lacan, *Le Séminaire, Livre VII: L'Ethique de la psychanalyse, 1959–1960* (Paris: Seuil, 1986); two chapters are entirely devoted to *das Ding*.

15　'L'approbation de la vie jusque dans la mort … En effet, bien que l'activité érotique soit d'abord une exubérance de la vie, l'objet de cette recherche psychologique, indépendante comme je l'ai dit, du souci de reproduction de la vie, n'est pas étranger à la mort': Georges Bataille, *L'Erotisme* (Paris: Minuit, 1957), pp. 31, 17.

16　La carte de Tendre ('The Map of Tenderland', literal translation), is a map attributed to 17th century French artist François Chauveau (see BnF website: www.expositions.bnf.fr/ciel/grand/sq11-06.htm), appearing in Mme de Scudéry's novel *Clélie, histoire romaine*. Accessed 30 September 2012.

17　*The Infinite Conversation* (*L'Entretien infini*) is the name of an essay written by Maurice Blanchot in 1969.

18　This theme is pursued by Barker in *Death, the One and the Art of Theatre* (Abingdon: Routledge, 2004).

19　Henri Meschonnic, *Pour sortir du postmoderne* (Paris: Klincksieck, 2008), p. 83 (my translation).

20　K. Gritzner, '(Post)Modern Subjectivity and the New-Expressionism: Howard Barker, Sarah Kane and Forced Entertainment', *Contemporary Theatre Review* (special issue on 'Beyond Postmodernism') 18/3 (2008), 328–40 (329, 332).

21　*Ibid.*, p. 328.

22　Kristeva, on Céline, in *Pouvoirs de l'Horreur*, p. 52.

23　Another clear example of this disinstitutionalisation of the unconscious could probably be Barker's treatment of Judith, either in *The Possibilities* or in the eponymous play. In the Apocrypha, the story of Judith reads precisely as an attempt to institutionalise Judith's unconscious. Barker's play powerfully resists this: 'Even his breath I longed to breathe. And take him in me, head and shoulders also, if I could

… I could not have cared if he dripped with my father's blood, or had my babies' brains around his boot, or waded through all Israel' ('The Unforeseen Consequences of a Patriotic Act', *The Possibilities* (*OP1*, 204–5).

24   A. Appadurai, *Après le colonialisme: les conséquences culturelles de la globalisation* (Paris: Payot, 1996, 2001).

25   'She says she's not a real character, not a real character like you get in a book or on TV, but a *lack* of character, an *absence*, she calls it, of character': Martin Crimp, *Attempts on her Life* (London: Faber, 1997), p. 25.

26   *Ibid.*, p. 26.

27   *Ibid.*, p. 59.

28   A somehow similar attempt at seizing this 'absence of character' is to be found in Sarah Kane's last plays: for example:
'— I gassed the Jews, I killed the Kurds, I bombed the Arabs, I fucked small children while they begged for mercy, the killing fields are mine, everyone left the party because of me, I'll suck your fucking eyes out send them to your mother in a bowl and when I die I'm going to be reincarnated as your child only fifty times worse and as mad as all fuck I'm going to make your life a living fucking hell I REFUSE I REFUSE I REFUSE LOOK AWAY FROM ME': Sarah Kane, *4:48 Psychosis* (London: Methuen, 2000), p. 25.

29   Zimmermann, *British Drama in the 1990s*, p. 190.

30   M. Morel, 'Women Beware Women, la stratégie de l'anachronisme', lecture at the symposium *Barker de la page au plateau*, Odéon/Sorbonne, 2 February 2009.

31   Giorgio Agamben, *La Fin du poème,* trad. Carole Walter (Belval: Circé, 2002).

32   Meschonnic, *Pour sortir du postmoderne.*

33   Jean-François Petit, *Penser après les postmodernes* (Paris: Buchet-Chastel, 2005).

34   Meschonnic, *Pour sortir du postmoderne,* p. 161 (my translation).

5

Institutions, icons and the body in
Barker's plays, 1977–86

Ian Cooper

Barker's plays of the seventies and mid-eighties dramatise the machinations of the state in recognisably English social and cultural institutions, environments and landscapes, such as burnt-out prisons, abandoned hospitals, bank vaults, mausoleums, battlefields and castles. In this political territory, Barker further identifies various forms of oppressive linguistic technology which the state employs to suppress individual pain, which may contain the spark of personal rebellion where individuals enact struggles for articulacy and self-definition. In this period of his writing, Barker dramatises the economic and political compromises of a post-colonial/industrial nation in decline, while reaching increasingly and identifiably towards the principally European contexts of his later work. His plays show the body as an essential dramatic territory to be fought over, abused and ultimately reclaimed, either by the oppressor or the subject. During this period, Barker also shifts perceptibly from his early uses of recognisable (usually contemporary) political contexts set in broadly satirical forms, to the defining personal catastrophes (of mythic history, and 'Anti-History') of his later work. His characters move, in distinctly physical terms, beyond ideologies of obedient allegiance as they search for a richer arena in which to define and explore the options which their experiences gradually and gruellingly expose.

'This soul's prison we call England': displacement and enclosure

Images of 'England' in Barker's plays, from *Fair Slaughter* (1977) onwards, are significantly revealed as repressive constructs of officialdom, in culturally pathological terms: historically conditioned individuals encounter and negotiate a self-perpetuating series of terms, symbols and rituals, an intentionally cohesive structure designed to institutionalise hierarchy and social stasis. However, the action of the plays also frequently involves the exhuming and anatomising of counter-images: surprising versions of experience, which significantly expose and alternatively re-vision 'the past' as a series of delimiting constructs. The action also provides chaotic events of extreme crisis, which provoke storms and upheavals in which characters can at least begin to engage in the construction of personal histories.

In *That Good Between Us* (1977), the Home Secretary, Orbison, declares 'our system relies entirely on consent' (*TGBU*, 23). However, here and elsewhere, Barker's drama shows how this consent is manipulated, enforced and maintained by those in power: they characteristically deploy and ordain the repetition of such abstracting phrases, to secure a superficial dressing of liberal humanism as a cosmetic for a *realpolitik* supported by totalitarian brute force. In *That Good*, Orbison's nominally socialist government attempts to assure others (and itself) of its own decency by invoking the civil system, but also straddles it in such a way that allows suppression and torture to quell riot and conspiracy. The corrosive rhetoric, enshrined by and within state terminology and discourse, ensures that, although violence and oppression exists and occurs in Orbison's Britain, the true forms of its manifestations are smothered beneath a very English sense of propriety, which Barker's plays of this period persistently expose as an endemic falsehood. Orbison clings to a purposefully reductive sense of what is appropriate and necessary, in order to justify the morality of her actions. The Special Branch agent, Knatchbull, also characteristically deploys euphemism to cloak his activities. Although Orbison condones his 'disappearance' of suspects, she expresses unease about Knatchbull's obfuscations of such unconstitutional atrocities: 'We have to get back to the personal pronoun. Stop hiding in the semantic wood' (*TGBU*, 53). Ironically, it is another character, McPhee, who will finally seize the nascent power of the personal pronoun, in the play's final lines.

Knatchbull's overly protective and paternalistic attitude to his daughter, Verity, succinctly provides a dramatic microcosm of this dominant political paternalism. When they stumble across the body of a murdered soldier on a common, Knatchbull attempts to deflect Verity's curiosity by repeating palliative myths about death, to prevent her confronting the actuality of the knowledge that the corpse was tortured. He appeals to an idealised state of innocence – a lack of knowledge – in the child, reflecting his implicit desires to inculcate this paralytic imaginative circumscription in the populace as a whole. In a moment which anticipates Barker's later dramatic invocations of the speaking dead, the body/corpse attempts to communicate his agony to the living; however, Knatchbull wishes to smother the pain and outrage which the corpse expresses: to nullify the power of the dead.

The epigraph of *That Good* is Matthew Arnold's phrase, 'Wandering between two worlds, one dead / The other powerless to be born'; this hints at the nascent worlds struggling within the cynical and exhausted belly of the English state. The excavation of possible alternatives is a major concern of the play, which opens with Billy McPhee, a thug, rapist and state spy, being thrown overboard from a rowing boat by Knatchbull and his lackey, after McPhee's embroilment in an army cell run by Major Cadbury. Indeed, the shifting and surprising depths of water provide a dramatic image of instability at various points in the play. The audience's first view of Orbison is also on a boat, on the Serpentine: Orbison's tense and volatile exchange with her own daughter shows how she despairingly attempts to grasp at meaning and to proclaim a sense of integrity, while never-theless claiming moral neutrality (which can also be potentially deadly to her enemies). She affects a frank awareness and examination of the methods which underlie such deadly euphemism, but her attempts merely expose a deeper despair about the possibility of any alternative; this contrasts with Knatchbull's unquestioning attempts to deflect and stifle inquiry and enforce impose an idealised 'innocence', which is limitation. Like Orbison, Cadbury is self-consciously aware of the power and importance of how language is wielded as a state weapon to stigmatise subversives, and isolate the terrorist in crushingly hermetic cells.

McPhee blunders into Cadbury's meeting, and is asked to articulate his loathing for the regime. He desperately wishes for Cadbury to place words in his mouth, and later seeks confirming support from Godber, who displays a patho-logical ambition to ascend through a Britain which he characterises as a prison. Godber's acceptance of, and reliance on, social hierarchy, to invest him with a sense of dignity otherwise denied him, makes him the perfect state servant. Significantly, Cadbury's insistence that McPhee describe himself, provides the terms for McPhee's self-overcoming. In the final scene, McPhee cries out 'I! I! I!' (*TGBU*, 59), expressing his ecstasy at his final escape from drowning. His use of this personal pronoun contrasts with Orbison's conscious despair at its removal from public affairs. The last scene expands the resonance of Nadine's earlier question to McPhee, 'Why weren't you born?' (TGBU, 46), to which the bewil-dered McPhee can only reply 'I was born, obviously'; he ultimately emerges from the water gasping and isolated, but *newly* born, without leaders or ideology, and at least potentially free.

Birth on a Hard Shoulder (1977, performed 1980) is a further dramatic analysis of a morally neutered political climate. In *Birth*, another secret society, this time of police chiefs and businessmen, is plotting to overthrow a newly elected Labour government. The election result and his own financial ruin have provoked Finney, a self-employed stockbroker, into personal catastrophe: he kills his family. He subsequently encounters two vagrant squatters, Hilary and Erica. Hilary seeks release by opting out of a system which precludes choice; however, she replaces it with a series of morally weightless postures. Her terms of endurance and abject acceptance cloak a kind of despair, by avoiding engagement with pain. Finney, who sinks into deeper despair, is re-inspired by his desire for Hilary and by a sense of obligation towards their unborn child; although his advances towards, and subsequent impregnation of, Hilary induce in her nothing but further abject acceptance. However, the intensity of his passion inspires Erica, who had hitherto slavishly modelled herself upon Hilary.

Finney attempts, in an absurdly hackneyed way, to develop his own personal cosmology in order to salvage some sense of dignity from the desensitising chaos which surrounds him. He makes contact with the conspirators who are plotting the overthrow of government; he initially feels some political affinity, but is subsequently disgusted at their willingness to ignore the death of Erica. A warehouse blaze, perpetrated by one conspirator, both demolishes an archaic symbol of the English free market tradition and represents his willingness to abandon his workers by relocating overseas. This further disillusionment, coupled with the cover-up of Erica's death, goads Finney into locating blame beyond his fearful demonisation of the Labour government. When he confronts his former co-conspirators, he identifies them as the morally bankrupt preservers of an ossifying and corrupt system through their attempted imposition of a conservative dictatorship.

Birth confronts an audience with dramatic consequences of the remnants of a political system sliding towards entropy under a Labour government which will align itself with capitalist order. Hilary and Erica try to dissociate themselves from this system, which they identify as offering only a pre-programmed and limited set of options, but they can posit no alternative imaginative possibilities. Another posthumous character, the Spectre, proves comically unable to communicate any sense of terms of urgency to Finney, whose stirrings of enquiry into the possible terms of dignity and commitment are ultimately stifled by his incarceration in a mental hospital. There, he is obliged to participate in the nullifying, repetitious act of therapeutic gardening. Thus, English institutional power (self-defensively) begets a sense of entropy in individuals, who sense a lack, but are unable to engage with others, or formulate alternative terms, in order to change the situation. This chaotic cacophony of characters, and their persistent highly idiosyncratic attempts to discover and derive terms of meaning in their world, raises Barker's plays above satirical 'state of the nation' commentary: the audience witness the desperate efforts of these inchoate, imperfectly re-birthed characters, striving to create a (temporary and doomed) coherence. Here (as in later and stylistically different Barker works such as *The Bite of the Night*), bids for political or ideological 'stability' manifest themselves in dangerously deluding and self-limiting forms of oppression which insist on ritual, habit and consumption. The audiences who follow the struggles of McPhee and Finney are invited to imagine beyond, and overcome, their reliance on ideologies of hierarchy; and these dramatic processes avoid the conventional postures of overt political interpretation or simplistic arrival at a cheering 'position'. No character is depicted as having the heroic status of ideological privilege, while any insights are won at dreadful cost in terms of despair or delinquency.

Barker repeatedly dramatises the ability of the state to assimilate and subvert fundamental criticism of itself through the ordering and representation of so-called 'facts', through fetishistic marshallings of information. Indeed, his plays show how political argument is increasingly displaced by terms of privatised realignment and adjustment to the (pre)assembled facts, leaving the fundamental rules of (dis)engagement finite and predetermined. In *The Hang of the Gaol* (1978), an inquiry is established and conducted in the bowels of the recently burned out Middenhurst Gaol. The purpose of this inquiry is to bandage over any sense of outrage at the effects of incarceration, and provide a preferable displacement of energy ('No-one ever died from two hundred pages of HM stationery', *HG*, 12). Both wardens attempt to deposit a turd in the debris - a superstitious, physically abjective attempt at ritualistic placation, in order to 'lay ghosts', to establish serene continuity. This exemplifies a recurrent motif in Barker plays of this period: the living use ritual or séance to establish continuities with the dead and stabilisations of the present; however, disorderly spectres tend to rise, demanding an audience for their mute participation in history.

The gaol is a material, institutionalised manifestation of Warden Cooper's ostensibly benign concern, the foundations of which are grounded in a patronising loathing of its population. Cooper wishes to bedazzle the inmates with the humanist principles exemplified by the refined pleasures of the canon of English Literature, barely concealing his contempt for the 'human animal' (*HG,* 72). However, the enquiry exposes Cooper's act of arson, and the despair on which his twisted humanist principles rest. The inmate Turk, who has hidden beneath a guise of inarticulacy, strategically unleashes his contempt for Cooper: 'Tell 'em in Whitehall there is no reconciling E.M. Forster with a kicking in the testicles' (*HG*, 66).

Turk claims responsibility for the blaze, hoping that his act will inspire further displays of disobedience, but his threat is promptly defused: the inquiry will smother Turk's gesture of defiance beneath its paperwork. The Labour Home Secretary, Stagg, shamelessly revels in his pleasure in wielding power for its own sake; he jettisons principles in the service of political expediency, and requires complicity in the production of a report that covers up the truth of the fire. Turk condemns as 'political things' those who inanely marshal the facts and repackage information, willingly subjugated into serving oppression. However, Stagg embodies and preserves Labour's political collusions and absorptions, in support of a decayed, collapsing system. The characters' brief ecstasies of personal rebellion are neutralised and concealed by Stagg's institutional compromises; they will be bureaucratically 'managed' into oblivion.

In *The Loud Boy's Life* (1980), the politician Fricker falls victim to the very values of restraint and maintenance of the status quo that he has elevated to mystical status. Significantly, Fricker uses an ornate and wilfully anachronistic language of classical allusion (built on torturous, elliptical imagery), yoked to a rhetorical deployment of puns and false modesty, to cloak his reactionary politics with donnish respectability. When he realises that the selection panel have failed to nominate him as Prime Minister, he tips himself into linguistic self-parody at an asylum's summer fete. His subsequent interring in St Paul's Cathedral - the final resting place of national heroes - is an act of absorption into a Westminster system he was once asked to destroy. Senior Tories orchestrate an act of cross-party consensus to celebrate Fricker's commitment to Parliament. This ritual of fragile unity is disrupted by the fervour of the schoolboy Natley, who embarrassingly eulogises Fricker by reading a self-composed poetic valediction to his hero, and then physically consumes Fricker's spilt ashes in a bodily enacted personal testament. The sham political unity of the wider event is designed to bury Fricker, not praise him; it represents the (more figuratively digestive) interring of an embarrassing demagogue whose personal sense of destiny is at odds with the outward facing consensus.

The Loud Boy's Life examines the absurd conservatism of the extreme patrician Right. *A Passion in Six Days* (1983) dramatises ways in which the institutionalised Left requires submission to received orthodoxies, and shows politics collapsing into managerialist gesture at an annual Labour Party Conference. Lord Isted, a ninety-year-old disarmament campaigner, makes an inspired plea for profound change, in his last conference speech; sidestepping debate, Isted relies on eloquent assertion, which would replace ideology with 'magic'. Leader Toynbee's calculated refusal to support Isted's resolution is a reflection of his growing authoritarianism; moreover, his opening address is, by comparison, devitalised and visionless. The language forces an entropic mood of suspension upon the conference. Its lack of vitality presages the political rise of his ambitious successor, Glint, who will suspend debate and expel the activists.

One such activist, Annie, proposes a resolution condemning the role of the property relationship between men and women in the institution of marriage. Her intention to follow through the new politics involves her rejection of her husband as sole sexual partner; however, her version of 'political correctness' is challenged by the exclusivity of the desire that her husband, Axt, feels for his wife. Annie nevertheless persistently attempts to shift the focus of Axt's longing from the subjective to the global/historical political context; this dramatises what Barker identifies as the 'Curse of Debate' (*PSD*, 3), where instinct is exhumed and dissected in the name of transparency and enlightenment: the exposure of private feeling to public scrutiny is crucial to its appropriation. Annie believes that desire can cross political boundaries at no personal cost. However, after her sexual rejection by Glint, she finds it is Axt who has been transformed by his (non-sexual) contact with: 'a woman. And she's stained me. And altered me. And I haven't touched her yet. And may not' (*PSD*, 51). Annie can only respond on the level of public debate: 'If it can't go into a resolution, it's not worth saying' (*PSD*, 51). The final image is of a Labour Party committed to arresting decline at the expense of a personal and politically transformative project; the delegates have fractured into individual visions of power, passion and despair, choosing either to unite around a sham social democratic unity, or to pursue new avenues to freedom. *A Passion in Six Days* thus develops a theme in Barker's drama: how the unpredictability of passion questions the divide between feeling and action, upon which political assimilation often depends.

In *The Love of a Good Man* (1978), one particular body acts as the focus for the national trauma of the First World War. On the battlefield of Passchendale, various characters seek, in various ways, to claim a soldier's body: his bereaved family seeks it as a personal totem, the royalist apologist would make it a national icon, and the capitalist entrepreneur would use it as an expedient talisman to further his own personal desire for intimacy or reward. The catastrophic setting promises the slackening of class restraints and traditional English boundaries of propitious behaviour and ingrained power relations. The bereaved mother, Mrs Toynbee, invokes the subjective promptings of her womb as a conservatively authoritative barometer of sincerity and certainty. Her daughter Lalage contrastingly wishes to change and improve the body's physical and spiritual circumstances in the brave new world she believes will rise from recent catastrophe. Hacker, undertaker and small-time cemetery contractor, becomes a broker of dead flesh, recovering a suitable facsimile of Mrs Toynbee's dead son, in return hoping for the promised access to her live body, which she offers as an incentive.

Thus Barker places the body both literally and symbolically at the centre of the play: it is alienated, used as an icon, and invested with mystic status in order to preserve hegemony in existing power relations. It can be commercially exploited (by Hacker), invoked to exert symbolical power (by the Prince of Wales), or treated as an object to be subjected to the imperatives of social engineering (by Lalage). The battlefield itself is eroticised by Mrs Toynbee who senses 'No two women have ever been surrounded by so much male flesh' (*OP3*, 269); the Bishop later conceives of it in terms of its orchestrated containment of pain, 'an Atlantic of stilled agony' (*OP3*, 316). Bride sentimentalises the setting as a monument or cathedral to the fallen; Hacker more prosaically treats it as a commercial opportunity for cost-effective sanitised disposal, dignified by appeal to the patriotic concepts of duty and of soil bought with English dead, but actually demonstrating the erosion of any ideals of physical sanctity: his desperation drives him to provide a German body to satisfy Mrs Toynbee's quest for her son's remains. However, Hacker proves ultimately unsuccessful and realises that the promise, even of this situation, will prove hollow: he will ultimately be redesignated Mrs Toynbee's social inferior. *The Love of a Good Man* is thus a notable early example of Barker placing characters in a landscape wracked by catastrophe, and tracing their tenuous attempts to impose order onto the chaos created by history and their own emotions.

The creative accommodations necessary to survival are explored in *Victory: Choices in Reaction* (1983), which shares with the preceding play the literal exhumation and repossession of the body as a central metaphor, for the retrenchments of order after the chaos of political and personal upheaval. The defeat of the radical Parliamentarian regime culminates in the disinterment and public humiliation of the body of a regicide, whose wife is expected to skulk in the shadows to avoid retribution. However, Susan Bradshaw refuses to behave as a figure of dignified defeat; her journey to recover her husband's 'bits' is both the performance of the reclamation of integrity and the demolition of a failed politics. She sheds received notions of dignity, which legitimise others' appetites for martyrdom, such as that demonstrated by Scrope, in accordance with his status as acolyte/secretary to Bradshaw's husband. Indeed, Bradshaw inflicts further pain on Scrope; when confronted with the spectacle of his mutilation, she witheringly baits his sense of misplaced intransigence and the sublimated erotic desire which he has invested in his hopeless gesture of accordance in victimisation.

Bradshaw's ability to reformulate her own set of personal imperatives contrasts with the despairing satire uttered by King Charles, wryly lamenting his loss of appeal to divine right to rule, and his replacement by a society of financially regulated conspicuous consumption. The newly ascendant bourgeoisie is represented by the technocrat, Hambro, a reconstructed republican who is now 'prime mover' in bringing back the monarch from exile: significantly, the Bank of England's currency bears Charles's name but Hambro's signature. Hambro's murder by Ball, who demands the restoration of absolute monarchy, is futile because of the unalterable shift of capital from the monarch to the state. A new Governor of the bank will be installed.

Bradshaw and (the now physically broken) Ball affect a union; she finally returns to her daughter Cropper with her husband's 'bits' and Ball's child. However, Cropper refuses to acknowledge the 'scrag' contents of Bradshaw's bag as her father. The play characteristically provides tentative opportunities for unity, which are then denied, compelling the audience to share the nausea produced by the contradiction of these 'correct' impulses. Accordingly, the traditional image of the home as haven and site of reconciliation conceals Cropper, resisting her mother's efforts to keep her 'bovine, religious and clean' (*OP1*, 19) by translating her father's supposedly defunct work from Latin into English. *Victory* develops Barker's avoidance of easy recourse to contemporary analogues, and his confounding of notions of characters as repositories for facile sympathy or ideological recognition.

The Power of the Dog (1984) moves outwards to another European battlefield, in Poland, to depict the failure of English language as control. Churchill meets Stalin to create the new map of Europe. Stalin appreciates the vertiginous enormity of the catastrophe which has befallen the continent, while Churchill clings drunkenly to the colonial mythologies perpetuated by his class, his language haunted by ponderous allusion. Stalin's faith in materialism enables him to orchestrate events, though he senses the moment's fragility, as he swings between senses of paranoia and omnipotence. Churchill meanwhile invests the moment with mythic and divine portents. The meeting breaks down irreparably as Stalin baits his guest and Churchill continues to treat him as a colonial heathen. Language, mediated through interpreters and hedged and adapted by attendant diplomats, proves to be hopelessly relative and the characters' ripostes become lost in a blizzard of approximations. Stalin merely issues a list of his territorial demands and sends the English delegation scuttling through their improvised notes, before the meeting collapses.

The play goes on to show the use of 'official' art and discourse to impose order on events, and its failure to imagine the incredible unforeseen. Matrimova, a film graduate, tries to synthesise personal testimony with objective events in the service of an ideologically correct notion of 'wholefilm'. Sorge, the arid ideologue, advises her that art needs to dispense more than pity, or a narrow 'proliferation of clichés' of warfare. Arkov despairs at this dry reductionism, which buries experience beneath ephemeral ideological totems. He resists Sorge's attempts at political indoctrination, asserting that events have an immutable moral dimension. Tremblayev asserts her passion for Sorge, and how this has altered her radically, but Sorge shelters within the terms of his role of regimental political officer. When Ilona demands the return of the body of her sister Hannela, Sorge does not allow this even to become a subject for conversation. Ilona wishes to negotiate the bureaucratic procedures to secure its release, but Sorge is self-absorbed, rationalising the problem of Ilona's improbable survival with his characteristic faith in the supposedly impeccable ideological instruments of collective values.

A group of soldiers hold a séance, in a parody of the 'witches scene' from *Macbeth*, adding a photograph of Stalin and a party card to the broth, to invoke the party's all-pervasive power. Surprisingly, they summon the spirit of an SS officer named Gloria, who is arrested and charged with Hannela's murder. However, while freely cataloguing her war crimes, Gloria refuses to take responsibility for Hannela's death. Like Richard Bradshaw, Hannela remains a totemic presence, her body providing or overshadowing the context in which others enter the dramatic arena. Like Susan Bradshaw, Ilona has submitted to the embrace of a murderer to survive, acting as the mistress of Heydrich; survival is equated not only with sexual submission but also with the temporary surrender of the self. Sorge's reliance upon his ideology to expunge contradictions is challenged by Hannela's assertion of an ethics based on desire. He berates her corpse, maintaining 'love is not to do with truth if it was there would be none …' (*CP3*, 49). Tremblayev realises Sorge's ruthlessness, suspecting that he drove Hannela to suicide, and intends to denounce him. However, Sorge has been driven by desire to insist that Ilona look beneath her protective blankness, and demand that she re-engage. Ilona struggles against this reactivation but is only partially effective. Sorge is arrested and Ilona is brought before Stalin to photograph him.

Ilona's struggles have exhausted her, leaving her open to further impositions from Stalin, who exerts a personal hegemonic power as embodiment of the absolute values valued by Sorge. Ilona reverts to her previous submissiveness. She struggles to retain her detachment before pleading for Sorge's life and collapsing exhausted into Stalin's arms. The comedian McGroot attempts to synthesise the cruelty of events with a comedy that drifts into impotent satire: he is occupies a precarious and marginalised position as Stalin's court fool, his attempts at humorous allegory collapsing beneath the gravity of Stalin's hegemony. The power of comedy to provide release through laughter is thus devitalised and finally splutters out, marking an end to the impulses and efficacy of farce and satire in Barker's work. While Ilona and Bradshaw's submissiveness exacts a terrible toll that excludes them from easy reconciliation, desire provides neither an escape nor a romantic haven; rather it renders the individual even more painfully vulnerable to the force of history. Ilona takes personal responsibility for Sorge even in the presence of Stalin. Thus, impulses and moments of 'Anti-History' persist even before the monumental face of the state.

'True like fuck': transformation through desire

In *The Castle* (1985), Stucley and his crusaders return from the Holy Land to find that the denizens of their medieval village have expunged the previously pre-eminent feudal values. The language initially used by the characters provides an immediate index to their respective sensibilities. Stucley expresses and amplifies the disappointment of his cherished ideals through escalating verbal arias of self-pity and sardonic humour; his spiralling sense of affront claims a justifiable violence in reaction to his serfs' and his wife's rejection of his control-oriented ideals. In contrast and counterpoint, the Turkish engineer Krak speaks with an outwardly cool restraint as he admires the hill of the demesne, 'an arc of pure limestone' (*OP2*, 12). Stucley's sense of disappointment and shame drives him further, to impose religious codes that reflect and codify his suffering. His rage builds to a tumescent manifestation in his impulse to erect the Castle, an edifice of impingement on all previous forms of social and moral order. Skinner, a witch who can 'see to the very end of things' (*OP2*, 38), apprehends the manifestation of the Castle as a ruthless extirpator of dissent and transformer of all social and unsanctioned personal relations, including her own with Stucley's wife, Ann. Accordingly, Skinner remains rigid and hopelessly resolute in her resistance to the consuming monolithic certainty of the edifice. Ann's abandonment to desire, first by reverting to Stucley and later by seducing Krak, throws these characters, together with Skinner, into identification with the Castle as a paradoxical metaphor for personal longing and concomitant sense of lack. Further, the (literal and imagistic) construction of the Castle as a multifaceted image denies it the controlled resonance of a single unified meaning: different characters identify with the edifice and seek to impose their own structures of meaning upon it. Skinner's ruthless and obsessive desire renders her immobile; Cant, then Ann and Krak, contrastingly find that desire impels them, or makes them succumb, to surprising reversals. Skinner's implacability leads her to a self-identification with part of the monolith – 'I am the Castle also' (*OP2*, 65) – and further allows her body to be canonised, turned into an image of worship, by the villagers.

Skinner's perception of the consequences inherent in events, and their most infinitesimal ramifications, is borne out by her subsequent mortification in the Castle's dungeons. The torturers' breaking through appalling barriers of injury inadvertently lends her an iconic quality of endurance. When they bind the body of her victim to Skinner's own body, they make a further mistake: her pain is in fact rendered emblematic, general and thus anodyne: the exhausted castle-dwellers abase themselves before her, regarding her as some kind of priestess. She is appalled, however, at her own sense of cruelty and refuses their submission, reverting instead to a sense of moral and political chaos. Thus, Skinner is unable to overcome her rendering of self as icon and so cannot immediately derive new knowledge or possibilities from her ordeals.

Stucley's increasingly desperate bids to co-opt various religious systems ultimately fail, and he resorts to outright physical coercion to maintain order and the ongoing construction of the Castle. The existence of the Fortress, the logical next step in military technology, and his betrayal by Krak, bring Stucley to breakdown as his personal sense of order disintegrates. Krak attempts to maintain personal equilibrium through the relentless exertion of the immutable laws of geometry and his aloofness from any passion. However, his seduction by Ann rekindles his sense of personal loss. The emotional blockages brought about by the slaughter of his family are destabilised by the knowledge that comes from the 'sacramental stillness born of hanging between pain and ecstasy' (*OP2*, 67), and by the realisation that Ann's offer of desire cannot be quantified:

> Where's cunt's geometry? The thing has got no angles! And no measure,
> neither width nor depth, how can you trust what has no measurements?
>
> (*OP2*, 67)

Unlike Ann, Krak realises that the ideal of hermetic retreat offers no haven from the implications of his construction. Ann commits suicide, and Stucley's certainty and sanity collapse. Krak's planting of the seeds of inevitable demolition in the heart of the Castle's design partly validates his declaration to Skinner that 'Demolition needs a drawing too' (*OP2*, 77). Less prosaically, Krak thus also hints at the potential germination of the re-creative impulses, and the imaginative strategies required to manifest them.

The body's role in Barker's work as the repository of political meaning is here stretched to breaking point, as the characters wrestle with the contradictory impulses of desire which prompt the 'wrong thinking' of acting on passion (as when Ann betrays Stucley for Skinner, Skinner for Stucley, and Stucley for Krak). By remaining attached to her confrontational political stance, which excludes any alternative possibilities, Skinner becomes a monument to her own and others' pain. The institutional abuse and mortification of her body brings her a shocking sensibility, impelled towards revelry in visions of cruelty and revenge, which she nevertheless cannot finally perform. Krak's final suggestion that she should help him engineer the demolition hints at his own exhaustion, as he tries to justify the destruction of the edifice by couching his words in the outlandish mysticism of the 'Wise Womb'.

In *Women Beware Women* (1986), Barker explores the contradictory impulses offered by desire that act as a maddening spur to change, and entry into the political arena. Barker's re-visioning of Middleton's play extends the Jacobean trope of using a story setting of Italianate passion as a provocative interrogation of contemporary English corruption, masquerade and coercion. Again, the body is dramatised as both a tool of oppression and a terrain of discovery. In *The Castle*, the characters are exhausted by the playing out of meanings encapsulated within the body; in *Women Beware Women*, the performance of inherent instability becomes a way of forcing the pace of change. This is succinctly dramatised by the Ward's soliloquy: a speech which overtly dramatises the process of establishing potential meanings and subsequently denying them (a characteristic trope in Barker's work). The Ward's narrative, of an encounter with a woman by a river, initially establishes a lulling sense of sex as a perfectly egoless transaction, bereft of the material greed and debasement of love and desire that characterises his society. His relish and control in sketching the idyllic image of this 'True story' is crucial to the performance of the speech and the final delivery of the punch line: 'True, like fuck it is' (*CP3*, 156). The Ward moves from his previous mockery of 'shallow ardours' to demonstrating the sensibility of a protagonist, capable of undermining conventional expectations, and thus preparing the ground for the play's later shocking performances of violation, prefiguring Sordido's disruption of equilibrium.

Livia expresses her own sense of sexual 'transformation', and instinctively contrasts it with the impotence of 'Repetition of the mundane life'; she extends this contrast to its furthest political reverberations: 'All hate your lives and change the world' (*CP3*, 153). The Cardinal realizes the potentially destabilizing effects of Livia's abandonment of propriety, and how this might 'undo whole cliffs of discipline' (*CP3*, 154), even as he acknowledges the Duke's political efficacy in licensing the purely sensual:

> Let all the population copulate, seduce daughters, bring out the waywardness of wives, whelps and growls from upper storeys all night long, good, satisfaction and quiescence everywhere, but this might lever up whole pavements and turn the fountains red. (*CP3*, 154)

The Cardinal concludes that Livia's personal resurrection/insurrection is also 'politics', much to the Duke's disgust; the Duke conceives of sex as the purely libertine grasping by the populace at satisfactions otherwise politically denied. He follows the political principle of flaunting sexual profligacy and using sex as a commodity, thus annexing ownership of what is most desirable and underpinning the state with 'pageantry and violence' (*CP3*, 162). This is a more confident variation on Charles's essentially populist gesture in *Victory*: 'there is no better stimulus to loyalty than for an apprentice to be molly shagging only minutes after I have left off. He grasps your flesh, he shares your monarchy' (*OP1*, 21). However, unlike the politically redundant Charles, the Duke is still able to maintain a synthesis between the state and capital, incarnated in a single, tangible, body. Indeed, the Duke's flaunted sexual and financial profligacy elicits not disgust but envy and a sense of vicarious participation from the populace. Thus he is able to contain and control the populist impulse, rather than sharing pleasure, and so enforce his potency ('I'll tell you what beauty is, it is what all men collude in desiring, and what all men desire I have, and fuck it, so there, silence your curiosity with that', *CP3*, 163). This is achieved principally by his enshrinement of Bianca as the unviolable and unobtainable symbol of the state, using the misleading promises of access(ibility) afforded by the media, which conjure a tantalising but ultimately unsatisfying sense of possession. The Duke annexes and incorporates marriage in the metaphorical power of state pageantry, which legitimises and licenses rituals of fertility, but actually denies any possibility that the populace might 'grasp the flesh' and share meaningfully in anything.

Livia's release and rebirth through desire impels her to seek knowledge beneath the populist street-bustle condoned by the Duke. Leantio's experience of sex with Livia has become a bolt-hole for his sense of impotent rage at losing Bianca; contrastingly, Livia's compulsive flaunting of her own deeper transformation through desire is a radically externalised performance of conventionally privatised or annexed experience. Her performance of personal alteration attracts the compulsively demonstrative outsider Sordido, who has maintained a sense of integrity undefiled by co-operation. Together they sense that the fetishising of the potency of the state in the body of the beautiful Bianca is reverberative only as long as power is demonstrated to rest upon denial; Livia plots with Sordido the enactment of an alternative, destabilising performance on the occasion of the Royal Wedding.

Bianca remains effective as a construct of the state: indeed, having no deeper intimation of personal autonomy, she swells with pride in the knowledge that she is the ratifier of the regime, fulfilling a dual role as emblem of endlessly deferred satisfaction ('always the thing that isn't', *CP3*, 174) and as the embodiment of the concentration of political power in the act of sex ('all the power of the state will huddle at my little, florid entrance', *CP3*, 174). Sordido's rape effectively undoes this delicate synthesis, dislocating her from the body politic of which she is emblematic. This flaying-off of Bianca's intoxicated self-rapture forces her into a perversely realised sisterhood with Livia, who remains transfixed at the appalling spectacle like a director in rapture at the autonomous lives of her actors.

Thus in *The Castle* and *Women Beware Women* the body is shown as vulnerable to possession by the state, and to annexation as a monument or icon to validate the state's own edifice. The body is endowed with a debilitating ideal of perfection which aims to smother discontent and suspend politics. However, the state's penetration of the individual falters in the face of the (conventionally and restrictively designated) 'wrong-thinking', which leads to impassioned action. Krak and Livia are both prised from their former lives as engineers of the ruling elite's fantasies and demands. Livia demonstrates how desire generates an ecstasy which can provoke profound dissatisfaction with 'mundane life'; she subsequently orchestrates the desires of others, offering them the opportunity to become protagonists. Expectations are established only to be uprooted as the audience witness characters resisting propriety and the enforced definition and equilibrium of others. Barker's characters, however, are not simple educators, as they carry no blueprints for, or maps to, enlightenment. Rather they prepare the ground and enact ruthless and painful searches for knowledge that leave them unsure and destabilised in their performances: as an audience will be, when witnessing them.

6

Access to the body:
the theatre of revelation in Beckett, Foreman and Barker

George Hunka

The speaking body on stage as the irreducible condition of theatrical experience is a trope so general as to verge on the meaningless. It is applicable to any theatrical event from a play by Neil Simon or Alan Ayckbourn to the farthest reaches of the work of the Complicite company, Jan Fabre or Romeo Castellucci. In some theatre of the late twentieth and early twenty-first century, however, it is this condition which itself becomes the focus for dramatic exploration. The speaking body's status as both subject and object, as both autonomous consciousness and as a spiritual artifact for the spectator's meditation and contemplation, becomes the basis for imaginative possibility. Schopenhauer's concept of the individual body as the 'immediate object', the source for all that can know and is known for the subject, acquires new significance with the threat by politics and culture to its autonomy.[1] Especially after the catastrophes of the two world wars, the decline of the nation-state in the years following and the rise of a corporatised post-capitalist ideology, the speaking body becomes a special issue of theatre as an art. As individuals themselves have been subjected to a catastrophic fracture of their autonomy in the community, the theatre has now become a self-conscious locus of individual redefinition.

This theatre represents an alternative post-Second-World-War theatre tradition, a tradition that exists parallel to both the social realism that arose on English-language stages in the wake of that war and the collectively conceived and politically progressive work exemplified in the United States by the Becks, in the United Kingdom by Peter Brook and Joan Littlewood and in continental Europe by Artaud and Grotowski. Beginning with Beckett's mature theatrical theory and practice, this theatre posits a unique triangulation of theatrical experience, from character to character to spectator, as the lyrical depiction of suffering, desire and love become, through the fracture of both social realism and collectivity, a means of poetic compassion. As this tradition develops through the work of the British dramatist Howard Barker and the American dramatist Richard Foreman, contemporaries in the English-language theatre, the body as autonomous perceptual and erotic object, known inwardly by the performer and outwardly by the spectator, is celebrated as the site of imagination. In the wake of the catastrophic twentieth century, the individual is encouraged to seize once again his or her body for him or herself, a body that has become a possession of the state under both totalitarianism and the post-capitalist culture industry.

Neither Foreman nor Barker, in their theoretical writings, explicitly point to Samuel Beckett's plays as a pervasive influence. Foreman's early work was based in an aesthetic borrowed from Gertrude Stein and Bertolt Brecht;[2] discussing the literature and music that informs his own practice, Barker cites Shakespeare and the Elizabethan and Jacobean dramatists, and as more contemporary influences he names the composers Bela Bartok and Karlheinz Stockhausen, as well as the writers Paul Celan, George Oppen and especially Louis-Ferdinand Céline.[3] And indeed, Foreman and Barker's work little resemble Beckett's pre-1962 dramatic writings. But they share with Beckett's post-1962 work a codification of the body as physicalised language, an explicit concern with the physical body in metaphysical space. It is not *Waiting for Godot*, *Krapp's Last Tape* or *Endgame* to which the plays of Foreman and Barker look back, but to *Play*, *Come and Go*, *Not I*, and radio plays such as *Cascando* and *Words and Music* – works that owe both form and content to a specific acknowledgement of theatrical metaphysics.

The body in Beckett's late work is not, at first, presented full-blown but as a series of fragments. The bodies in his early plays, as innovative as these plays were, still existed in a recognisably quotidian world: the two tramps on the road, four figures in a post-apocalyptic landscape. *Happy Days* of 1961 ends with Winnie buried to her neck in sand, only her head visible. *Play* of 1962 begins with these speaking heads, disembodied, rehearsing the memory of an extramarital affair. It is only with *Play* that Beckett's dramatic and theatrical practice seizes upon the innovations of his fiction. The man and two women of *Play* are wrested from any recognisable realistic context and trapped now in urns, in some non-realistic, unspecified locale.

What draws the spectator's attention, more radically than before, is the condition of the body and the speed, inflection and vocabulary of the expressed spoken word. Language, like the body, is a series of disconnections, fragments that remain to be experienced and reassembled by an individual auditor. *Play*'s spotlight, a self-consciously theatrical technology, becomes a fourth character in the performance, the object through which the suffering of the characters is brought forth to consciousness. If the light is a ray of recognition, of consciousness, what then lies within the darkness that surrounds both the figures and the shaft of illumination?

Light sculpts the disembodied heads in *Play*, as well as the hands of *Come and Go*, the mouth of *Not I*. But it also sculpts the negative space of the darkness that surrounds these speaking heads. In his later plays like *Footfalls* and *That Time*, words emerge from this darkness as well, rendering the body on the stage itself an auditor. The space in which these plays transpire is not a crossroads, or an underground bunker, or a searing desert, but the theatre auditorium itself. The second half of the theatrical subject/object equation, the spectator, is now consciously assumed in the theatrical experience. The fourth wall is not so much broken as moved to a place behind the spectator as well.

Bodies in a darkened space, perhaps conceived as an unconscious. But not, it is important to note, as a collective unconscious. As extraordinary as *Waiting for Godot*, *Krapp's Last Tape* and *Endgame* were, the notion of audience as collective was still an element of Beckett's dramaturgical practice, and elements of popular entertainment such as the music hall and the silent film shaped the structure and performance of these plays. As Beckett explored the more profound implications of the speaking body as primary element in theatre, however, these popular cultural accretions were shorn away from his practice, leaving mere presence and physicality as the severely restricted palette for his theatrical explorations.

Language, the means by which Beckett's characters tell their stories in the late plays, is no longer an avenue towards intelligibility. Instead, words become experiential, riven by anxiety and catastrophe, fragmented and unable to contain physical experience. Nonetheless, in the theatre, these words are the only means by which his bodies can define themselves, can present themselves to the spectator. The mouths sputter their words out ceaselessly as if driven by a need to define the bodies that express them.

The written text serves as origination for Beckett's theatrical work, as it does for that of American dramatist Richard Foreman. In both his written plays and his directorial and design work for his Ontological-Hysteric Theatre founded in 1968, Foreman's explorations of the dynamics between two bodies begin in his work with the word. Most instructive in terms of the body in the theatre and the triangulation of desire is Foreman's description – perhaps better described as an epiphany – that led to his theatrical practice:

> I saw a particular static moment from my seat in the Circle in the Square where I watched a rather dreadful production of *The Balcony*. And I remember seeing [Shelley] Winters, on one side of the stage, and Lee Grant on the other, and it was just a moment of stasis, and a moment of a kind of tension between them, and I just wanted to make a whole play that had nothing except that unresolved tension between them. And I wrote out of that. I said that's what I want in the theater, just that moment, and it doesn't develop into any of the other awful stuff, the psychological stuff, the narrative stuff, the adventure stuff that it always develops into. But it's just that.[4]

If Beckett fragments and deconstructs the body in post-war Western culture, Foreman attempts to reconstruct it, particularly within the politically progressive culture that surrounded his downtown New York theatre in 1968. Foreman's practice is presentational rather than representational: his performers often face squarely towards the audience, their dialogue often prerecorded and played through loudspeakers (by which means, Foreman said, he frees his non-professional actors from the rigours of memorising his elliptical dialogue to concentrate on stage placement and movement). His style aims explicitly to triangulate what he refers to as 'tension' between performers and spectators. Within a few years, his stage work was eroticised with the appearance of Kate Manheim, Foreman's second wife, who frequently appeared naked, tension then gaining the additional quality of erotic desire, the dynamic of which was then introduced into the performance space.

As the name of his theatre suggests, Foreman's primary concern is the nature of reality as constructed by a subject, particularly within the context of emotional, physical, and psychological extremity. His project is to introduce, through the bodies onstage and his own gnomic, lyrical language, a fracture between the world inside and the world outside the theatre. Seemingly hermetic, Foreman's work also has a cultural dimension that he does not disclaim:

> My plays are an attempt to suggest through example that you can break open the interpretations of life that simplify and suppress the infinite range of inner human energies. … The strategies I use are meant to release the impulse from the straitjacket tailored for it by our society. Character, empathy, narrative – these are all straitjackets imposed on the impulse so it can be dressed up in a fashion that is familiar, comforting, and reassuring for the spectator. But I want a theater that frustrates our habitual way of seeing, and by so doing, frees the impulse from the objects in our culture to which it is invariably linked. … It's impulse that's primary, not the object we've been trained to fix it upon. It is the impulse that is your deep truth, not the object that seems to call it forth. The impulse is the vibrating, lively thing that you really are. And that is what I want to return to: the very thing you really are.[5]

If Beckett theorises the body as a site of expressed suffering, Foreman restores to the experiencing body a creative and imaginative function. The body-as-object, as a physical thing to be contemplated in Beckett's work, reacquires a consciousness that reconstructs and, more important, can act upon the world that surrounds it. A case in point is Foreman's 2003 play *Panic! (How to Be Happy!)*, in which four characters, two men and two women, find themselves in a forbidding natural landscape as they attempt to scale a mountain.[6] Three of the characters hopelessly hurl themselves against the given landscape with little success; only one, a woman given to physical stillness, is granted any sort of peace, a peace generated not from understanding but from an ability to reconceive her surroundings. Her body is just as real, just as challenging an object, as the given mountain. We can take the mountain as a metaphor for the theatrical work itself (and why not, given the perspectival freedom that Foreman seeks to encourage in his audiences?). The ordeal of the Beckettian body leads to the imaginative freedom of Foreman's female bodies:

The artistic experience *must* be an ordeal to be undergone. The rhythms *must* be in a certain way difficult and uncongenial. Uncongenial elements are then redeemed by a clarity in the moment-to-moment, smallest unit of progression. … But CLARITY is so difficult in the smallest steps from one moment to the next, because on the miniscule level, clarity is muddled either by the 'logic' or progression (which is really a form of sleepwalking) or by the predictability of the opposite choice – the surreal-absurdist choice of the arbitrary & accidental & haphazard step.

Of course

ORDEAL

is the only experience that remains. And clarity is the mode in which the ordeal becomes ecstatic.[7]

This experience of ordeal is shared by the character with an individual auditor or spectator, a specifically theatrical experience that confronts the performing body with the perceiving body, the object with the subject. It is necessarily a challenge. In Foreman's theatre, the challenge is presented by the performer exhibiting his or her body as a site of imaginative speculation, inviting the audience to share in that imaginative journey, not knowing its outcome. Foreman writes:

Only one theatrical problem exists now: How to create a stage performance in which the spectator experiences the danger of art not as involvement or risk or excitement, not as something that reaches out to vulnerable areas of his person,

but rather

the danger as a possible decision he (spectator) may make upon the occasion of confronting the work of art. The work of art as a contest between object (or process) and viewer.[8]

The performer's body, as well as the spectator's, remains inviolate – the work of art does not 'reach out to vulnerable areas of [the] person', but invites speculation that the process of perceiving the work of art itself originates.

Foreman's theatrical project restores to Beckett's bodies under siege the individual's ability imaginatively to remake the world and the culture that has led to this siege, and simultaneously redefines comic possibilities of theatrical form. In his three mid-career plays that inaugurated his Theatre of Catastrophe, *Victory*, *The Castle* and *The Europeans*, Howard Barker explores the same imaginative remaking of the body in the world, this time however restoring to it a tragic consciousness, perhaps more Europeanised, it could be said, than Foreman's brighter, more optimistic American perspective. Indeed, these three plays arguably form a tragic trilogy of the European body, specifically the female body (and it must be noted that of the three dramatists of whom I speak today, the female body is far more central to their work than the male: females are protagonists in most of Beckett's work for solo performers and Foreman's character Rhoda led the casts of nearly all of his early and mid-career work). At the same time, Barker's characters find in confronting and performing their suffering a path to reconstitution and freedom.

In *Victory*, the first of these three plays, the reconstruction of the human body is the explicit subject matter of the play. Bradshaw roams Restoration England in an attempt to collect the body parts of her late husband, a Republican who is arrested, tortured, and finally decapitated by the King's soldiers in the final days before the Restoration. For Scrope, her husband's assistant, this journey is a mere act of mourning for a death, but for Bradshaw herself it is this and more: the reconstruction of her husband's dead body leads to a reconstruction of her own living identity. Indeed, by the end of the play, she has the justified audacity to physically lash out at Milton, an exemplar of the Republican ideology.

The risks are greater in *The Castle*. In the aftermath of a war, male soldiers return home to find that women have created a matriarchy based in compassion and collectivity, a situation that Stucley responds to with the construction of an impossible fortification against the natural world itself. The architect Krak is associated by Barker with an expertise in rectilinear engineering and defense. Rationality and hierarchy are specifically male interests in this play. Krak's rectilinear imagination is threatened when he falls in love with Ann, Stucley's wife, whose very body has introduced chaos into his own expertise. 'Where's cunt's geometry?' he exclaims; 'The thing has got no angles! And no measure, neither width nor depth, how can you trust what has no measurements?' (*OP2*, 67). Nonetheless he has become obsessed, and the obsession is a threat to the continued stability and construction of the castle. As David Ian Rabey notes in his discussion of the play:

> Krak is engulfed in new drawings, shunning calculation of angles, bending himself to pursue new form: 'Drawn cunt ... In 27 versions'. Even Stucley is swayed momentarily from his course: 'The representation of that thing is not encouraged by the church. ... It's wrong, surely, that ... I have never looked at one before'. This recalls the ... authoritarian tendency to separate, designate something a polar opposite and then to proceed in denial of confronting its existence, inevitably [producing] the counter-pressure of upheaval, making war necessary.[9]

Of the women in the play, the witch Skinner bears the suffering of genital mutilation and torture, finally condemned to have the rotting corpse of Holiday, whom she has killed, tied to her own body for the rest of her natural life. In this grotesque bonding of dead body to mutilated body, however, 'Skinner finds a strength and freedom', Rabey observes; placed 'outside the community and normal boundaries of human experience, she is free of desire for Ann, recognises her vanity and rediscovers an autonomy, if only to accept punishment and remain where she pleases, claiming, "I belong here. I am the castle also"'.[10]

It is simplistic to say that Barker's women 'embrace' bodily suffering, despite this explicit embrace of death and life in Skinner's punishment. Instead, as for Beckett's and Foreman's women, this suffering – often associated with the marginal status of women in a paternalistic and authoritarian society, whether it's the seventeenth or the twentieth century – offers an avenue to imaginative autonomy and freedom. Skinner finds it in a newly acquired wit and individuality. What makes this treatment tragic, however, is that there is ultimately no sure redemption in freedom or autonomy. Skinner's condition is a condition of recognition, not reconciliation. Beckett's heroines may be left to their status as objects trapped within memory or trauma, Foreman's find themselves somehow redeemed and encouraged. Neither is the case with Barker's speaking bodies.

Even the possibility of love as experienced by Katrin in *The Europeans* is not necessarily redemptive – though love provides new possibilities and new imaginative worlds, it does not for that reason redeem tragic experience. In large part this lies at the heart of Barker's conception of tragedy. Katrin is the most theatrical of the female protagonists in these three plays, self-consciously exhibiting herself in childbirth in the public square, an exhibition which attracts Starhemberg, her future lover, to her. Read, again, as a metaphor for the theatrical experience itself, the co-optation of Katrin's exhibition by Leopold when he names the child (who is a product of Katrin's rape by the Turks) Concilia, a co-optation of the imaginative offering Katrin makes to her audience. Her child can become a property of the state if she herself cannot. It is her own suffering physical body to which Katrin ultimately lays claim even in the trauma of the abandonment of the child at the end of the play. This suffering, and the new imaginative freedom it has engendered, is beyond Leopold's and the culture's reach. In her suffering is no reconciliation or redemption, but there is in it a freedom from the authoritarian state, and finally a freedom to love.

This alternative theatrical tradition reunites the two halves of the Cartesian human being, joining body to spirit once again. And it was from a rejection of this Cartesian thought that Beckett's work most notoriously sprang. In one of his final plays, Beckett took on the theatre itself – not merely as metaphor but as explicit subject matter. A theatre director and his assistant arrange the body of an aged, pale, voiceless man for public exhibition. The director and his assistant are busy, crude, and self-important; the director is in a hurry for he has a meeting to attend (what's more, a government meeting: 'Step on it, I have a caucus', he exclaims).[11] But the body around which they scurry remains, at centre stage, raising its head only at the very end to stare the applauding audience in the face. The applause stops; the man keeps staring, though he remains silent. Barker and Foreman's project is to re-equip this suffering body with a voice and movement, to start out from this individual human body without which there can be no theatre whatsoever. Beckett's play *Catastrophe* came at the close of his career, though it comes as an opening to a new theatre for the next century.

Notes

1 I cite Schopenhauer here with quite deliberate intent. The three dramatists under consideration in this paper are frequently discussed in connection with contemporary continental philosophies such as those of Adorno, Lacan, Bataille and Badiou, but it seems to me that their work clearly emerges not from the Hegelian strain of post-Cartesian and especially post-Kantian thought, but from the alternative strain that leads from Schopenhauer to Nietzsche (despite Adorno's dismissive comments on Schopenhauer). Most contemporary continental philosophy, such as Zizek's, emerges from a closer emphasis on the Hegelian rather than the Schopenhauerian stream of influence. In the avoidance of a discussion of Schopenhauer's metaphysics, these critics it seems to me offer an incomplete – and occasionally blinkered and narrow – consideration of the European aesthetic tradition that lies beneath these plays. (I also urge that, apart from Beckett, Foreman and Barker may or may not agree with this assessment of a Schopenhauerian dimension in their work; I'm unaware of any specific reference to this philosopher in their theoretical writings.)

2 Richard Foreman, *Plays and Manifestos* (New York: NYU Press, 1976). See especially editor Kate Davy's introduction.

3 Interview with Howard Barker, *Private Passions*, BBC Radio 3, 11 June 2006.

4 Richard Foreman, 'Interview with Ken Jordan' (1990), p. 6. Accessed 20 June 2009 at www.ontological.com/RF/rfinterviews/ForemanJordan1990.doc.

5 Richard Foreman, *Unbalancing Acts: Foundations for a Theater* (New York: Pantheon Books, 1992), p. 4.

6 Richard Foreman, *Panic! (How to Be Happy!)*. In *Bad Boy Nietzsche! And Other Plays* (New York: Theatre Communications Group, 2005).

7 Richard Foreman, *Plays and Manifestos* (New York: New York University Press, 1976), p. 74.

8 Foreman, *ibid.*, p. 70.

9 D.I. Rabey, *Howard Barker: Politics and Desire An Expository Study of his Drama and Poetry*, second edition (London: Macmillan [1989] 2009), p. 167.

10 Rabey, *ibid.*, pp. 166–7.

11 Samuel Beckett, *The Complete Dramatic Works* (London: Faber & Faber, 1986), p. 458.

7

'Not nude but naked': nakedness and nudity in Barker's drama

Eléonore Obis

The theatre is, etymologically, what makes us see; more precisely, the theatre exposes what is usually hidden. In Peter Brook's words, the theatre makes visible the invisible.[1] In this sense, the representation of the naked body is highly theatrical: the stage can reveal the body without clothes in public, although society, conventions and morals forbid it in 'real life'. The naked body is a *leitmotiv* in Barker's plays. It is a crucial moment of the theatrical experience for the playwright: 'The anxiety created by nakedness is intensely theatrical in the ways in which it arises both sides of the curtain: tension on the stage is so swiftly transmitted by an empathy that can't be found in, say, film. The self-consciousness of the naked actor is electrifying, and the spectacle of her nakedness wounds us in some way, even where it is erotic in intention, and perhaps effect'.[2]

In his plays and essays, the words 'nude' and 'nudity' are hardly ever used, while 'naked' and 'nakedness' are recurrent. This could be surprising considering the influence of painting and visual arts in Barker's works: while 'naked' and 'nude' both refer to the unclothed body, the word 'nude' refers more specifically to the world of art, and is more generally used for an artistic representation of a human figure (usually female and especially in sculpture and painting). Barker gives us a number of clues to understand this choice in his works and essays, but when it comes to representation, a tension arises between nakedness, the body unclothed, and nudity, the body clothed in art. First, I will develop the protean meanings of 'nakedness' for Barker so as to address, in a second part, the representation of the naked body in some productions. The tension between nakedness and nudity echoes an ancient debate in art history, which I will briefly develop in this second point.

Nakedness in Barker's drama

'Naked' comes from the archaic verb, 'to nake', which means 'to strip'.[3] This active, verbal meaning of the term can be opposed to the more stable meaning of 'nude', which is both adjective and noun referring to the nude in art, the unclothed body stabilised in a way, or even controlled through art. Hence Barker's choice of the word 'nakedness', privileged over 'nudity', can be defined as a sort of iconoclastic gesture that can be applied to four different fields: characters, actors, the audience and finally language.

Characters

In Barker's work, the characters are thrown into catastrophic situations. These extreme situations push them to the limit, which allows them to explore their identities and their capacities. One of these situations is when the body is naked: the body can exist, be present through the gaze of others, and be released from the moral and political powers that suffocate the individual. In an interview, Barker claimed that 'The body is a symbol of liberty, of disorder. Free sexuality, the liberty of desire is a threat to political power, to the order of the state. The human body is the object of all political power. It is the control of each body that is the object of the state'.[4] Echoing here the theories of Michel Foucault,[5] Barker places the body at the centre of his aesthetics as a disruptive element of all pre-established order. Being naked is a 'revolutionary' act, as Queen Caroline illustrates during her trial at the end of *The Gaoler's Ache* (1998). Loosely based on the life of Queen Marie-Antoinette during the French Revolution, the play describes the incestuous relationship between Queen Caroline and her son who are in jail during the French Revolution. At the end, when the queen has to go before the court, she shows her breasts as an act of defiance. She then says: 'To be naked is to reveal which was yours. And these breasts were never mine for the simple reason that I don't exist' (*CP4*, 242). Through nakedness, the character can find herself again through her own body and her desires as a woman instead of as queen. Caroline no longer exists as a queen because of the 'ordering' forces associated with History and the Revolution – but also, moreover, because of her history and revolution against order, as an individual who privileges her private life and desires.

Nakedness is also a part of the characters' quest for knowledge. Whether the characters are trying to undress another or unclothing themselves, the same message can be derived from the gesture: to unclothe is to look for some revelation about either the self or the other. In *The Twelfth Battle of Isonzo* (2000), the nakedness of Tenna is the main thread in a battle where two characters try to assess each other's powers through a ritual of seduction. Nakedness is an ordeal for both: for Tenna, as Isonzo stresses, 'Nakedness / It's not just no clothes is it ... It's pain / it's fear / it's horror' (*CP5*, 266). The ordeal also affects Isonzo, who is 'stretching the pleasures of anticipation to their breaking point' (*CP5*, 270). One cannot help but think this undressing is metaphorical. Indeed, although it is ambiguous whether Isonzo is blind or not – for he says: 'I'm not blind/ I merely shut my eyes' (*CP5*, 269) – to undress leads to the real encounter with the other, or at least makes this encounter possible, because Isonzo and Tenna may perceive beyond outward appearances, even beyond the surface of the skin, thanks to their heightened senses:[6] 'Is it not the virtue of our sightlessness that we make no distinction any more between the surface and the depths' (*CP5*, 242).

The desire to penetrate, to look inside the other's body is taken to the limit in *He Stumbled*. At the end, Doja, a famous anatomist, cuts himself open for his lover Turner. Turner uses her nakedness to manipulate Doja until he has to die by dissecting himself. Doja seems to have an inkling of this when he sees Turner naked, for he says: 'And nakedness … far from being … a testament to truth is … further – […] manipulation' (*OP3*, 223). In this particular play, nakedness is not enough for lovers, because it reveals nothing; rather it excites the desire to look for what lies underneath the flesh. Barker has suggested that 'the act of exposure enervates itself and therefore demands the discovery of another area of exposure: in the end, this destroys life, I think it's self-destructive'.[7] From this perspective, nakedness often reveals itself as a dead end to the quest of knowledge in his work.

When the naked body appears, it becomes the driving force of the *agon*, a main dynamic in the underlying conflict that defines the relationship between characters and presides over the way they communicate: nakedness implies both the vulnerability of the naked character as well as its power on others. Characters hesitate between modesty and shamelessness. In *The Bite of the Night*, Gay puts it this way: 'If I am naked and you are not, what then? One of us has the advantage but who?' (*CP4*, 97). While the word 'naked' often means 'vulnerable' or 'defenceless' in Barker's plays, it can also turn into an instrument of power, as in *Gertrude – The Cry*, scene 19. When Gertrude and Claudius poison Hamlet, Gertrude lets her dressing gown fall in '*a gesture of self-assertion*'; while naked, she orders her son to drink the poison. Hamlet cannot but obey, repeating: 'So many things I do not understand' (*OP2*, 158). The nakedness of Gertrude, symbolising her passion and desire for Claudius, belongs to the irrational for Hamlet. He cannot understand this nakedness but it imposes itself on him and makes him die.

Actors

In *A Style and its Origins*, Barker's alter ego Eduardo Houth stresses that 'Barker thought seriously about nakedness in theatre and used it cautiously, with discretion and never to humiliate' (*ASIO*, 38); on Victoria Wicks playing Gertrude, for instance: 'the demands he made on her lay as much in what he caused her to say as in the actions she so skilfully demonstrated, words which, spoken in nakedness, might lacerate an actress' (*ASIO*, 67). The sense of danger in acting naked is part of the demands made on the actors of The Wrestling School, along with the physicality of the acting. David Ian Rabey notes how the characters can frequently be 'explicit body performers', dramatically fictional but at least to some degree authentically theatrically manifested by the courage of the performer, as in efforts of will involving speech, action and physical disclosure (such as nakedness) which throw notions and criteria of authenticity into play'.[8] Indeed, while nakedness is a sign of both vulnerability and power for the characters, it is also a disruptive sign in the acting since it blurs the frontier between fiction and reality, between the stage and the real world.

When the naked body of the actor is exposed, it reveals what makes the theatrical experience so essentially different from any other: the body of the actor is present, and as Roland Barthes reminds us, the spectator could try to touch it if he/she dared. It is what he calls '*la vénusté*',[9] the fact that the theatre presents us with a body that is both the body of the actor and that of the character he plays.[10] It is this ambiguity, this instability of the body as sign that allows for the creation of anxiety: 'in theatre the living body has a hazardous potential unavailable to the makers of film, and nakedness is its crisis point' (*ASIO*, 108). Nakedness is therefore the epitome of the catastrophic state of the body since it disturbs the relations between the characters and the relations between the actors and the audience.

The audience

The naked body can still shock, and disturbs the audience. In our Western societies, the influence of biblical taboos concerning nakedness is still valid. The shame of Adam and Eve when they discover their nakedness in the book of Genesis, or the taboos listed in Leviticus still have an impact on the structure of society nowadays. Leviticus emphasises: 'None of you shall approach to any that is near of kin to him, to uncover their nakedness' (Lev, 18:6).

Barker constantly plays with these taboos, reinterpreting Genesis in *I Saw Myself* or multiplying the dangerous liaisons in the same family (in *Dead Hands, The Fence in its Thousandth Year, Gertrude – The Cry*). In addition, since it is still forbidden to be naked in public, and since the audience has to look at the naked body, the experience is one of anxiety: the spectator has to participate in a voyeuristic game, where his/her own gaze is questioned, while the morality and the legality of the act are suspended in the plays. Nakedness puts into question the oppositions between presentation and representation of the body, between a theatrical experience that is experiential, based primarily on the senses, and one that is mainly intellectual. It partakes of the creation of 'moments of loss' (*AT*, 53) and of an art of theatre that is an art of secrecy; to quote Barker again, 'nakedness is the great secret of the stage, and the stage an art of secrecy' (*ASIO*, 110).

Language

Nakedness can also apply to the way Barker handles language, since it must be stripped of its 'ethical garments', just like the audience. Barker writes that '*the art of theatre* aspires to moral nakedness. It is the antithesis of education, which is clothing, which is a suffocation in *ethical garments*' (*DOAT*, 33). Through this allusion to Nietzsche's *The Gay Science*,[11] Barker suggests the need to find another poetical language, stripped of all stable meaning so as to create anxiety. The repetition of words or sentences in the plays makes for the unclothing of language so as to endow it with a plethora of meanings, making the very notion of meaning itself unstable. For instance, the repetition of the phrase 'bad news' in *The Dying of Today* can be stripped of its ethical garments, in that it is the meaning of the expression, what is behind those words, which is the target of constant speculation for the two characters of the play. 'Bad news' is the subject of the play as well as its object, what it is trying to define.

Barker's aim is also to make his characters speak 'nakedly', to borrow an expression used by Hippolito in *Women Beware Women* (*CP3*, 162): 'Since what cannot be expressed cannot exist dramatically, the attempt to abolish the word becomes an attack on the body itself – a veiled attempt to remove the body from dramatic space' (*AT*, 30). Barker tries to take off the ethical garments of language and to bring the body back to language – through obscenity for instance. The most emblematic example is Barker's use of the word 'cunt'.

Nakedness in representation: a debate in art history

Barker's focus on nakedness in his aesthetics is fascinating because it revives an ancient debate on nakedness and nudity in art history. The main reference on the subject of the nude in art is Kenneth Clark's *The Nude, A Study in Ideal Form*, which dates back to 1956, and where the author makes a clear distinction between the naked and the nude:

> The English language, with its elaborate generosity, distinguishes between the naked and the nude. To be naked is to be deprived of our clothes, and the word implies some of the embarrassment most of us feel in that condition. The word 'nude', on the other hand, carries, in educated usage, no uncomfortable overtone. The vague image it projects into the mind is not of a huddled and defenseless body, but of a balanced, prosperous, and confident body: the body re-formed.[12]

Nakedness implies a sense of anxiety and instability that, of course, suits Barker's purpose much better than the concept of nudity as defined by Clark, which is associated with stability and conventions. Clark's analysis was later revised by John Berger in *Ways of Seeing* (1972): for Berger, 'To be naked is to be oneself. To be nude is to be seen naked by others and yet not recognised for oneself. A naked body has to be seen as an object in order to become a nude. [...]

Nakedness reveals itself. Nudity is placed on display.'[13] Here, an ambiguity arises: for while the characters in theatre tend to reveal themselves through nakedness, as it is associated with a catastrophic situation most of the times, they are also objects placed on display on the stage, hence always potentially nudes according to Berger's definition.

Finally, Lynda Nead reopened the debate with her book *The Female Nude: Art, Obscenity and Sexuality*, published in 1992, where she addresses, more specifically, the question of the representation of the female body:

> To formulate a feminist history of the female nude (in response to Clark for instance) the representation of the female body within the forms and frames of high art is a metaphor for the value and significance of art generally. It symbolises the transformation of base matter of nature into the elevated forms of culture and the spirit. The female nude can thus be understood as a way of containing femininity and female sexuality.[14]

According to Nead, the procedures and conventions of art are one way of controlling the unruly female body and placing it within the securing boundaries of aesthetic discourse. Barker's iconoclastic aesthetics seem, at first, to go against the idea of transforming the female body into a nude, a body controlled through art.

'Not nude but naked'?

Barker's potential awareness of this debate appears very clearly in *Terrible Mouth*. In this opera, Alba has to agree to being raped by a character called the Captain in front of the painter Goya, her lover. While undressing herself for the rape, she states that she will be 'not nude but naked' (*TM*, 12). The sentence conveys a double meaning, in the light of the definitions given by Clark, Berger and Nead: first, she is no longer Goya's model during the rape but a defenceless, exposed woman. Secondly, her body is put into a catastrophic situation that enables her to escape from the control of art and hence to be herself. In order to escape from any sort of control, be it artistic or political, the female character has to go through a rape, which is very extreme, so as to reach a kind of ecstasy, taken literally as to be 'outside oneself'. But one could point out that although she is naked, she is still an object for the Captain. However, it is the experience of such catastrophic moments that Barker advocates so that the subject can escape the rules and constraints imposed on him/her to remain a 'nude'.

One is tempted to say that the quote from *Terrible Mouth*, 'not nude but naked', could be applied to all the scenes where the naked body appears, in accordance with Barker's choice of nakedness over nudity. However, two elements contradict this idea.

First, the treatment of the naked male body is different from that of the naked female body in Barker's plays. The later plays constitute resurgences in dramatisations of male nakedness, in *Ursula, Animals in Paradise* or *I Saw Myself.*[15] This could be understood as another iconoclastic trend in Barker's aesthetics: since nakedness is more often linked to women in our society (in advertisements, on television but more generally in the visual arts), having naked male bodies on the stage could be a new shock tactic to go against the grain of the audience's expectations. But the male body is never as disruptive as the female body in the context of the plays. In *I Saw Myself*, the naked body of Modicum, imprisoned in the closet, is never attacked or in a position to be threatened. It is limited, as his name suggests, and he is not as central to the play as the female heroine Sleev. In the production of *Ursula* that was staged at the Théâtre de l'Odéon in June 2009 (directed by Nathalie Garraud and Olivier Saccomano, for the Paris Barker season), the actor playing Lucas naked was full of confidence and his nakedness was not disruptive at all: there was no sense of shame or danger. In *Animals in Paradise*, the naked body of Practice, the old servant, contrasts with Tenna's. His nakedness is a symbol of decline and only disturbing in the contrast. Hence, these naked males are not disquieting to the audience, because they are not main characters and their nakedness is not a main step in their own catastrophic situations. In *Gertrude – The Cry, The Fence in its Thousandth Year* or *The Twelfth Battle of Isonzo* on the contrary, female nakedness stresses the charisma and potential of the women as heroines. In Barker's theatre, female nakedness is usually very powerful and it is acted out by physically attractive actresses so that nakedness is at the height of its visual power. Although the female naked body may initially seem to be an object under the gaze of the male spectator, in the terms identified both Berger and Nead in the field of art history (where the representations of female nakedness is usually interpreted in terms of subordination to social and artistic male conventions), Barker often subverts these conventional power relations by making his heroines' nakedness triumphant.

Finally, a second element hinders the 'not nude but naked' strategy on the stage. It is Barker's great sense of pictorial stage composition (and that of the more successful other directors of his work), in which the naked body is stylised, staged with particularly subtle lighting effects and, above all, framed by the stage itself: arguably, all the naked bodies turn into 'nudes' in Clark's sense of the term. This is true for instance of The Wrestling School's production of *I Saw Myself* in 2008 where frames kept recurring in the play: the closet where Modicum stood was a kind of frame, while the tapestry itself was represented by frames on the stage and the architecture of the theatre seemed to frame the characters. In Giogio Barberio Corsetti's production of *Gertrude – The Cry* in the Théâtre de l'Odéon, the naked body of Gertrude was also in a way 'clothed in art': the first scene, where Claudius and Gertrude appear and make love was staged in a kind of shadow, at the back of the stage. When Gertrude is naked in front of Hamlet to poison him, blue and red lights stylised the exposed body of the actress, which was on the far left side of the stage. Of course, this can also be interpreted as a safeguard against a naturalistic representation. The architecture of the theatre, which is that of the Italian theatre, also framed the characters. In the picture frame formed by the proscenium arch, the characters cannot but be nudes, as in a painting.

However, when nakedness is frontal and/or in full light, just like that of Algeria in the final scene of *The Fence*, or that of Tenna in front of Taxis in the French production of *Animals in Paradise* in Rouen in 2005, the white body of the actresses first attracts the voyeuristic gaze of the audience. Nevertheless, nakedness can be achieved because the audience senses the danger for this exposed body on the one hand and on the other, because the naked body is like a screen: the image of the dazzling white naked body remains a mystery, a secret. It exists at the frontier between the naked, the body exposed, and the nude, the body clothed in art, since its stillness and whiteness remind of a sculpture and flesh becomes stone, as Clarissa reveals in *Seven Lears*: 'nakedness can be so cold. Can be so granite' (*OP5*, 115).

Perhaps the tension between nakedness and nudity is a sure sign of Barker's concern with the particular, not to say almost sacred, condition of the actor. The sometimes sculptural quality of the bodies on stage also remind us of the Pygmalion myth, the body at times coming to life, at times becoming statuesque,[16] as Isonzo remarks: 'I know how hard it is / To be adored / To stand unflinching under scrutiny / As statues washed by fountains' (*CP5*, 259).

Barker has remarked how the naked body 'commands silence',[17] just like a work of art. This silence embodies the suspension of meaning lying at the heart of the representation of the naked body, which remains a mystery. The unveiling of the naked body on the stage is the act of revelation itself and does not reveal anything. One could call it an 'immaculate suspension' along with Isonzo (*CP5*, 276). Barker's fascination with the naked body probably lies in this suspension of meaning: 'it is such a mobile surface of concepts, the unclothed body, a surface which, no matter how overwritten, still has the power to be discovered *differently*' (*Theatre of Catastrophe*, 34); and, one could add, whether naked or nude.

Notes

1 P. Brook, *The Empty Space* (London: Penguin, 1990), p. 45.
2 H. Barker, letter to David Ian Rabey, 12 March 2010.
3 A late use of the verb appears in Cyril Tourneur's *The Revenger's Tragedy*, Act V, scene 1, 60: 'Come, be ready; nake your swords ...'. I am grateful to Charles Lamb for finding this quotation.
4 Barker, interview with Gilles Menelgado, 'Challenging Conventions. An Interview with Howard Barker', *Sources* 3 (1997), 157–71 (169).
5 See Michel Foucault's three volumes *The History of Sexuality* (*Introduction*, *The Uses of Pleasure* and *Care of the Self*), translated by Robert Hurley (New York: Vintage Books, 1988–90).
6 For much more on this subject and the meaning of 'nudity' in Levinas's philosophy, see Elisabeth Angel-Perez's article, 'Facing defacement: Barker and Levinas', in K.

Gritzner and D.I. Rabey (eds), *Theatre of Catastrophe: New Essays on Howard Barker* (London: Oberon, 2006), pp. 136–49.

7   Barker, quoted in C. Kiehl, 'Le Corps dans le théâtre de la Catastrophe de Howard Barker' (PhD thesis, Université de Metz, 2006), p. 453.

8   Rabey, in Gritzner and Rabey, *Theatre of Catastrophe*, p. 20.

9   Barthes:'la fonction érotique du théâtre n'est pas accessoire, parce que lui seul, de tous les arts figuratifs (cinéma, peinture), donne les corps, et non leur représentation. Le corps de théâtre est à la fois contingent et essentiel : essentiel, vous ne pouvez le posséder (…) ; contingent, vous le pourriez car il vous suffirait d'être fou un moment (ce qui est en votre pouvoir) pour sauter sur la scène et toucher ce que vous désirez. Le cinéma, au contraire, exclut, par une fatalité de nature, tout passage à l'acte: l'image y est absence *irrémédiable* du corps représenté' in Barthes, *Roland Barthes par Roland Barthes* (Paris: Seuil, 1975), p. 81.

10   *Ibid*.

11   F. Nietzsche, *The Gay Science*, translated by W. Kaufmann (New York: Vintage Books, 1974), Book V, §352:'*With morality the European dresses up.*'

12   K. Clark, *The Nude: A Study in Ideal Form* (Princeton: Princeton University Press, 1972), p. 3.

13   J. Berger, *Ways of Seeing* (London: Penguin, 1972), p. 54.

14   L. Nead, *The Female Nude: Art, Obscenity, and Sexuality* (London, Routledge, 1992), p. 2.

15   Male nakedness occurs in the early Barker plays *That Good Between Us* (1977), *Downchild* (written 1977, staged 1985) and *No End of Blame* (1981) – as well as female nakedness in the first and third of these – as a significantly reversible index of power and vulnerability.

16   I am very grateful to Heiner Zimmermann for this particular insight on the Pygmalion myth in relation to my essay. For further development see his essay, 'Die Frau als Erziehungsobjekt des Mannes: Der Pygmalionmythos und Shakespeares *The Taming of the Shrew*', in D. Schulz and T. Kullmann (eds), *Erziehungsideale in englischsprachigen Literaturen – Heidelberger Symposion zum 70. Geburtstag von Kurt Otten* (Frankfurt am Main, Peter Lang, 1997), 79-98.

17   Barker, in Kiehl, 'Le Corps dans le théâtre de la Catastrophe de Howard Barker', p. 454.

18   Barker, in Gritzner and Rabey, *Theatre of Catastrophe*, p. 34.

8

Places of punishment: surveillance, reason and desire in the plays of Howard Barker

Michael Mangan

We required Michel Foucault to elaborate what most Europeans have always suspected about dark places and speaking: that confession comes easiest in the dark, and that it is vastly more sexually stimulating to tell than to keep silent.

Howard Barker[1]

The relationship between rationalisation and the excesses of political power is evident. And we should not need to wait for bureaucracy or concentration camps to recognize the existence of such relations. But the problem is: what to do with such an evident fact?

Michel Foucault[2]

Introduction: the place of punishment

The idea of a place of punishment seems to have a strange hold on the human imagination altogether – and nowhere more vividly so than in the traditions of the Abrahamic religions. Polytheistic and Eastern cultures, it is true, have their places of posthumous punishment as well: the ancient Greeks had Tartarus, Buddhism has *avici* – and both of these, like the Jewish Gehenna and the Islamic Jahannam, are places where sins committed by the mortal flesh are punished. But in none of these systems of thought is the place of punishment so vivid, or so absolute in its promise of eternal and inescapable punishment, as it is in Christian thought. In its imaginings, its moral systems, in its nightmares and in its corresponding hopes of salvation, the European imagination of the last two thousand years has been drawn again and again to the idea of Hell, to the image of the underworld as the infinite prison/dungeon. We see countless images of this in Western art: the Last Judgement and its aftermath, in which the holy, the righteous and the saved are separated from the profane, the damned, the sinners, and the latter are dragged down to eternal torment, to be hanged, skewered, spitted, roasted, devoured, dismembered, boiled, flayed or flagellated according to their sins, each punishment fitting its corresponding crime – usually one of the seven deadly sins. And each of the traditional seven sins – *superbia* (pride), *avaritia* (avarice), *luxuria* (lechery), *invidia* (envy), *gula* (gluttony), *ira* (anger), *acedia* (sloth or apathy) – is related to an emotional state, and largely to versions of desire. In the iconic representations of Hell, emotions themselves become the source of guilt and damnation, opposed to the rational law that is God. With this kind of hold on the imagination, it is perhaps little wonder that the societal model for punishing crimes begins, at certain points in history, to reflect this cosmic one: the prison, the place of punishment and sometimes of torture, or the analogical 'theatre of punishments'[3] where retribution can be seen to fit the crime according to a poetic logic of symbolic justice.

In the plays of Howard Barker these places of punishment become a way of addressing one of the great themes of Western drama: that of the relationship between emotion, rationality and the law. It is a theme whose iconic images include the many versions of Antigone, standing defiantly before Creon the law-giver, and Shakespeare's Lear, who misunderstands the relationship between emotion and the law to the extent that he demands declarations of affection as part of State ceremony. Lear's world is torn apart when the powers of his own long-suppressed emotions rise up in unexpected sympathy for those 'poor naked wretches … that bide the pelting of this pitiless storm'[4] and whom his own laws have marginalised; and he realises, as a result, that the law is not as absolute as he once believed: 'See how yon justice rails upon yon simple thief. Hark in this ear: change places, and handy-dandy, which is the justice, which is the thief'.[5]

Theatres of punishment

In exploring Barker's contributions to this tradition I shall be using as touch-stones not only the work of Michel Foucault (to which Barker himself alludes in the quotation from *Arguments for a Theatre* which I am using as an epigraph for this essay) but also another key – and contrasting – cultural narrative concerning the prison. To begin, though, with Foucault: it is in his writings on prisons, imprisonment, punishment and surveillance that we see some of his most telling insights into rationalisation (or rationalism) and political power. As Christopher Balme puts it:

> Foucault's theory of 'power' undertakes a fundamental revaluation of the concept itself. In contrast to a Marxist understanding which sees power in pejorative terms as an instrument of repression in the hands of the ruling classes, Foucault argues that power is a productive force regulating all levels of social relations. He makes this argument most clearly in his study *Discipline and Punish: The Birth of the Prison* (1979), where he calls for an end to the negative application of the word 'power'. Power does not just negate, he argues, it also produces and manifests itself more thoroughly, albeit

covertly, in everyday social and cultural practices than in centralized state institutions … Foucault repeatedly drew attention to the fact that power can be studied in the way changing discourses construct our understanding of the body differently – the body is one of the main locations of power in the Foucauldian sense.[6]

In *Discipline and Punish* Foucault elaborates a theory of power, analysing the 'birth of the prison' in terms of three phases: the first it characterises by describing in detail the horrors of a mid-eighteenth-century public execution, in which the power of the State (in fact the monarch) is graphically inscribed on the body of a hapless failed regicide. This is followed by a middle phase, roughly chronologically concordant with the French Revolution and its aftermath – a 'gentle way' which sees the punishment fit the crime in a plethora of minor symbolic theatres of punishment. Finally, taking the cue from Jeremy Bentham's Panopticon, the modern-style prison emerges in the nineteenth century, a system in which control is established through isolation and (apparently) continual surveillance. But, Foucault proposes, this prison is not merely an end in itself: it is part of a larger 'carceral system'[7] – a vast network, involving society as a whole: schools, hospitals, military institutions and factories, all share in this 'panoptic' system of social control. If Marx's dominant image for society is the factory (with owners of means of production exploiting labourers who are the real producers of wealth), Foucault's dominant image is the panoptic prison and its regime of hidden surveillance. It is an image whose aptness and prescience might have startled even Foucault himself. A major study entitled *A Report on the Surveillance Society* suggested that technological advances have made Foucault's metaphor a reality: in 2006 there were something in the region of 4.2 million closed circuit television cameras operating in the United Kingdom – one for every fourteen people.[8] That proportion may well be greater now.

Foucault, of course, has not been alone in seeing the prison as an image for society: Hamlet, after all, recognised that 'Denmark's a prison'.[9] But the richness of Foucault's analysis (even setting aside his prescience in identifying the panoptic prison as a precursor of the technologically-driven surveillance society) has been extraordinarily influential in a number of academic disciplines beyond his own 'history of systems of thought'. Philosophers and sociologists, historians and literary scholars all cite *Discipline and Punish* as a matter of course – while the admirably succinct summary of Foucault's work by Christopher Balme which I quoted above, comes from an introductory book to theatre studies. So ubiquitous, in fact, is the influence of *Discipline and Punish* that it has tended to eclipse a very different image of the prison which was paradigmatic for European and American historians, political scientists, philosophers and cultural critics during the third quarter of the twentieth century. Auschwitz, Dachau, Buchenwald: these are the images of incarceration which haunted the work of a generation of intellectuals. In particular, intellectuals of Jewish descent such as Hannah Arendt, Primo Levi, George Steiner and Elie Wiesel were concerned with the question of how to develop a discourse capable of handling not only the actual horrors perpetuated in these places, but also their implications for our understanding of the human and of human culture. Theodore Adorno's much-quoted phrase, 'To write a poem after Auschwitz is barbaric' in his 'Essay on Cultural Criticism and Society',[10] sums up this sense of rupture. A whole branch of Jewish and Christian theology – known collectively as Holocaust Theology – attempted to come to terms with the implications of the Holocaust for religious belief. Auschwitz (standing metonymically for the Holocaust as a whole) came to be seen as the dark core of the twentieth century and the task of looking into that deep abyss became a prerequisite for understanding modern history and identity.

In the first decade of the twenty-first century, that passionate despair of the Holocaust theologians and philosophers seems oddly distant. The passing of time in general, and the specific events of the history of the last half-century, not the writings of Michel Foucault, are the causes of that; it would be naïve to posit a simple paradigm shift by which one analysis renders another redundant. Yet Foucault's focus on the notion of prison as an iconic social norm stands in sharp contrast to, and may in some way have helped to lessen the impact of, the image of Auschwitz as the hell on earth which George Steiner described:

> The concentration and death camps of the twentieth century, wherever they exist, under whatever regime are *Hell made immanent*. They are the transference of Hell from below the earth to its surface. They are the deliberate enactment of a long, precise imagining.[11]

If I take the liberty of placing Foucault's panoptic prison of rationalism in some kind of binary opposition with the nightmare irrationalism of the concentration camps, it is because there has recently been a sense expressed by an increasing number of scholars that events have now rendered Foucault's model, too, effectively outdated. In *Precarious Life: The Powers of Mourning and Violence* (2006) Judith Butler writes about the 'Indefinite Detention' of Guantanamo Bay:

> On March 21 2002, the Department of Defense, in conjunction with the Department of Justice, issued new guidelines for the military tribunals in which some of the prisoners detained domestically and in Guantanamo Bay would be tried by the US. What has been striking about these detentions from the start, and what continues to be alarming, is that the right to legal counsel and indeed the right to a trial, has not been granted to most of these detainees … In the name of a security alert and a national emergency, the law is effectively suspended in both its national and international forms. And with the suspension of law comes a new exercise of state sovereignty, one that not only takes place outside the law, but through an elaboration of administrative bureaucracies in which officials now not only decide who will be tried, and who will be detained, but also have ultimate say over whether someone may be detained indefinitely or not.[12]

Others have not been slow to take up the implications of this – implications which concern 'the limit and scope of legal jurisdiction itself'.[13] And even when, with the election of Obama, there emerged the political will to undo the effects of the 2002 guidelines, it turned out to be both politically and practically harder than was expected. The real-world effects of all this are yet to be measured. In terms of cultural theory, however, it seems that some of the apparent certainties of the late twentieth century are now less certain. Caleb Smith is not alone when he says:

> We see, especially, how the tremendously influential thesis of Michel Foucault's *Discipline and Punish* – that prisons produce self-governing subjects through isolation and surveillance – loses its explanatory power in the age of Guantánamo. As sovereignty eclipses subjectivity as the key analytic concept, incarceration seems to concern not the 'soul' but war, citizenship, and the boundaries of the body politic. In the war prison, we find none of the techniques of training, labor discipline, or rehabilitation associated with the penitentiary. We confront, instead, detention without subjects: a captivity that strips away rights and mortifies subjectivity.[14]

Thus Foucault's sophisticated and influential discourse stands, not by itself as a monolith, but in dynamic relation to other discourses of the prison. It is with this in mind that I now turn to the way in which Barker has engaged with discourses of the prison.

'A place which licensed no pity': prisons in Howard Barker's Theatre of Catastrophe

Several years ago Barker coined a term for that rhetorical kind of theatre which he himself was in the process of rejecting. He termed it the 'Critical Theatre':

> The Critical Theatre, which for the sake of argument I shall take to be that of Brecht, Shaw and the bulk of our contemporaries, is essentially a theatre of clear objectives. It is predicted on the idea of 'saying'. In the Critical Theatre the play 'says' something to the audience and the elucidation of this 'saying' is the function of the production, the aim of the director and actors alike … [and] it brings with it the demand that the play should 'say' unambiguously.[15]

This unambiguous 'saying' is contrary to Barker's own view of what theatre should be, and contrary to his own dramaturgical and directorial practice. Against the Critical Theatre Barker sets his own vision of what he calls the Theatre of Catastrophe, a theatre which 'willingly divests the dramatist of his divine status as dispenser of truth and harmony',[16] whose 'ecstatic possibility lies in the denial of the possibility of Solution'[17] and whose method is 'the erosion of narrative',[18] with the result that 'the production must become, in essence, a poem, and, like a poem, not reducible to a series of statements in other forms'.[19]

Barker's 'poetic' Theatre of Catastrophe deals compulsively with prisons. David Ian Rabey talks about the way in which 'Barker's landscapes are frequently overshadowed by a "Big House", an edifice of authority';[20] and he uses the term 'Big House' in the sense of manor house or mansions, governor's houses or castles. But in American slang the Big House is the prison, and the gaol is a particular version of the authoritarian edifice which dominates the psychic as well as the scenic landscapes of the plays. We see them in the titles of his plays: *The Hang of the Gaol, A House of Correction, The Gaoler's Ache for the Nearly Dead, Ten Dilemmas: The Incarceration Text*. Sometimes these are metaphorical: one of the plays which saw Barker's breakthrough as a recognisably major dramatist was *The Hang of the Gaol*, in which the prison becomes a metaphor for Britain. Captivity was the theme of Barker's earliest publicly performed play, *One Afternoon on the North Face of the 63rd Level of the Pyramid of Cheops the Great* – a radio drama about the slaves who built the Pyramid. But it is really in the late 1970s that he began to use the image repeatedly, at a time when, as Rabey says, his plays begin to articulate a sense of 'the disjunction between social institutions and the ideals which they ostensibly embody'.[21] Dramaturgically, Barker's prisons are frequently places to escape from – or to be released from – in order to permit a subsequent journey, as happens in plays such as *Fair Slaughter*, *A Wounded Knife* and *Ten Dilemmas: The Incarceration Text*. In *Seven Lears* the gaol becomes a choric character, calling out to Lear, offering him some of the ambiguous wisdom that the Fool offered his Shakespearean predecessor. In plays such as *The Poor Man's Friend* and *The Hang of the Gaol* the prison haunts the action of the play as a whole – as it does in *Brutopia*, Barker's dystopic riposte to the romantically heroic picture of Sir Thomas More which Robert Bolt depicted in *A Man for All Seasons*. In *Brutopia* Barker places a prison for heretics, literally, at the heart of More's apparently idyllic garden. This haven of calm and intellectual contemplation contains within it the place of punishment and torture; and as the play develops, we come to understand that the prison is a necessary component of the garden, that it actually makes the garden possible. It comes as no surprise when, by the end of the play, the heretic imprisoned in the garden-gaol has become More himself.

There are many other Barker plays that could be added to the list. Not only does prison feature repeatedly as an image or setting for the Theatre of Catastrophe, Barker has also written insightfully about theatre in prisons. One of his most moving essays is 'On Watching a Performance by Life Prisoners': this was a performance of one his own plays in Wormwood Scrubs, by a drama group formed in the prison. Barker describes how

> in the performance, they affirmed the drama as freedom … and a necessity … They felt gratitude for the existence of speech and metaphor and made it their own, though it was not the language of the gaol … In a place which licensed no pity, they found it possible to express pity. They guarded this closely, as a privilege. They shielded it from others, who would have derided it, and exposed it only in the room which was called a theatre … It was considered by the authorities that the bulk of the prisoners would object to the play. They would disrupt the production and might

attack the actors. In a prison the active power of morality, its coercive intolerance, is expressed most violently ... The gaol was thus a society as tightly regulated as the outside by relativist morality.[22]

The final sentences show Barker's kinship, on one level at least, with Foucault. I use the term kinship because Barker's relationship to Foucault is an oblique one. We can see this quite clearly if we compare Barker's writing to the way in which, for example, Caryl Churchill adopts and adapts the philosopher in her explicitly Foucauldian play *Softcops*. Churchill enters into a direct relationship with *Discipline and Punish*: she takes a work of philosophy and history, and turns it into a play. When we look at Barker's dramaturgy, however, we need to think of Foucault's work as providing a 'con-text' – a text to be read *alongside* the subject text, rather than as source material or influence.

One Barker play in which this Foucauldian con-text is particularly evident is *The Gaoler's Ache for the Nearly Dead* (1998). Although the world in which the play takes place predates Bentham's designs chronologically, the idea of the panopticon is dominant: much of the action takes place in a cell of some kind – a cell in which people are under constant but intermittent surveillance. The play's governing image is that of the execution of Marie Antoinette – or more precisely the events leading up to her execution; its theme is the way in which the Revolutionary Tribunal mythologised the queen as a debauched figure, in opposition to the Revolution's own 'Virtuous ' nature. In particular, it is concerned with Hébert's notorious and damning charge that Marie Antoinette had committed incest with her own son.[23] For Barker this itself is an instance of the way in which the State uses a supposed dichotomy between reason and desire as a means of political control.

> Those whom the state wishes to destroy must first be vilified. Because revolutions are sexually reactionary, the most efficacious calumny is that of sexual delinquency. Thus Marie Antoinette, last Queen of the French, not sufficiently guilty by virtue of her birth, required to be revealed as a debauchee to ease her progress to the guillotine ... If the Revolution is the apotheosis of a myth, Marie Antoinette, slandered by the revolution, must be the myth of its opposite – depravity against cleanliness, licence against order. In incest – invented, imagined, confessed, the crime of crimes, the ultimate transgression over the collective, hope and horror become inextricably mixed.[24]

Barker's Theatre of Catastrophe is a theatre of extremes and of ambiguities, and one which takes great liberties with history. Thus its setting is not the historical French Revolution, but some sort of imaginative parallel reality to that, and the historical characters are displaced into imaginative correlatives of themselves. Marie Antoinette becomes 'Queen Caroline', the Dauphin becomes 'Little Louis' – and in the process they become simultaneously tragic and grotesque.

The opening stage direction stipulates '*Darkness. A panel opens high in the wall.*

A face appears in the aperture. It surveys. It disappears. The panel shuts with a clap.' This surveying face becomes a repeated motif in the play, and we discover that the surveillance is carried out by Trepasser, the Hébert-like Republican, and his minions. The austere Trepasser is Caroline's chief persecutor; however, he is also sexually obsessed with the Queen, in much the same way as Angelo in Shakespeare's *Measure for Measure* was obsessed with Isabella. The surveillance which he organises and undertakes is both repression and adoration.

> CAROLINE: Do we have to be observed? What is this constant observation? .. Day and night we are observed.
>
> TREPASSER: *(turning to look up, as if surprised)* Observation? Perhaps it is not observation, Caroline, but… Perhaps the thing you experience as observation is not observation at all. Perhaps in actual fact … it's love … The gaze is never without its ambiguities … One cannot overlook the possibility … the very real possibility … The State is infatuated with you, Caroline.[25]

Significantly, Trepasser projects his own infatuation onto the convenient abstraction which is 'the State'. This constant state of surveillance in which the characters in *A Gaoler's Ache* exist both contains and also to some extent produces Caroline as a sexual subject. In *Measure for Measure*, it was Isabella's purity that attracted the corrupt Angelo. In *The Gaoler's Ache*, on the other hand, Caroline, the object of Trepasser's infatuation, is both sexual and – according to any conventional morality – corrupt. Barker responds to the Revolutionary Tribunal's demonising of Marie Antoinette, not by defending her innocence, but by imagining a fictional counterpoint, Caroline, who fulfils all their imaginings and more. In *The Gaoler's Ache* the imaginary incest becomes real – but in the process it also challenges the most intense taboos of Trepasser's morality. Rabey again: 'Caroline discovers in her intimacy with Little Louis a defiant, unbreakable resolve which recalls that of Webster's imprisoned and persecuted Duchess of Malfi.'[26] We are offered Caroline as a tragic heroine – but in order to relate to her on that level, we must also accept the subversiveness of her perverse sexuality. The audience, like Trepasser, is implicated.

Barker may not be engaging – as Churchill is clearly engaging – in a direct dialogue with the text of *Discipline and Punish*, but the Foucauldian resonances are unmistakeable. Barker's dramaturgy, however, creates a world which does not just demonstrate the truths of Foucault's analysis, but which develops them. In the real-life history of Marie Antoinette, the State employed the eroticisation of the body in order to demonise the Queen – to vilify her before destroying her. In Barker's metaphorical history, this logic is turned upside down: the body – specifically, Caroline's body – both disrupts and subverts the totalising power of Trepasser's surveillance. This works as a poignant reminder of Balme's secondary point about the implications of Foucault's analysis which I quoted earlier: 'Foucault repeatedly drew attention to the fact that power can be studied in the way changing discourses construct our understanding of the body differently –

the body is one of the main locations of power in the Foucauldian sense.'[27] Barker's unique dramatic style creates a powerful discourse which enables the implications of this to be played out and explored.

In *The Fence in its Thousandth Year* (2003), this logic is taken still further. In several ways *The Fence* may be seen as a companion piece to *The Gaoler's Ache*. Its primary protagonist is the Duchess Algeria; like Caroline, she is an aristocrat, a powerful and paradoxical woman who is characterised by her compulsive eroticism and the implicit challenge she presents to conventional morality – even the morality of the State of which she is the head. Like Caroline's, too, Algeria's eroticism has an incestuous dimension: her lover is the blind youth Photo, apparently Algeria's nephew but actually her son. The play is written in Barker's characteristically poetic (and now largely unpunctuated) language as a deliberate strategy to create a linguistic environment, a discourse, which resists the demands of dramatic realism. The result is an extraordinary rich and complex text – too complex to do full justice to it here, for it weaves together an extraordinary variety of themes: the personal and the private; intimacy and power; limits and taboos; blindness and perception; freedom and constraint. For the purposes of this essay I want to unpick just one of the strands of that weave: the image of The Fence itself.[28] This operates on the levels both of metaphor and of reality. A steel wire and concrete structure, it is a boundary which, like the Berlin Wall or the security fence in Gaza, and like countless historical frontier walls, serves to delineate 'them' from 'us'. And like the barbed wire of Guantanamo or Auschwitz it stands as a metaphor for the way we define ourselves as human by *de*humanising 'them'. It separates Algeria's duchy from the outside world, enabling the privileged ones within to define themselves (the 'farmers') in opposition to the shadowy figures beyond the wire (the 'thieves'). An intrinsic part of the set design, The Fence itself is visible throughout the play. It dominates the stage, and dominates, too, the thoughts of Algeria and her subjects: they perform serio-comic rituals to celebrate it, and they talk about it incessantly, probing its paradoxical meanings:

> ISTORIA: There is nothing funny in the wire … thank the wire … look in the mirror is your face beautiful and your limbs how straight are they you owe it to the wire.[29]

> PHOTO: The Fence is not beautiful nonetheless it is a condition of beauty you cannot understand this only when you have penetrated The Fence will it be understood but not by you only by your children they will then erect a Fence … It is only The Fence that allows us to contemplate The Fence …[30]

> KIDNEY: I was shaving this morning and I thought is there anything sillier or sadder than a fence with a hole in it its not like a hole in anything else is it … if there is a hole in a fence the entire fence all three hundred miles of it is as if it were abolished[31]

KIDNEY: High is The Fence (*He walks towards it*)
Long is The Fence (*His shoulders heave with laughter. The searchlight swoops and falls on him*)
HOW DEEP IS IT THOUGH[32]

PHOTO: Beautiful is The Fence more beautiful than the castles of our forefathers […] but … this beauty of The Fence a beauty at this moment apparent only to me is possibly an aspect of its redundancy[33]

I have spoken of 'The' Fence – but in fact there are several fences in the play; or rather The Fence metamorphoses, more than once, during the play. At first it is the effective frontier boundary I have already described. However, time passes and Algeria's power wanes, Oedipus-like, with the discovery of her incest; her State degenerates, the boundaries between Inside and Outside become blurred, and The Fence itself becomes, as Photo describes it above, redundant. We see it '*rotted and thick with clinging litter*'[34] and it is eventually replaced onstage with a new 'pristine'[35] fence which drops suddenly into place. The function of this new fence, though, is not to keep the 'Thieves' out, but suddenly to imprison Algeria herself. The theatrical space which the fence defines metamorphoses into a very Foucauldian mental institution: a place of control and a place of punishment.

Algeria (like Queen Caroline) becomes the victim of political enemies who use her scandalous sexuality as a weapon against her, labelling her. Once more Algeria is defined by the boundary, but this time she is the subject of it rather than the beneficiary. Yet even as she recognises her new state she resists being oppressed by it. She is not destroyed by her incarceration:

ALGERIA: I am do look at me I am beyond the reach of all …
BEYOND ALL GRIEVANCE BEGGARY OR THREAT
MADNESS ALSO IS A FENCE
… I am not a duchess, I am the inmate of my own asylum and I think the fence is beautiful beautiful is the fence …[36]

Algeria's claim to be 'beyond the reach' of worldly troubles may resonate with the transcendence which is associated with the heroes of classical tragedy. But *The Fence in its Thousandth Year* is not, ultimately, a tragedy, nor is Algeria a classic tragic heroine. She survives her institutionalisation and the final ambiguous scene sees her free once more, exhausted but alive, watching from a hillside as in the distance workmen build yet another Fence. More to the point, Algeria's resistance is not a matter of transcendence. She is and remains a creature of the body. Like Caroline, the site of resistance to authoritarian structures (even her *own* authoritarian structures) is the body and the mode of resistance is desire. This had been demonstrated in the very first moments of the play, in the stage directions which describe the startling and taboo-breaking tableau with which it begins:

Algeria's nocturnal copulation with three impatient thieves, through the wire of the fence, and her exultant remorselessness when '*fixed in her pose*' by a traversing searchlight.[37] This act of subversive eroticism is performed in defiance even of the laws and customs which uphold her own State and keep it separate from the domain of the Thieves – although we know none of this as yet. This enigmatic open image encapsulates the oppositions on which the play is based: the rational structures of laws, boundaries and frontiers come into immediate juxtaposition with desire, eroticism and emotion. The image is repeated later in the play: when Algeria is in the asylum she is visited by her lover, with whom once more she couples through the wire.

Earlier in this essay I made a distinction between two images of the prison. On the one hand, I suggested, there is Foucault's analysis of the rise of the Benthamite, panoptic prison, with all the implications that contains for a 'surveillance society'. Against this I set the mid-century response to the horrors of the concentration camps, and the more recent responses to Guantanamo and Abu Ghraib. The world of *The Fence* is not the world of the concentration camp, but the shadow of the concentration camp hangs over it, and the post-9/11 fences of both Gaza and Guantanamo are implicated in its landscape. Barker's Theatre of Catastrophe exists in a dialogue with Foucault – but it is also an implicit response to Adorno. The poetry of catastrophe is that poetry which it is possible to make 'after Auschwitz' without being barbaric, because it is a poetry of extremes, in which the inevitable conflicts between reason and emotion are acted out in the bodies of its protagonists.

The image of the woman copulating through the wire of the prison/frontier fence is not a real-world answer to the question of definition which Barker poses here: the play is not proposing a thesis that love (or even sex) will conquer all, for one of the characteristics of his Theatre of Catastrophe is 'its denial of the possibility of Solution'.[38] But in its poetic imaginings of the encounter between the Law and the Body – a body which is intensely eroticised and sexualised – this typically Barkerian image challenges us to look once more at Foucault's concept of the body as one of the main locations of power.

Notes

1 H. Barker, *Arguments for a Theatre*, third edition (Manchester: Manchester University Press, 1997), p. 162.

2 M. Foucault, 'Omnes et Singulatim: Towards a Criticism of Political Reason' (*The Tanner Lectures on Human Values*, Stanford University, 10 and 16 October 1979). Archived online at http://foucault.info/documents/foucault.omnesEtSingulatim. en.html. Accessed 26 August 2009.

3 M. Foucault, *Discipline and Punish. The Birth of the Prison*, translated by Alan Sheridan (New York: Vintage Books, 1979), p. 110.

4 W. Shakespeare, *King Lear* III, ii, ll. 28–9.

5 *Ibid.*, IV, v, ll. 147–50.

6   C. Balme, *The Cambridge Introduction to Theatre Studies* (Cambridge: Cambridge University Press, 2008), p. 114.
7   M. Foucault, *Discipline and Punish*, p. 271.
8   D. Wood, *A Report on the Surveillance Society* (London: The Information Commissioner's Office, 2006) p. 19.
9   W. Shakespeare, *Hamlet* II,ii, l. 239.
10 T. Adorno, *Prisms*, translated by Samuel and Shierry Weber (Cambridge, MA: MIT Press, 1967), p. 34.
11 G. Steiner, *In Bluebeard's Castle* (New Haven, CT and London: Yale University Press, 1971), p. 47.
12 J. Butler, *Precarious Life: The Powers of Mourning and Violence* (New York and London: Verso, 2006), pp. 50–1.
13 *Ibid.*, p.51.
14 C. Smith, 'Detention without Subjects: Prisons and the Poetics of Living Death', *Texas Studies in Literature and Language* 50, 3 (2008), 243.
15 H. Barker, *Arguments for a Theatre*, p. 119.
16 *Ibid.*, p. 121.
17 *Ibid.*, p. 122.
18 *Ibid.*, p. 121.
19 *Ibid.*, p. 123.
20 D.I. Rabey, *Howard Barker: Politics and Desire An Expository Study of his Drama and Poetry*, second edition (London: Macmillan [1989] 2009), p. 121.
21 *Ibid.*, p. 42.
22 H. Barker, *Collected Plays Volume Four* (London: Calder 1998), pp. 65–6.
23 G. Walter (ed.), *Actes du tribunal révolutionnaire* (Paris: Mercure de France, 1986), pp. 74ff.
24 Barker, *Collected Plays Volume Four*, p. 186.
25 *Ibid.*, p. 213.
26 D.I. Rabey, *Howard Barker: Ecstasy and Death: An Expository Study of his Drama, Theory and Production Work, 1988–2008* (Basingstoke and New York: Palgrave Macmillan, 2009), p. 86.
27 Balme, *The Cambridge Introduction to Theatre Studies*, p. 114.
28 In the text *The Fence* is sometimes capitalised and sometimes not. In the interests of consistency I have used capital letters throughout – except where a more general notion of 'a fence' is introduced.
29 H. Barker, *The Fence in its Thousandth Year* (London: Oberon, 2005), p. 15.
30 *Ibid.*, p. 17.
31 *Ibid.*, p. 24.
32 *Ibid.*, p. 29.
33 *Ibid.*, p. 35.
34 *Ibid.*, p. 45.
35 *Ibid.*, p. 56.
36 *Ibid.*, p. 59.
37 *Ibid.*, p. 7.
38 Barker, *Arguments for a Theatre*, p. 122.

9

Barker, criticism and the philosophy of the 'Art of Theatre'

(including 'Twenty-one Asides on Theatre Criticism')

Mark Brown

Introduction

There is an eclecticism within mainstream theatre[1] which is at odds with the singularity of vision required of a great theatre artist. This would certainly appear to be the case in the very difficult relations which have long existed between the mainstream theatre in England and the drama of Howard Barker.

Barker argues in his 'Fortynine Asides for a Tragic Theatre' that, 'The authoritarian art form is the musical' (*AT*, 17) and he castigates what he calls the 'ideology' of London/English theatre, which is, he asserts, 'liberal humanism';[2] that is the politically determined expectation that theatre subject itself to a project of moral and/or social improvement/reassurance of its audience.[3] Neither of these positions endears him to the leading critics in London.

It will be my purpose here to examine the nature and scale of the chasm which exists between Barker's theatre – and also his theatre theory (which I maintain is better described as a *philosophy* of theatre) – and what might be termed the directorial and critical 'establishment' of London/English theatre. Furthermore, I will consider why Barker's theatre appears to fare better in the Scottish theatre milieu, in which I work as a critic and teacher.

A response to attack: the basis of Barker's theory

Barker describes the motivation for his theoretical writings on theatre as being primarily defensive. He began writing theory, he explains, because he had been, 'under sustained attack from the English [theatre] establishment for a very long time, over the last 15 years or so …'.[4] The dramatist also asserts that the only alternative he could see to the self-defence of his theory was 'suicide'.[5] He comments that this statement might appear self-dramatising. However, it would seem to be undeniable that an artist can be driven to the point of suicide by overwhelming critical hostility and the neglect of their work by the artistic establishment of their society. A notable example is that of the great Japanese filmmaker Akira Kurosawa, who attempted to commit suicide in 1971 following the considerable hostility shown towards his work within Japan; hostility which was largely motivated by the notion that his films were 'too Western'.[6]

The hostility of the London critics

It is unarguably the case that there has been, for some years, a virtual consensus among the leading theatre critics in London where hostility to Barker's theatre is concerned. A brief consideration of the positions taken by the lead critics on the *Guardian* (Michael Billington), *The Times* (Benedict Nightingale) and the *Daily Telegraph* (Charles Spencer)[7] puts the situation beyond doubt.

In 1996 Billington announced himself, 'an admirer of much of Barker's work'.[8] However in 2001, in a comment which revealed a great deal about Billington's general outlook on theatre, he wrote the following:

> What alarms me is that [Torben] Betts says he is abandoning 'social realism' and is now under the influence of Howard Barker. I know it sounds much sexier to say one is a theatrical poet rather than a domestic realist, but the observation of quotidian truth is the hardest of all theatrical tasks. On the evidence so far, I'd say it is the one for which Betts was born.[9]

Leaving aside the highly dubious assertion that 'the observation of quotidian truth is the hardest of all theatrical tasks' (I would have thought it was the easiest!), Billington's comments do, at least, have the virtue of clarity. He prefers 'domestic realism' to 'theatrical poetry'; a preference which (his appreciation of Harold Pinter's domestic *anti-realism* notwithstanding) seems to be a driving force in Billington's criticism,[10] and is certainly at the heart of his ambivalence towards Barker's theatre. As we see in his review of Barker's play *He Stumbled* in 2000:

> [The play] is pithier, sharper, infinitely more accessible [than Barker's epic drama *The Ecstatic Bible*]. But, for all the stylishness of Barker's production and the pungency of his language, I was still left wishing he would once more apply his dramatic gifts to a realistic situation. With Barker we are increasingly in the land of myth.[11]

Billington's protest that Barker takes us into 'the land of myth' is illuminating. If the London critics' antipathy to Barker is rooted partly in the dramatist's eschewal of social realism, it is also largely an expression of a closely related concern, namely their frustration over the lack of easily identifiable *meanings* in Barker's Theatre of Catastrophe. This frustration is reflected in Nightingale's almost comically dismissive comments, *en passant*, regarding *Scenes from an*

Execution (which, ironically, is one of Barker's most nominally 'accessible' plays). In 2001: 'Howard Barker's bizarre *Scenes from an Execution*';[12] and again, the following year: 'Howard Barker's eccentric *Scenes from an Execution*'.[13] Indeed, Nightingale has long nurtured a contemptuous disgust towards the ambiguities in Barker's theatre.[14]

In his review of the Colchester production of Barker's *The Europeans* in 2002, Spencer opined that the play's reflections on the clash of cultures between Christian Europeans and Muslim Ottomans during the Siege of Vienna in 1529 had been given a new relevance by the terrorist atrocities in the United States on 11 September 2001. However, the review is only grudgingly positive, returning us, on numerous occasions, to the London critical fraternity's demand for clarity of meaning and its distrust of theatrical ambiguity. It is worth quoting Spencer's review at some length:

> You have to tip your hat to the Mercury Theatre in Colchester. Even the RSC and the National Theatre baulk when it comes to staging Howard Barker, the wild man of contemporary British theatre and traditionally regarded as box-office poison ... Barker isn't an easy dramatist, believing he honours an audience by making his art hard. You cannot grab handy nuggets of truth or hope out of his work, and he is often deliberately ambiguous about what his characters' actions mean. And there are, as always, moments when Barker appears merely barking. How seriously can one take his apparent approval of a corrupt priest who murders his dear old mum because 'if I did not know cruelty, I could not know pity ... Beauty, Cruelty and Knowledge, these are the triple order of the Groaning God' ... In the final analysis, I'm not at all sure what Barker is banging on about, still less whether what he writes is sane. However, there's no doubt that, on this occasion, his reckless visionary ranting makes for thrilling theatre.[15]

Is there a single dramatist, apart from Barker, and perhaps the late Sarah Kane, who could simultaneously be described as the author of 'thrilling theatre' by a major London newspaper, whilst also having their sanity questioned? A distrust of and hostility towards Barker appears to be almost an article of faith among the lead critics in London.[16]

There is a perfect match between Barker's characterisation of the prevailing 'ideology' of English theatre and the basis for the London critical fraternity's hostility towards his theatre. The critics' complaints centre precisely on demands for naturalism, social realism, liberal humanism, functionality and, above all, *meaning*. Yet, as Barker writes:

> Very great plays yield no meanings. They move like the mouths of the dead on the banks of the Styx. 'Meaningful' plays are soiled/spoiled by their *meanings*. What is the meaning of death?   (*DOAT*, 20)

Found in the Ground: a brief case study

In keeping with the London critical pattern, when Barker's company the Wrestling School staged his play *Found in the Ground* at the Riverside Studios in London in the autumn of 2009, none of the lead newspaper critics attended. Nevertheless, for the most part, the depute critics who reviewed in their stead proved perfectly capable of responding to the piece with the necessary derision.

The drama – which, uniquely in Barker's oeuvre, is expressed as an impressionistic theatrical landscape, rather than as a narrative – focuses primarily upon a retired Nuremberg judge, Toonelhuis, who is in a condition of seeming madness and definite disgust for his culture. The consequence of this disgust is that the great lawyer is systematically burning his library. Given the play's distinctiveness from the narrative dramas which previously characterised Barker's Theatre of Catastrophe, one might have thought that *Found in the Ground* would have required critics to adjust their critical perspective somewhat. In most cases, however, and with sometimes astonishing honesty, the reviews returned to the comfort of established prejudices.

Fiona Mountford's review in the London *Evening Standard* was especially proud of its contempt: 'Howard Barker is back in town and it's time to run for cover'.[17] Continuing, with the offended sensibility of a traditionalist outraged by the music of Leoš Janáček or the paintings of Georges Braque, Mountford asserted: 'What, if anything, this may or may not be about is anyone's guess'.[18]

Writing in *The Times*, Dominic Maxwell was equally eager to display his anti-Barker credentials, writing: 'Howard Barker has always occupied a territory somewhere between total theatre and total cobblers'.[19] Complaining, in familiar terms, about the 'wilfully opaque'[20] nature of Barker's characters, Maxwell concluded:

> On its own terms I dare say this succeeds. Sadly, those terms are locked in a safe, sealed in concrete then immersed in the deep dark oceans of Barker's imagination.[21]

Awarding the production a contemptuous two stars out of five, the *Guardian's* Lyn Gardner continued with the London critical fraternity's obsession with meaning:

> It is one of those theatrical experiences where everyone around you seems to be genuflecting at the altar of radical theatre, while you are left scratching your head and feeling like a bear of very little brain.[22]

Whilst acknowledging that the presentation 'reeks brilliantly of sex and death', Gardner translated her personal frustration with her inability to extract sufficient meaning from the play into an ultimately negative critical judgement:

> It feels both monumental and unassailable, like a vast piece of theatrical granite. If only Barker would allow us near.[23]

In the midst of this entirely predictable chorus of critical disapproval, Andrew Haydon, writing in *Time Out* magazine, expressed concerns about the production which were of a different nature from the standard complaints of London criticism. He began:

> I am an enormous fan of Howard Barker and his project – to challenge the idea that theatre must be comprehensible or useful. So I was puzzled and even shocked by how much I didn't like his new play ...[24]

Expressing his disappointment with the lighting, sound and the cohesion of the acting performances (which, he suggested, 'hadn't quite gelled'[25]), Haydon concluded that the production was a case of an 'aesthetic that has misfired'.[26]

Given his apparent pain in his inability to engage with the presentation of *Found in the Ground*, it is, perhaps, unsurprising that Haydon, alone among the London critics,[27] felt the need to explore further his response to the production. In a blog for the *Guardian* website, which deserves to be quoted at some length, he wrote:

> [W]hen I went to see [Barker's] latest play, *Found in the Ground*, I was shocked and disturbed to find myself in the 'really didn't enjoy it' camp. But was I meant to like it at all? In *Arguments for a Theatre*, Barker is unequivocal about enjoyment, reward or understanding. It is a manifesto for a theatre that we are not meant to understand, he argues. If I'd been enjoying his plays for the last 10 years, was that actually a good thing? I liked their sense of humour; I had a rough idea that I'd been following them reasonably well, that I'd understood what they were about. In short, my appreciation of them was possibly contrary to the way they were meant to be received. Barker's intention, after all, hadn't been to give me a nice night out – and yet somehow I'd managed to have one.[28]

Haydon's honest self-examination regarding his relationship with Barker's theatre will be recognisable to many who consider themselves to be *Barkerista*.[29] Even audience members, such as myself, for whom *Found in the Ground* was a deeply affecting and, in the broadest sense, fulfilling experience can empathise with his dilemma:

> I was annoyed because this play [*Found in the Ground*] wouldn't let me [experience enjoyment]. Or because my bourgeois notions of enjoyment and reward were unfulfilled, as Barker might have put it. Thus, in a curious way, I'm more grateful to the production than I thought. More than any other show I've seen, it has made me think about the way I experience theatre. The extent of its jarring, dissonant juxtapositions; its refusal to map on to a received world view; its complete indifference to my enjoyment; even its refusal to be part of 'contemporary theatre' – all have continued to fascinate me.[30]

There is a striking similarity between Haydon's difficulty with the quasi-abstract, non-narrative form of *Found in the Ground* and the critical crises caused by the works of various modernist artists in the early-to-mid twentieth century; for instance, the English-language premiere of Beckett's *Waiting for Godot*, in London in 1955, was famously met with incomprehension by most of the critics.[31] However, unlike the majority of the London theatrical press pack, then as now, Haydon's response was not the aggressive negativity of a frightened cat, but a considered reflection upon his own expectations of theatre and of the norms which have become established – almost as a set of ideological shibboleths – for theatre going in England.

Liberal humanism on the London stage

Barker has said that the motivation for writing his plays has often been a 'nausea'[32] induced by the liberal humanism of the mainstream theatre. That liberal humanism might be said to have found particular expression in the adaptations of modern classic plays for the National Theatre in London by David Hare (as adapter) and Howard Davies (as director).

If we take the examples of their versions of Federico García Lorca's *The House of Bernarda Alba* (2005) and *Bertolt Brecht's The Life of Galileo* (2006)[33] we can see very marked distortions of the plays to fit the requirements of theatre as 'massage' for the National Theatre audience. In *The House of Bernarda Alba*, the titular grand villa was illuminated beyond endurance. The darkness which dominates the house, on the orders of the eponymous matriarch, was entirely absent. The sense of prevailing denial and uncertainty and the subjection of the erotic to the exigencies of religious and social propriety and social class were replaced by a project to enlighten. The various and powerful expressions of Bernarda Alba's control over her daughters were diminished. Whatever Lorca requires to be covered or invisible, was exposed violently by Hare and Davies.

Something similar occurred in the production of *The Life of Galileo*, the following year. Although Simon Russell Beale played Galileo with great skill and passion, Hare and Davies contrived to turn Brecht's play from a work of 'epic theatre' into a naturalistic thriller. The moment in which Galileo's acolytes await the tolling of the bell that will herald the astronomer's recantation of his Copernican beliefs was vulgarised to fit the Hare/Davies liberal doctrine. Where Brecht would have us contemplate the implications of the recantation, Hare and Davies had the acolytes pointing melodramatically towards the bell tower, as if we, the audience (ignorant, of course, of the history), should join them in rooting for a silence which would articulate Galileo's resistance (and probable death).

When such an emasculating recasting of classic plays is the fashion in London, it is little wonder that Barker's theatre inspires such loathing and fear.

Why no such hostility in Scotland?

The hostility faced by Barker in England is not replicated in Scotland. There have been no fewer than eleven productions of Barker's plays[34] at Scotland's national conservatoire, the Royal Scottish Academy of Music and Drama.[35] Further to those presentations, the Royal Lyceum Theatre, Edinburgh staged an acclaimed production of *Victory*[36] in 2002, and Dundee Rep's presentation of *Scenes from an Execution*[37] in 2004 swept the boards at the Critics' Awards for Theatre in Scotland in 2005.

Barker himself compares his reception in Scotland to the appreciation of his work in continental Europe, observing a broader cultural phenomenon at work:

> I always think of Scotland as a European country, and England as, unfortunately, not one. The prejudice against my work in England, I think, is predicated on something that probably goes back to the Reformation, which is the idea of the utility of works of art. These plays have no use.[38]

Barker explains what he means by being 'European' elsewhere: 'To be European is to hold to opposites and live, if not rejoice, in the contradictions.'[39]

Without entering into the quagmire that is the historical debate regarding the Scottish Reformation, its attitude to theatre and the general weakness, or almost absence, of a historical Scottish theatre tradition, one can detect in modern Scottish theatre a continental aesthetic which might explain, in part, Scotland's more receptive attitude to Barker's drama, as compared with England. There is in Scottish theatre a contrast, perhaps even a paradox, between what might be considered to be two identifiable strands; the 7:84 Scotland/Wildcat strand,[40] on the one hand, and the Communicado strand,[41] on the other.

The latter has been hugely influential on such leading contemporary Scottish theatre companies as Vanishing Point and Wee Stories, and might be considered to have contributed hugely to a theatre environment which has brought forth a generation of celebrated dramatists, such as Gregory Burke, David Greig, Zinnie Harris, David Harrower and Anthony Neilson. This strand in Scottish theatre, which is at least as interested in European and international theatre is in live drama in London, might be considered to be the basis for Scottish theatre's warmer embrace of Barker, in comparison with England.

In conclusion

I hope I have succeeded in establishing that there is, among the leading theatre critics in London, a consensus of hostility where Barker's theatre is concerned; it is not a figment of Barker's imagination. That this hostility has its basis in a liberal humanist ideology within London/English theatre is, of course, open to debate (although it seems clear to me that Barker is correct in his diagnosis).

In any case, any observer of theatre trends internationally can see clearly that

Barker's theatre is received with enthusiasm in many parts of the world, and faces more hostility in England than anywhere else. My own experience, speaking with theatre critics and practitioners at festivals and conferences around Europe and elsewhere in the world, is of Portuguese, French and Americans who are perplexed that Barker, an eminent English dramatist of his generation, should be less celebrated in his own country than in theirs.

Twenty-one Asides on Theatre Criticism

The following set of aphorisms can be read as one critic's personal manifesto. They represent a series of conclusions I have come to in the course of sixteen years as a professional theatre critic within Scotland, the UK and internationally. These conclusions have many influences, ranging from (their key influence) the theatre and the theoretical writings of the great, contemporary English dramatist Howard Barker, to the principles of criticism offered by the nineteenth-century English critic William Hazlitt (by way of his latter-day disciple Tom Paulin), and the lyrics of the Australian singer-songwriter, musician, novelist and screenwriter Nick Cave.

Personal though it is, however, no manifesto worthy of the name has ever been written for an audience of one. Like Barker's uncompromising, painfully beautiful vision for theatre (expressed, of course, in his exceptional plays, and articulated in his collections of theory *Arguments for a Theatre* and *Death, The One and the Art of Theatre*; the latter of which, I insist, is also a book of poetry and philosophy), my 'Asides' are addressed to the 'impatient' (*AT*, 18).

As Barker asserts, 'The critic must suffer like everyone else' (*AT*, 71), and so, like all ideology, this manifesto is 'the outcome of pain' (*AT*, 17). It is painful, and nauseating, to observe and comment upon an arena of cultural practice which is under increasing pressure to infantilise itself. We find this pressure in the commentators and practitioners who deride as 'elitist' the assertion that the art of theatre must eschew the commercial and cultural imperative to 'entertain'. We find it in the liberal critic who wears as a badge of honour his or her belief in the socio-political *functionality* of the theatre.

These 'Asides', therefore, are a personal response to the pain induced by this pressure. They are a cry, an ideological assertion, in defence of 'radical elitism'.[42]

1   The critic is a privileged member of the audience.
2   The critic's pen is a wand, a quill and a dagger.
3   Criticism exists in the discrete space between journalism and art.
4   I write here of true criticism; there are other kinds.
5   The only true critical agenda is the pursuit of quality, and so the critic is a radical elitist (*AT*, 32).
6   'Without mercy or malice':[43] the motto of the true critic.

7   The critic is subjective. She does not deny her subjectivity. Her only responsibility is to be worthy of it.

8   The demand that the critic 'reflect the collective view of the audience' nauseates.

9   When he asserts the 'equal value' of all genres, the critic slits his own throat with his pen.

10   The critic is not a human 'clapometer'.

11   Criticism abhors equivocation (which is distinct from nuance).

12   The bad critic: a fence sitter, deferring to personal sentiment, social propriety or cultural fashion.

13   The true critic: suspicious of consensus, prepared to be in a minority, even of one.

14   Synopsis is not criticism, although it often masquerades as such.

15   All theatre is political. So the critic is suspicious of the term 'political theatre'.

16   The critic is not a doctor, she gives no prescriptions.

17   The prescription is a noose around the neck of the free artist.

18   Criticism, like poetry, is not a job, but a vocation; but the critic, like the poet, has bills to pay.

19   'Polemic is for the street. The theatre is not the street'.[44]

20   The critic has to be a pugilist, prepared to give and take blows.[45]

21   'The critic must suffer like everyone else' (*AT*, 71).

(The 'Twenty-one Asides on Theatre Criticism' were originally published in the second edition, of *Critical Stages*, webjournal of the International Association of Theatre Critics, Spring 2010.)

Notes

1   Howard Barker calls the mainstream theatre '*the theatre*', as opposed to 'the art of theatre', asserting, 'I do not know *the theatre*, and *the theatre* does not know me' (*DOAT*, 1).

2   Barker, from the symposium, 'The Theatre of Howard Barker', Royal Scottish Academy of Music and Drama (now Royal Conservatoire of Scotland), Glasgow, 24 May 2008. An audio stream of the interview which I conducted with Barker at the outset of the symposium can be heard at: www.theatrevoice.com/listen_now/player/?audioID=606. Accessed 28 March 2013.

3   Barker refers to this as theatre as 'massage', *AT*, p. 208.

4   Barker, RSAMD symposium, 24 May 2008.

5   *Ibid.*

6   Jerome F. Shapiro, *Atomic Bomb Cinema: The Apocalyptic Imagination on Film* (New York: Routledge, 2002), p. 300.

7   Through my work as a theatre critic I have met Billington, Nightingale and Spencer on numerous occasions, and I find them to be most agreeable men. I have no personal agenda here, but, rather, a profound intellectual and critical disagreement.

8   Michael Billington, *Guardian*, 1 May 1996.

9   Billington, *Guardian*, 20 January 2001.

10 The twin preferences for social realism and overt, usually left-wing politics seem to me to be the determining factors in Billington's criticism.

11 Billington, *Guardian*, 3 November 2000.

12 Benedict Nightingale, *The Times*, 7 September 2001. Nightingale retired as critic of *The Times* in May 2010.

13 Nightingale, *The Times*, 8 July 2002.

14 The following is typical of Nightingale's casual contempt for Barker's theatre: '[I]t [audience participation at a production of Dick Whittington] is probably healthier than inwardly growling at some worthily incomprehensible play by Howard Barker, Howard Brenton, or Howard something else.' Nightingale, *The Times*, 29 December 1998.

15 Charles Spencer, *Daily Telegraph*, 13 November 2002.

16 Whilst the lead critics in London appear to have boycotted Barker's theatre in recent years, some of their deputies, such as Sam Marlowe (*The Times*) and Dominic Cavendish (*Daily Telegraph*), have engaged with his work in a more thoughtful fashion; albeit that, in Marlowe's case, at least, a resentment of Barker's ambiguities persists.

17 Fiona Mountford, *Evening Standard*, 2 October 2009.

18 *Ibid.*

19 Dominic Maxwell, *The Times*, 6 October 2009.

20 *Ibid.*

21 *Ibid.*

22 Lyn Gardner, *Guardian*, 7 October 2009.

23 *Ibid.*

24 Andrew Haydon, *Time Out,* 8 October 2009.

25 *Ibid.*

26 *Ibid.*

27 Dominic Cavendish of the *Daily Telegraph* also wrote a thoughtful piece for his newspaper's website regarding the *21 for 21* celebrations of twenty-one years of Barker's company The Wrestling School; although his description of Barker's core audience as 'fawning acolytes' was both gratuitous and inaccurate: www.telegraph.co.uk/culture/theatre/theatre-news/6396396/International-Howard-Barker-day.html. Accessed 7 February 2013.

28 Andrew Haydon, Guardian theatre blog: www.guardian.co.uk/stage/theatre-blog/2009/oct/22/howard-barker-play-pleasure. Accessed 7 February 2013.

29 Just as the great theatre critic Kenneth Tynan proclaimed himself '*godotista*' in his famous review of Beckett's *Waiting for Godot*: *Kenneth Tynan: Theatre Writings*, ed. D. Shellard (London: Nick Hern Books, 2007), p.72.

30 Haydon, Guardian theatre blog.

31 The notable exceptions being Tynan in the *Observer* and Harold Hobson in the *Sunday Times*.

32 Barker, RSAMD symposium, 24 May 2008.

33 See my review of *The Life of Galileo*, *Socialist Worker* (15 July 2006): www.socialist-worker.co.uk/art.php?id=9203. Accessed 7 February 2013. Also quoted in the *Guardian*'s review of the reviews (13 July 2006): www.guardian.co.uk/stage/2006/jul/13/theatre4. Accessed 7 February 2013.

34 All of which were directed by the Academy's now Dean of Drama, Hugh Hodgart.

35 Further to these productions, the RSAMD contributed to the *21 for 21* events, on

21 October 2009, with a performed reading of Barker's *(Uncle) Vanya*, directed by Neil Doherty, and on which I was invited to be dramaturge.

36 Directed by then Lyceum artistic director Kenny Ireland, who was a founder of the Wrestling School.

37 Directed by Dominic Hill, now artistic director of the Citizens Theatre, Glasgow.

38 Barker, RSAMD symposium, May 24, 2008.

39 Barker quoted K. Gritzner and D.I. Rabey (eds), *Theatre of Catastrophe: New Essays on Howard Barker* (London: Oberon, 2006), p. 37.

40 7:84 Scotland and Wildcat were companies, established in the 1970s, with an emphasis on live music, rooted in the Scottish folk tradition, and left-wing politics. Neither company now exists.

41 Communicado is a theatre company established in the 1980s, which has a performative aesthetic which is widely perceived to be inspired by many elements in continental European theatre.

42 An 'elitism' which is based upon no factor other than the pursuit of quality, beauty and profundity in the theatre, as expressed in Barker, *AT*, p. 32.

43 Nick Cave, from the lyric 'Get Ready for Love' (2004).

44 Barker, *DOAT*, p. 3.

45 Tom Paulin, *Guardian*, 4 April 2004.

10

Staging Barker in France 2009

Christine Kiehl

Introduction

The Odéon theatre in Paris, also called the Théâtre de l'Europe,[1] seeks to promote new forms of writing. Howard Barker was first invited there in 1995 with his production of *Hated Nighfall* and with Kenny Ireland's production of *The Castle*, both presented by The Wrestling School. Fourteen years later, Barker's Theatre of Catastrophe returned to the Odéon. A season of four plays was presented from January to April 2009, opening with two plays from the 2000s, *Gertrude – The Cry* and *Knowledge and a Girl* (*Le Cas Blanche-Neige*), and ending with two plays from the 1980s: *The Europeans* and *Scenes from an Execution* (*Les Européens, Tableau d'une exécution*). Additional independent productions ran parallel to the Odéon festival: the premiere of *Lot and His God* at the Théâtre de l'Atalante for a whole month, and a production of *Ursula* in Marseilles.

The Odéon theatre organised a series of venues on that occasion, with readings,[2] talks, interviews and a conference under the aegis of the Sorbonne University.[3] A special issue of Barker's latest reflections on drama was commissioned by the Odéon – *These Sad Places, Why Must You Enter Them?* (*Ces tristes lieux, pourquoi faut-il que tu y entres?*[4]), a booklet illustrated with photographs by Barker's alter ego Eduardo Houth.

Since 1995, no fewer than thirteen Barker plays have been staged in France (including *Brutopia, Gertrude, Knowledge and a Girl, (Uncle) Vanya, Judith, The Possibilities, Seven Lears, The Twelfth Battle of Isonzo, Animals in Paradise, The Love of a Good Man, Wounds to the Face, The Dying of Today*). Though the productions were generally successful, the name of Barker has remained unfamiliar to a wider audience, owing to the conspicuous reticence of major French theatres towards a form of theatre they consider complex and non-political.

The Barker season in Paris gives us the opportunity to examine the response to his Theatre of Catastrophe by the various stage directors, the audience and the drama critics. In this essay, I want to broach several questions: how can Barker's unique dramatic language and aesthetics accord with a variety of distinctively different staging propositions? Does the concept of Catastrophe demand a specific aesthetic treatment? And, to what extent is Barker's poetic and tragic theatre of obscurity congruent with wider public production?

Barker at the Odéon theatre: Olivier Py and the project

For the 2008/09 season, Odéon director Olivier Py's project was to focus on the work of, and invite the participation of, a dramatic poet, as Py claimed 'great poetry is the hallmark of a grand dramatic opus when the poetical and the political interlock'.[5] Barker was nominated to fulfil this 'messianic role' for Py, who added that 'putting on four plays is hardly excessive in an effort to suggest the diversity of his work, [its] lavish inventiveness, […], its unique combination of a cultural heritage and formal innovation'.[6]

Py describes the Odéon theatre as an austere construction, built like a temple, with its stucco caryatids, the two statues of Tragedy and Comedy, the bust of Antoine, its staircase and its terse, stone foyer, and finally, its Italian-style theatre, a cavern of gold and purple. Olivier Py 'opened the doors to his theatre to splendour, to insolence';[7] claims which represent both an honour and a challenge for Howard Barker, knowing the somewhat tedious reactions to his work by conventional establishments in his own country.

Py insists his passion was born from his reading Barker's drama so let us consider whether the four productions staged constituted an appropriate tribute to Barkerian poetic drama.

Programming

Four productions, by three directors, were programmed at the Odéon. The opening production stood apart from the rest of the season for several reasons: *Gertrude* was a French premiere whereas *Knowledge and a Girl/Blanche-Neige* and *The Europeans/Les Européens* were not. Second, *Gertrude* was the only play to be performed in the Odéon Italian theatre itself, the other three plays being staged in the outskirts of Paris.[8] Third, *Gertrude* had the largest press coverage, a coverage which gradually waned as the season progressed. Finally, the actress Anne Alvaro was awarded the French Molière[9] award as the Best Actress of the Year for her leading role in *Gertrude*. Was *Gertrude* a better artistic production than the other three, or did it thrive on the central cultural and media promotion of the Barker season? As a director, Olivier Py is a staunch devotee of long epics; he resists the sociological pessimism which valorises short plays, and he has found a public for his four- or even twenty-four-hour long creations.[10] But Py admits that even these are 'bourgeois drama' whereas Barker writes tragedy, a genre which continues to be less attractive.

Giorgio Barberio Corsetti's Gertrude

As I suggested, *Gertrude* was the Grand Opus of the season, unsurprisingly so: the Italian director Giorgio Barberio Corsetti is also a distinguished opera director.

His *Gertrude* was a scenographically virtuosic production based on a gigantic machinery system: changes of location were indicated by partitions crossing an open black stage and gliding along a rail, shaped in a figure eight to symbolise infinity: the infinite mechanism of entrapment in the labyrinth of power and morals that the play depicts. A whole set of manoeuvring mirrors were arranged along the wide bare stage, with a tree and a man descending from the flies, upside down, reflecting a man and a tree onstage. The magical potential of this mechanical system was highlighted in the climactic scene of the play with a stupendous illusion: the façade of a massive eighteenth-century building appeared spread over the entire width of the stage with the actors dangerously scrambling up and down the front: this was actually a mirror effect, as the wall was designed horizontally on the floor, with its perfect reflection projected on a vertical mirror sheet backstage. The effect was both breathtaking and self-consciously aesthetic, emphasising the tragic dimension of the play whilst sustaining dramatic distance. Corsetti's scenographic presentation of a stage strewn with ashes could be seen as an illustration of Adorno's vision of the world after Auschwitz.[11] The production's visual splendour was completed by the powerful but minimalistic lament of a plaintive viola, played live from the first balcony: Corsetti explained 'its sound was as close as could be to Ann Alvaro's voice'.[12] A carefully rhythmic arrangement between stage effects and sound counterpointed the vocal poetry of the dramatic text. The press generally acclaimed the play's organic and crude language, the actors' excellence, the mixing of tragedy and humour. However different from The Wrestling School's aesthetics it may have been, this breathtaking and arresting composition offered a striking response to Barker's Theatre of Catastrophe, expressing many of its objectives.

Other productions in the Odéon season

Knowledge and Girl, originally written and directed by Barker as a radio play companion piece to *Gertrude,* nevertheless inspired diametrically opposed aesthetics to Corsetti's baroque. The stage director Frédéric Maragnani, who first staged *Le Cas Blanche-Neige* in 2005,[13] proclaimed 'innovation as a response to Barker's innovative writing born from the combination of two traditions, that of a poetic text proffered frontally and the realistic tradition of the fourth wall'.[14] Maragnani filled out the physical indeterminacies and suggestiveness of the play's radio production, with his own visual inspirations from the images of the photographer Martin Parr, famous for his original portrayal of ordinary British life, both documentary and bizarre; and more particularly from a 1950s picture of a mental asylum. Maragnani identified Parr as:

A chronicler of our age. In the face of the constantly growing flood of images released by the media [...] he enables us to see things that have seemed familiar to us in completely new way. The motifs he chooses are strange, the colours are garish and the perspectives are unusual. His weapons to counter the propaganda of published images are: criticism, seduction and humour.[15]

Blanche-Neige's stage design was conceptual, geometrical and highly stylised with partitions arranged symmetrically to serve functional purposes – 'the dramatic space on stage is not contextualised, it is an open area to be crossed and traversed' claimed Maragnani.[16] The postmodern abstraction of the stage design was completed with garish colours; the occasional use of emblematic objects like a plastic tree, or glowing red apples, stood out like a Magritte or Andy Warhol item against the brightly lit set. The female costumes were stylishly basic and kitschy, with primary reds or turquoise blue, reminiscent of the 1950s. Maragnani argued that Barker's revisioning of the Snow White tale was a pretext to open up vistas for our present times: the stage director wished to excavate the myth so as to emphasise the madness of the tragic protagonists and their violent turmoil: to that effect, the actors were urged to physicalise their characters and to release an unrestrained delivery of speech.

However, the deliberate distance achieved by the markedly elegant staging weakened the depiction of the characters' emotions, which was at times chilly, at times humorous, but not as disquieting as one might expect from an awe-inspiring text. The performance of the Queen by Marie-Armelle Deguy was convincing, powerful and complex, but that of Snow White was tongue-in-cheek and hence less potent.[17]

The next two productions in the season, *The Europeans* (as first staged in 2001) and *Scenes from an Execution* (commissioned for the occasion) were constructed as a diptych, using the same stage machinery. In accordance with director Christian Esnay's conception of drama as 'work in progress', the stage was turned into a theatre workshop, with set changes in full view of the audience. The wings were visible on each side, isolated from the acting area by light curtains hastily drawn for costume changes. With rhythmic fluidity the actors manipulated adjustable scenes, and mobile elements delimited the various acting spaces: two movable staircases were combined to create alternatively a suspended platform, a scaffolding or even a parody of an Episcopal see. The distance effect was compounded by a choric form of acting intended to avoid both naturalism and psychology, with the character of Galactia portrayed by no fewer than five actors. The dialectics of art and politics, dramatised in both plays, found a harrowing and buoyant treatment on a stage swarming with life and yet avoiding demonstrative illustration. The actors sustained a rhythmic dramatic tension, combining crudity and humour in the (sometimes exaggeratedly expressive) articulation of the lavish and riotous texts.

Scenes from a critical reception

The season had a significant, well-documented and celebratory coverage, in newspapers and radio alike, before the event started. The Odéon theatre coordinated a large educational initiative, providing online academic documents for students as preparation and follow-up work to the plays. Barker was hailed as the 'Superb Desperado',[18] *Gertrude* was described as an exploration of '*Le cri qui tue; petit traité d'une logique de l'extase*' ('The murderous cry: a short treatise on a logic for ecstasy').[19] However, the other plays had less coverage as the season went on. I will focus specifically on two reviews, which, beyond their authors' hasty and at times inaccurate statements, are emblematic of a distinctive discomfort of the journalist profession when tackling Barker's productions; and I wish to interrogate the terms of this unease. The French critic Fabienne Pascaud rejected the conspicuous exuberance of *Gertrude*'s scenography as well as a 'lack of steering' of Barker's text. I think that what Madame Pascaud considers a deficiency, a 'lack of steering',[20] may be associated with a distinctive expression of Theatre of Catastrophe in its conspicuous avoidance of rational argumentation or overt thesis, preferring the exploration of a poetical landscape. Some art forms – and particularly Barker's Theatre of Catastrophe – cannot be comprehended by a journalistic approach which ultimately persists in serving the economic priorities of cultural production and consumption. Pascaud criticised 'Corsetti's pedantic staging, its sterile and vain aesthetics'[21] as if it failed to bring the text to light (when Corsetti himself took a poetical inspiration from a poetical text). One can sense the journalist's underlying imputation of artistic narcissism, when in fact both Barker and Corsetti share a rejection of the sensationalism and narcissistic regression induced by cultural marketing in our hyperindustrial society.[22] Pascaud wrote of *Gertrude* as Barker's 'neo-Shakespearian drama' in which the character of Gertrude is 'a bitch, an Elizabethan Lulu, the caricature of a monstrous queen which is highly improbable today'; the play was accused of 'cheap psychoanalysis, scandalous misogyny', and its use of nakedness considered 'old-fashioned as a scenic device'.[23] Here, Pascaud uses arguments applicable to bourgeois comedy, and she fails to differentiate the politics of narcissistic regression and Barker's return to individuation as an essential and vital form of narcissism necessary to build one's resistance to totalitarianism. Corsetti described his work on *Gertrude* as poetic: he aimed to approach staging as organically as Barker approaches writing. This organic quality was identifiable beyond the horizontal and vertical interplay of his baroque scenery: the play's recurrent image of the cliff became an archetypal emblem materialised in the scenic wall, but also manifested in the actors' risk-taking, which involved keeping the audience uncomfortably suspended in the imagistic dynamics of ominousness and threat. Corsetti observed: 'The cliff is inside the characters themselves' when 'each word has a particular direction, a musical notation', adding that his staging was 'not a description but an act'.

I dwell on this article exclusively because I think it is representative of a media politics in which theatre reviews generally lack an adequate vocabulary to address Art in general, and Barker's theatre in particular. Journalists all too often profess a need to 'make sense' of any and every art form, in pre-established and dominant terms; Barker's theatre of 'obscurity' is at purposeful variance with this urge for (ostensible, but selective) clarity. As Barker explains:

> Le dramaturge révèle par accident, jamais par calcul. [...] Nous devons tendre l'oreille non pas à ce qui est dit mais à ce qui *énonce*, et ce qui énonce est peut-être le contraire de ce qui est proposé ...[24]

Catastrophe, within and beyond elaborate sophistication, permeates the plays as a paradoxically coherent design, necessarily elusive to reason, but organically consistent. Critics like Pascaud are compliant with cultural consumerism's terms of swift efficiency in dispensing an immediate gratification and an overtly profitable 'customer satisfaction'; they use a risk-averse, defensive and infantilising journalistic idiom which is at odds with Barker's essentially poetic work. His Theatre of Catastrophe defies categorisation, for example, between the two extremes of Brechtian distance and Artaud's total adhesion: two constant, because convenient, references for critics. The audience is probably more comfortable than such journalists with the unnameable quality of a Barker play. Barker is not the only artist today who, in Rancière's terms:

> does not want to instruct the audience, and refuses to use the theatre as a means to convey a message. These artists are intent on inventing a form of consciousness, an intensity of feeling, energy for action.[25]

Like other contemporary artists sometimes tagged as postmodern, Barker resorts to an aesthetics which becomes politically significant although it does not advance a political message. The Theatre of Catastrophe counters 'the process of production and consumption whose aim is to channel our desires and reduce every singularity and every existence to mere subsistence'.[26] In today's world, our most profound desires – our libido – are regulated by a politically controlled merchandisation of society: via consumerist models and media, politics regulates our tastes, our senses; in other words politics regulate aesthetics (the etymology of the word 'aesthetics' denoting 'sensation'). Barker's writing is relentlessly resistant to the widely pronounced and assumed 'fact that the aesthetic and symbolical dimensions of life are now entirely subservient to industrial consumption [...] whose interests have altered the economy of desire, contributing to the loss of individuation', and how 'artistic practice as well as political practice is also altered in the process'.[27] Indeed, Barker's theatre distinctively aims to explore and show how social and political authorities have sought to alter, in their own interests, 'the economy of desire'.

This awareness is at the heart of Barker's innovative aesthetics of Catastrophe. Many critics still fail to consider aesthetics as an ethical area which may be more efficient than explicit ideological statements. Whenever a theatre play perturbs our sensations, our senses, and questions our understanding, it becomes political by asking us, through the dramatised fiction on stage, to revise our preconceived perceptions of the society we live in, of our place in it and of others' places in it.

Barker's political aloofness (in relation to the surfaces of conventionally familiar social politics) is existentially frightening as a visionary testimony to an ethical loss that language finds impossible to tag. The unnameable abyss of Catastrophe, the noisy silence of aporia – wrongly interpreted as pessimism – is as frightening as death (which as we know, is a recurrent motif in his plays). Barker's baroque eloquence disturbs just as much as Beckett's bareness and silence. Another reason why Barker is disturbing is that his characters' actions are urged by the supreme desire which rests inside our unconscious, unknown from us: the characters of Catastrophe address our unnameable 'singularity', the 'animal person'[28] in us, as Alain Badiou calls it. I wish to qualify the recurrent notion that Barker is not a political writer: his Theatre of Catastrophe owes as much to the classicism of aesthetic 'distance' – that is the ecstatic contemplation of beauty – as to the postmodern efficiency achieved through aesthetic 'rupture', in the terms of Rancière, where 'rupture' means 'the production of the form of art as dissociated from the direct production of a determined effect on a determined audience';[29] Rancière asserts that this breech becomes 'efficient dissension' in that it 'goes beyond conflicts of ideas or feelings'; 'Before being the exercise of power, politics is the activity which reconfigures the concrete context in which common objects and subjects find their places'.[30] Barker's Theatre of Catastrophe is political in that sense: it is both a confrontational presence (as all drama is) and it allows the liberating process of thought and reflection (a process which defines both politics and philosophy[31]).

Deductions on staging catastrophe

In the Odéon season, Barker's drama inspired three highly diverse productions, from the flamboyance of the operatic *Gertrude*, to the realistic workshop of *Scenes from an Execution*, via the postmodern abstraction of *Knowledge and a Girl*. More and more stage directors turn to Barker's theatre; but can his Theatre of Catastrophe sustain such diverse dramatic and aesthetic conceptions? Barker has both conceptualised Catastrophe and directed The Wrestling School company to dramatise its distinctive language. But should this imply limits to performance choices? The very notion of restriction is obviously at odds with the questioning which is essential to the physics and metaphysics of Catastrophe, its aporia.

The test of the appropriateness of a production of a Barker play staged outside the Wrestling School is the audience affect. By 'audience affect' I do not mean the consumers' verdict on the performance that has just taken place, but the stage director's continuous reflection all through his staging process on the affects generated in the spectator. The first pitfall to avoid for any stage director is to try and illustrate the notion of Catastrophe: Catastrophe is no theory but a driving dramatic force, a compelling creative process, a paradoxically intimate experience of harrowing pain without conventional complacent empathy. Catastrophe is emotionally powerful, whilst producing the distance of solitude, so that the audience feels both a sensorial closeness and an eerie distance to the dramatic experience onstage. Such effect can only be achieved through a unique bodily and mental commitment on the part of the actors, keeping us at bay but almost addressing us privately.

Such was the impression I had when I saw Nathalie Garraud's outstanding production of *Ursula*, performed at the Odéon, but after Py's Barker season, in which the audience experienced both an uneasy proximity to the characters' inner emotions and an awesome distance from the operatic beauty of the production, the forcefulness of which stemmed from this strange combination of unrestrained passion and sober nobility. Garraud's production was visually enthralling, dramatising the pictorial beauty of Renaissance paintings, with their nuanced ebony and deep red, and their chiaroscuro effect recreated through stage lighting. The final arresting image of the train of Placida's long robe, bathing in blood and tracing on the floor the final red line of tragedy as she left the stage, was particularly memorable.

This production was a highly poetical and dramatic response to the painter Lucas Cranach, but also a tribute to Barker as a poet and a painter. Nathalie Garraud successfully staged Catastrophe with a baroque magnificence which emphasised the operatic music of the text. The audience's attention was invited to a 'willing suspension of understanding', on edge between a harrowing tension and a state of active 'pensiveness' opening to the obscure part of our inner selves.[32]

Barker's immediately subsequent current French productions included another production of *Gertrude*[33] and Guillaume Dujardin's production of *Deep Wives, Shallow Animals* in Paris, September 2009. Lyon's entry in the '21 for 21' event was a reading of *Und*.[34]

The capitalist economy has shown its limits since the financial collapse of winter 2008. In the wake of this downfall, I would like to believe that presentations of art, including those in theatres, will further manifest the collapse of the current capitalist economy of art.[35]

Acknowledgment: I would like to thank the Odéon theatre, who agreed to make the substantial press review digest, together with some magnificent photos, available to delegates at the 2009 Aberystwyth conference, 'Howard Barker's Art of Theatre'.

Notes

1 Le décret du 1er juin 1990 qui donne à l'Odéon son titre de Théâtre de l'Europe, consacre son indépendance en tant que 'maison commune du théâtre européen' et

renforce sa mission de 'vivifier le patrimoine dramatique de l'Europe' in www.theatre-odeon.eu/fr/l-odeon/histoire. Accessed 25 March 2013.

2   Howard Barker reading his poetry. Recorded on www.theatre-odeon.eu/fr/file/2166. Accessed 25 March 2013.

3   Olivier Py, Colloque *Howard Barker, du mythe à la scène, de la page au plateau*, 2 February 2009, Paris, Odéon Théâtre.

4   Howard Barker, *Ces tristes lieux, pourquoi faut-il que tu y entres*, traduction et postface de Daniel Lozaya, *Actes Sud*, 2009. Original title: Howard Barker and Eduardo Houth, *These Sad Places, Why must You Enter Them?*

5   Py, Colloque *Howard Barker*.

6   *Ibid.*

7   *Ibid.*

8   Les Ateliers Berthier, a former warehouse, is the Odéon's second theatre.

9   26 April 2009 was the twenty-second *Night of the Molières* – the French drama award celebration.

10 Olivier Py, *La Servante, histoire sans fin*, a twenty-four-hour performance of five plays and five shorter plays, Avignon Festival, 1995. Other productions include Claudel, *Le Soulier de satin*, 9 March, eleven hours.

11 See Adorno (1966), *Negative Dialectics*, translated by E.B. Ashton (London: Routledge, 1973).

12 Interview with Giorgio Barberio Corsetti, Théâtre de l'Odéon Paris, 2 February 2009.

13 *Le Cas Blanche-Neige* was first created by Frédéric Maragnani in 2005 at the Théâtre Jean Vilar in Suresnes.

14 Frédéric Maragnani, Colloque *Howard Barker*.

15 www.martinparr.com/index1.html. Accessed 7 February 2013.

16 Maragnani, Colloque *Howard Barker*.

17 Further critique on http://www.lestroiscoups.com/article-27889223.html. Accessed 25 March 2010.

18 Jean-Pierre Léonardini in « La chronique théatrale » for *L'Humanité*, 5 January 2009.

19 Fabienne Arvers's report for *Les Inrockuptibles*, 27 January 2009.

20 Fabienne Pascaud, *Télérama n° 3079*.

21 *Ibid.*

22 Bernard Stiegler, *De la Misère symbolique, La catastrophe du sensible* (Paris: Galilée, 2005), pp. 281–2.

23 Fabienne Pascaud, *Télérama*.

24 H. Barker, *Ces tristes lieux, pourquoi faut-il que tu y entres?*, *Actes Sud*, 2009, p. 18.

25 Jacques Rancière, *Le Spectateur émancipé* (Paris: La Fabrique éditions, 2008), p. 20.

26 My translation of « [...] les processus de production aussi bien que de consommation [...] qui vise à capter et à canaliser la libido des individus, et à réduire toutes singularités, c'est-à-dire toutes existences, à de simples subsistances », in Stiegler, *De la Misère symbolique*, p. 279.

27 Stiegler, *De la Misère symbolique*, p. 186.

28 Alain Badiou, *L'Ethique, Essai sur la conscience du mal*, Nous, p. 75.

29 Rancière, *Le Spectateur émancipé*, pp. 63–6.

30 *Ibid.*, pp. 66–7.

31 See Denis Guénoun, *Livraison et délivrance* (Théâtre, politique, philosophie), (Paris: Belin, 2009).

32 See Jean-Christophe Bailly reflections on « Le Pensif » in *Le versant animal* (Paris, Bayard Jeunesse, 2007).

33 Théâtre du Corbeau blanc, Juillet 2009, Festival Nous n'irons pas a Avignon du 1er au 26 Juillet 2009, Vitry sur Seine, France.

34 *Und*, a reading by Juliette Mézergues, staged by Mathieu Dufourg with an original music arrangement by El Kinki, Compagnie Nés Sous X, Université Lumière Lyon 2, Cultural Theatre, 21 October 2009.

35 Adapted from Stiegler, *De la Misère symbolique*, p. 158.

11

21 for 21:
a breakthrough moment in
international theatre-making?

Sarah Goldingay

And I ask
Does anybody want them?

The answer comes back
Nobody at all

So I go on
The Forty[1]

21 for 21: a redemptive action?

As with the other chapters in this book, this reflexive examination of my work with Barker over the last five years began as a paper at the July 2009 Aberystwyth University conference, 'Howard Barker's Art of Theatre', developed by David Ian Rabey and Karoline Gritzner. It was a significant moment for me. I was in the process of organising an event called *21 for 21*.[2] Ostensibly, *21 for 21* set out to mark the twenty-first birthday of Howard Barker's collaboration with The Wrestling School in the form of a one-day international festival of his work. In aspiration however, it was designed to re-energise the perception of Barker and The Wrestling School both nationally and internationally. Many of those who were in attendance at the conference had already agreed to participate in the event that would take place on 21 October of the same year, and I was keen that many other of the international conference delegates would also choose to take part. The desire to re-energise the perception of Barker, and his work, had come about after a meeting with Barker where I agreed to develop new strategies for the financially beleaguered Wrestling School (the company devoted to producing his theatrical work). This was the result of an email exchange with Rabey in June of 2007, which was in turn prompted by Mark Evans at Coventry University. Evans had emailed members of the Standing Conference of University Drama

Departments (SCUDD) drawing our attention to a *Guardian* newspaper blog. It was written by Barker, and explained that The Wrestling School's application for Arts Council England (ACE) funding to present Barker's new play, *The Forty*, had been denied. It was entitled 'The Olympics Killed my Theatre Company'.[3] At the time of Barker's blog, the Olympics were some far distant folly, akin to the Millennium Dome, and cuts of this consequence were hitherto unimaginable since the days of Thatcher. With the hindsight of three years however, this action hardly seems surprising at all.

There is an interesting debate to be had about why The Wrestling School project should fall in the first round of ACE cuts, which are continuing in 2013.[4] The subsequent success of the Olympics in terms of 'medal haul', public engagement, legacy and positive media coverage means that it is difficult to engage with this issue without sounding either churlish (by challenging the language, form and enjoyment of the event) or reductionist (by suggesting that for the Department of Culture, Media and Sport (DCMS), the former, culture, was only left in the Minister's portfolio in order to serve the latter, media and sport). Yet, there is an important issue here. The argument that suggests it was the shift in money from culture to support sport which meant *The Forty* was not funded is convincing. However, we cannot be certain of that causality. Regardless of the shifting funding landscape, and in particular in a time of economic contraction, The Wrestling School may not have been successful in its project application. I would suggest that in the case of Barker the clarity of his artistic vision, that in its development and articulation neither seeks to be avant-garde nor responsive to shifts in funding fashions, does not sit comfortably within how both arms-length and charitable funding organisations operate. It is not responsive, and nor are their criteria. The organisational boundaries of each, artist and funder, can only be occasionally porous to allow a compromise that can accommodate the other. It is even rarer for this porosity to coincide at a mutually beneficial point. This oppositional operation of boundaries and frontiers was the catalyst of my work with Barker, and forms the spine of this chapter's exploration of what breakthroughs, frontiers and futures might be for him and The Wrestling School.

With frontiers as its spine, hindsight and reflection will be the form of this chapter. My paper at the 'Art of Theatre' conference was entitled '*21 for 21*: Redemption, Persistence and Optimism' and in many ways one could argue that the subsequent success of *21 for 21* – in combination with other important interventions such as a significant donation by an anonymous American patron to The Wrestling School and Barker's Arts and Humanities Research Council funded Creative Fellowship at the University of Exeter – is indeed proof of the power of persistence and optimism. On reflection, these interventions, the processes by which they were enacted, and their effects are not clear cut; however, they are still clearer in my mind than the question of redemption with which the paper led. Dominic Spencer in the *Daily Telegraph* described *21 for 21* as 'a breakthrough moment in international theatre making'.[5] And as a 'breakthrough', we might then see this as a redemption of sorts. Yet this idea of redemption continues to trouble me. It places a complex, multifaceted, trans-cultural event within the singularity of an insider/outsider dichotomy. In so doing, it implies two things: first, that there is a boundary to 'break through' enabling the one who was once on the outside to be welcomed back to the inside, and second that there were once clear frontiers to behaviour and practice which were transgressed, a transgression which was subsequently forgiven to allow re-entry to 'the fold'. This simplistic model suggests that there is only one frontier with the majority on the inside and the Other(s) on the outside. Moreover, it assumes that there is a desire by those on the outside to return to their 'origin' in order to be with the majority. And in terms of funding, it is this majority that the organisational parameters of large organisations such as ACE are set up to serve. This frontier-based binary assumes that there is a common point of origin and a majority which are in some way fixed with self-generating frontiers that can be broken through. When working with Barker, all of these assumptions are troubled.

In my attempt to find new ways of supporting the work of Barker and The Wrestling School, my early thoughts were focused on developing non-standard approaches to funding and which would require as little compromise as possible to the integrity of Barker's artistic vision. This vision was, and is, tangible, concrete and well articulated. In 2007 it did not fit well with the vision of the ACE: the frontiers of neither party were sufficiently porous to accommodate the other. This is unsurprising in the work of a practitioner who we might more closely associate with an 'Arts for Arts Sake' discourse than one concerned with 'target audiences'. It was clear to me that to pursue a funding strategy which more closely sustained Barker's artistic vision would mean leaving ACE behind. At the time, this was a paradox. For the last twenty years ACE, in all its iterations, had been The Wrestling School's principal funder and by his association as auteur, a key supporter of significant elements of Barker's practices. The sensible thing to do was to revise the application and resubmit. However, this would have required a further compromise of Barker's vision and The Wrestling School's own practice. In a courageous action, along with Wrestling School Company Manager Chris Corner, Barker agreed that we should try a new approach. It has since been suggested to me that if Barker expected funding from the State, as he articulated in 'The Olympics Killed my Theatre Company',[6] then he 'should have been prepared to compromise'. From a commonsensical perspective there is merit in this *quid pro quo* argument. However, the ACE operate at 'arms length' from the DCMS who distribute funds on behalf of the State. The DCMS explain that this means the ACE work 'independently' of them. Therefore ACE selection criteria should operate distinctly from the ebb and flow of Government. If this were the case then one could assess the question of the rejection of *The Forty* bid simply against the artistic criteria of the time. However, the DCMS continue to explain that their arms-length operation also means that ACE also follow DCMS 'guidance criteria'. The appropriateness of this format is being debated elsewhere, but suffice it to say that what is described as arms-length detachment is, unsurprisingly, neither full nor fixed. I am not suggesting that there is a conspiracy against Barker and The Wrestling School at work, but I am describing this conflict between independence and influence to emphasise that for an artist like Barker, with a clear vision which develops over a forty-year career, it is unlikely he will ever be in sufficient vogue to find funding effortless. And, as we continue, I will return to this point to suggest that this experience will necessarily affect how artists self-narrativise and are narrativised by others in response.

As time went on, it became clear that because The Wrestling School had never been fully on the inside of traditional core or repeat-funding paradigms, developed in order to more fully meet ACE criteria, they were an idiosyncratic organisation. On the one hand this had been detrimental: this was why the removal of the funding of a single project could cause the company's closure. Yet on the other hand, they were a flexible, responsive organisation able to travel fast and light. Although this meant they lacked 'resilience' – an increasingly key term for ACE – in the form of a permanent building or full-time administrator, they had great stores of tenacity and innovation.[7] The new holistic funding approach I developed built on Barker's existing rapport with the Academy across the globe. It set out to be mutually beneficial. Increasingly UK academic institutions are looking for high-profile ways of connecting their research to an external audience through processes that have been termed as impactful or translational. This expansion effort by the Academy has increased the porosity of its frontiers, which meant Barker did not need to compromise his artistic vision to an unacceptable level where integrity was lost. Moreover, Barker's intellectually rigorous, high-quality, practice-led approach was valued. What to another backer was dissonant, resonated deeply with his academic collaborators. Regardless of this synergy, this was an innovative and therefore risky funding strategy. However, for Barker and The Wrestling School who were already on the outside, it was a risk they were prepared to take. *21 for 21* was an early expression of the overall strategy: it was intentionally high-profile, sought media coverage and collaboration with significant participants like the Royal Shakespeare Company. Understandably, this change of approach was difficult for Barker.

Yet, on the night before *21 for 21* opened with its first productions, which were to take place in Murdoch and Perth in Australia while we in Europe slept, Barker gave a gift to those who were taking part. He wrote a poem.

We were outside, always outside, like heretics or lepers forbidden to pass the city gates.

Then one night, by agreement, we lit fires at the same hour, and the extent of the light showed us were not alone, as we had thought, but we were numerous, and not only numerous, but inspired, and could both *move* and *speak* in the light, and be beautiful …

H.B. 21 – X – 09[8]

This poem troubles further the insider/outsider dichotomy set up by Spencer's referral to the event as 'a breakthrough moment'. In his use of 'we' Barker challenges the power structure sustained by the frontier model – he subverts it. In so doing, he is constructing a new group, one that operates as beacons of light that hold open an environment in which beauty can occur. Now one need not be on the outside, longing to get in back to one's origin, because of a transgression: instead, there is another collaborative existence. With hindsight, the beauty of this collaboration was its transient and fragmentary nature: groups knew of one another's existence, but by taking part in the one-day event could not, necessarily, experience other events. As the world turned and the sun rose on each continent the lights were extinguished one by one. This transient collaboration's form is interesting. In the terms of Surowiecki, we might see it, and its members, as 'wise'. The collaboration did not require them to cascade their collective knowledge into a single homogenised output, nor did the flawed and economically driven tenet of Western liberalism lead to 'methodological individualism'.[9] The individuals and organisations who collaborated in *21 for 21* were remarkable. To take part required risk and sacrifice. All of them, in their own way, were outsiders because of geography, politics, economics, passion and curiosity. All were profoundly resourceful and worked hard to find ways of facilitating their event. In the co-creation and co-design of what might take place we were never sure of what would take place. All participants could be certain about was their own project, and for many these were in a fragile and vulnerable state. We would not know until after the event what had happened and that would be fragmentary knowledge. And, because of its simultaneous nature, no one could ever know the totality of this event: it could not therefore be placed inside a single frontier. These were all outsiders. And yet, these participants were optimists who perhaps shared an affinity with Eduardo Houth, and by inflection Barker himself. Houth said in *A Style and its Origins*: 'Artists are sometimes redeemed by the upheavals of their time.' (*ASIO*, 85) Perhaps *21 for 21* was an event for a time of upheaval, an event that offered a redemption for this Artist, Barker. But what of this redemption? What form would it take? Would it be a return to inside the frontier, to a point of origin imagined by the majority? And is this point of origin a problematic conception of 'mainstream British Theatre'? And importantly, if Barker crossed this frontier, how long would it last for?

In my paper, two years after my first meeting with Barker, I suggested the conference was taking place in a time of redemption, in particular for Barker. It appeared to be a time of socialist potential: a place where the people owned the banks, where the board of the Peggy Ramsay foundation rewarded Barker's persistence and where a philanthropist from the United States of America recognised the power of art and funded The Wrestling School's remarkable theatre from 2008 to 2010. This took the form of *I Saw Myself*, *The Dying of Today*, *Found in the Ground*, *Hurts Given and Received* and *Slowly*. This generous donation from a 'fan' was administered via the University of Exeter in the form of the Howard

Barker Research Fund,[10] and led to the creation of the Howard Barker archive assembled with scrupulous attention by Peter Hulton.[11] In this case Wrestling School artefacts were literally redeemed from the decay of fading video-tape and disintegrating paper to be digitised and held in perpetuity. This strengthened the case for an Arts and Humanities Research Council funded Creative Fellowship for Barker, which was to follow in October 2009 to October 2012. Here again the feeling of redemption was buoyed further by the reviewer's surprising response to the application when they described its funding as 'a no-brainer'. During the fellowship Barker explored plethora and bare sufficiency in relation to his practice. It has now reached its successful completion: the staging of a new work *BLOK/EKO* by The Wrestling School, a summary of further outputs, along with critical commentary and a new script, *Charles V*, is mapped and explored in a special edition of *Studies in Theatre and Performance*.[12] And *21 for 21* saw forty-six performances of Barker's work in seven languages in one day (for the most part). They occupied four continents and realms, including second life and embraced a multitude of performances, staged readings, poetry recitals, salons, improvisations, adaptations and celebrations. They even included perform-ances by companies who might have, before the event, been perceived as adver-saries, such as the Royal Shakespeare Company (RSC). I will return to the frontiers of the perception shaped around 'national theatres' below. But to close this section, I want to suggest that each of these projects and events could be termed redemptive in terms of Houth's vision: where eminent scholars gather to celebrate Barker's work and people across the globe join together with the estab-lishment – companies like the RSC no less – in order to perform wholes and fragments, comprehensions and misunderstandings of Barker's plays and poetry. *21 for 21* both sustained and ignored frontiers because on the same day lovers of persistence, optimism, Tragedy, pain, poetry and sorrow left their homes to make theatre in celebration of the twenty-first birthday of The Wrestling School. They gave themselves for no reward other than to share their embodiment of Barker with those who watched. This was remarkable. On paper these last five years have been a time of significant redemption, and there have been several event that we might describe as breakthrough moments in theatre making as Dominic Spencer does. However, as Barker and The Wrestling School move forward again, I wonder how significant these breakthroughs are. Do they have longevity? Where are we now? What might the future be?

21 for 21: an amateur event?

As an academic I also teach. In preparation for the Creative Industries Management class this term, a student – let us call her Anita – had read Barker's blog in the *Guardian* entitled 'The Olympics Killed my Theatre Company',[13] we had watched films from the archive, read a rich range of literature and discussed *21 for 21*. Against the complexity of this material it was the simplicity of her statement that struck me: 'If people weren't paid for it then it was an amateur event and not professional.' It was one of those conversations with a young, and possibly, idealistic creative practitioner that troubles your understanding of arts, culture, society and economics. The dominance of late-modern discourses, like post-positivism and subjectivism, place binaries such as Anita's at the periphery of our thinking: quite properly these approaches emphasise that we should be sceptical of absolutes. And yet, the frontiers provided by these binaries give shape to provocative edges which challenge us to reconsider the fluidity of our position. My conversation with Anita gave new impetus into this exploration of the complexity different frontiers, and how they operated in the creation and delivery of *21 for 21*; how they catalysed the event, when we crossed them, removed them, desired them and found them to be lacking. But Anita's concern was not about the importance of 'Arts for Arts Sake' or the strength of Barker's artistic vision, which although it matched her own commitment to her practice she found challenging. It was instead a question of money. And this in turn troubled my own earlier identification with Houth's world where the people owned the banks and integrity mattered more than cash. This tension brings us back to the long-contested question of the social, political and economic 'value' of theatre.

Based on Anita's measure, *21 for 21* was indeed amateur: in economic terms I, as its Executive Producer, was not paid nor were many of the remarkable people who gave their time and energy to make the four-continent event a success. But this was not true of everyone taking part. For example, members of the RSC who were directed by Roxy Silbert in a challenging reimagining of *The Castle* (1985), were paid to perform as part of their stipend as salaried ensemble members.[14] Therefore, like much theatre, *21 for 21* does not lie quite in the economically articulated binary of amateur versus professional: in several ways its participants and expressions were too omnifarious for any such simplistic taxonomy. There is also considerable literature that uses the amateur versus professional binary to make distinctions about aesthetic quality; it is one way of giving shape to complex notions of production values. This question of performance quality cannot be neatly divorced from questions of economics: the 'increasing emphasis on professionalism in all sectors of society', Cochrane notes, are a 'consequence of advanced capitalism'.[15] However, this question of aesthetic quality cannot be simply reduced to an expression of economics and a matter of product differentiation.[16] It has an important role the play in how theatre, in all its complexity, imagines and describes itself. These descriptions frequently operate *via negativa* and set out to articulate one form by placing it in opposition to another; thus, frontiers are built. Such a process is an important aspect of Barker's work and the development of The Wrestling School: virtuosic performances, exceptional writing, the authority of the director's vision, beautiful scenography and self-consciously elitist practices are central to narratives used by, and about, Theatre of Catastrophe. We have already seen that with a single poem to the participants of *21 for 21* Barker catalysed a self-identification process. These frontiers of quality and identity are core values that need to be sustained for The Wrestling School to be distinctive: therefore, we might see Barker's work with them as both the creator and manifestation of self-identifying narratives around professionalism. Yet, at times, like with *21 for 21*, Barker and The Wrestling School work for little or no payment. This leaves us then with a challenge. To be on the outside of the frontier of mainstream practice, as articulated in response to the dominant funding paradigm, enables independence of thought and the space to pursue a vision. However, to be an outsider is to place oneself in a position of economic lack and resultant limitations on how that vision can be expressed. Barker and The Wrestling School have long had a capacity to slip between economically shaped definitions like professional or amateur and not-for-profit or paid. They have however maintained a core of values that make them cohesive and distinct against this shifting context. We might see them as creators of their own frontiers.

These frontiers are problematic. They are not absolutes, but porous and shifting constructions that respond to the evolution of Barker as an auteur and individual. These frontiers are redesignated as boundaries by particular scholars because they are understood as a means of keeping out those who would ask questions, rather than as sustaining those who feel beleaguered within. They are seen as constructions created to limit the capacity for external critical enquiry, audience engagement and even mitigating the work's capacity to challenge dominant forms because they are 'controlling, mediating, and ultimately explanatory'.[17] Yet, *21 for 21* troubled the idea that Barker and The Wrestling School could only operate within the confines of elitist frontiers where those on the inside operated *via negativa* to those on the outside. As Barker's poem to its participants describes, 'we were not alone, as we had thought, but we were numerous and not only numerous, but inspired, and could both move and speak in the light, and be beautiful'. The Wrestling School contribution to the event included a staged reading by the company of *Hurts Given and Received*. This was within Barker's artistic control. However, the event also grew to include a range of full productions and readings by students and performers who would self-identify as amateur. In the co-design of the event this issue presented a significant challenge. As I scoped the project with Barker, along with much-needed insight from his agent Howard Gooding, we discussed the question of who might be invited to participate and who would not. At times it felt like I was speaking with Houth, as we recognised that this was an atypical moment for Barker and The Wrestling School and for such an event to succeed typical frontiers would need to be re-envisioned and become porous rather than exclusionary. Barker and the company had always engaged generously and been welcoming to those interested in its work, but they had not needed to compromise typical practices in these situations. However, Barker's work had never been simultaneously interpreted by such a dynamic range of people in diverse settings:

quality control and professional standards would necessarily mean something different.

In the first instance, we invited those who had already collaborated, corresponded and engaged with Barker, Gooding and The Wrestling School to take part. Melanie Jessop, Gerrard McArthur and Chris Corner of The Wrestling School as were invaluable in generating and consulting on this list as were a group of friends and colleagues, scholars who became known as the Inner Circle – another self-identifying frontier. Academic-practitioners Steve Nicholson, David Ian Rabey, Mick Mangan, Colin Chambers and Christopher McCullough were tireless in their support of the project and many of them created beautiful *21 for 21* events. Luke Beattie who was the regional producer for Canada and the USA and Sophie Hickman who was the regional producer for the UK, Europe and Iceland were also invaluable in their passion for and commitment to the event. Both brought both calm and vigour, sophistication and simplicity to its delivery. Hickman even managed to secure the West End's Fortune Theatre for a reading of *The Road, The House, The Road* which she directed. As time went on, the list of participants moved from the clear linearity of those we first invited to a diffuse cloud of half-remembered names, which became more complex as event was publicised through word of mouth. There was a Barker underground already well established. Quickly, we exceeded our original hope of eight, and then twenty-one participating companies. This gave me confidence that the project might well be viable. But also at this point Barker and I needed to discuss what this expansion would mean in terms of the quality of the event. This was challenging. Our discussion spread over several days until Barker concluded, with a laugh: 'In the words of Chairman Mao, let a hundred flowers bloom.' And Howard Gooding, along with Henriette Baker, a colleague at Judy Daish Associates, arranged for the free licensing of Barker's work for each event. With this action Barker challenged those who assume the frontiers of his artistic vision are singular. They are porous, shifting and multifaceted. He chose to sustain the frontiers of integrity that are paramount in his articulation of his own artistic vision, while facilitating the exploration of his canon by a diverse range of other practitioners. In the face of such evidence, some may even choose to see this as a redemption of sorts.

Finally, at the frontier offered by the amateur-professional binary we are presented with another provocation. This is perhaps the most complex of all the provocations we have considered thus far. It involves economics and quality, but is principally centred on questions of identity and narrativisation in a wider context. If we return to Cochrane, she explains that '[m]uch of today's state-funded theatre […] ostracizes the amateur [which] has its roots in early twentieth-century amateur/professional collaborations'.[18] *21 for 21*, like much work that could be catagorised under the term amateur, is problematic when reviewed with Cochrane's astute observation. It was saturated with virtuosic practioners and world-class companies who were not paid for their contribution.

It also saw them readily collaborate with self-identifying amateur and student ensembles – not in a homogeneous singularity but under a single banner. Instead, this was another frontier of those who locate themselves either inside or outside a theatre-of-utility. I noted earlier that Baker's perceived annexation by the National Theatre has become a key strand in his self-narrativisation and its reporting by others. He is absolute about its motivations in *Arguments for a Theatre* where he states that:

> the exclusion of my work from the National Theatre of England is the past 18 years can only reflect its hidden moral function – common to all national theatres by definition – 'the serving of the community', as if the community were served by conscience in the first place.

In this statement we see him clearly articulating the frontier of mainstream practice, as articulated in response to the dominant funding paradigm shaped by government policy. He is embracing this exclusion and placing himself, and his work, outside such utility. This exclusion enables independence of thought and the space to pursue a vision. As he continues, in a moment of uncanny foresight he points to:

> one of the flawed conventions of my accessible play *Scenes from an Execution* that the protagonist, the artist Galactica, with whom all critics find it easy to sympathize, is a pacifist. (*AFT*, 89).

His identification of *Scenes from an Execution* is telling because it is this play that the National Theatre have chosen to stage in 2012 as their first work by Barker. It is directed by Tom Cairns: the National is engaging with Barker the dramatist, in part; or at least the still-artefact of his work, the playtext. This turn of events however challenges the self-narrativising frontier that places Barker, and by association The Wrestling School, outside the mainstream in general and state theatre in particular. Perhaps this is his real breakthrough moment, his moment of redemption?

Barker does not offer such an easy resolution. In an insightful interview with Maddy Costa of the *Guardian* entitled 'Howard Barker:"I don't care if you listen or not"' he is clear that there are important frontiers in his work and its production, and that these do not fall across simple binaries. While he writes 'from ignorance. [...] I don't care if you listen or not',[19] he cares that his work is seen, but is also frustrated that it is his most accessible work that is being shown. This nuance suggests Barker will always be set against those who would seek utility in the arts – whether that is an audience who require meaning from their theatre or a funding body who need to fulfil criteria shaped by a government who is held only at arms-length. The clarity of Barker's vision means that his work has clear artistic frontiers which protects it, and by extension him, from those who would put it to 'good use'. He intentionally is an outsider, and artist who has generated frontiers that are significant in how he, and others, describe his work and practice. These are not to primarily to keep others out I would suggest, although Barker is clear that he values his solitude, but rather to sustain the beleaguered within.

I have been struck by how over the last twenty years or so we continually point to the change in value-narratives that construct the discourse that bemoans the loss of the significance placed on the importance of art as an articulation of inspired, creative-intervention, and the shift to an expression of how the arts' value are measured not in terms of their capacity to express something supernatural; that is to say, that which goes beyond the quotidian, but rather they are expressed in their socio-economic value: these values are often articulated through the terminology of business and economics. I wonder how new this is, are we like generations past idealising artistic 'production'? There has always been a tension between the painter and the patron, the utility and the Art. The American government gives us a neat four-part definition of how this language is clustered that offers insight into its twenty-first century manifestation. It explains, in response to the question, 'Why are the Arts a good public sector investment?', that 'in addition to their inherent value to society, the arts offer a distinctive blend of benefits [...as] economic drivers [...] educational assets [...] civic catalysts [...and creators of] cultural legacy'.[20] It is important here that the argument is not simply reduced to a question of the imposition of the American model onto the UK system. In fact, there is a clarity here that is often lacking in the documents that support the aspirations of the DCMS and by extension ACE. The UK is going through a significant change where a return for former levels of state funding of the arts appears increasingly unlikely, and pseudo-philanthropic models such as the Big Society and Crowd Funding come to the fore, the space for the intangible value of art is changed: Barker has something important to contribute to how we might respond to this shift.

From his moments of 'breakthrough' and hints of 'redemption' Barker's important frontiers remain, and broadly these see him again cast as an outsider. In 2009 a double issue of *Cultural Trends* identified 'the tension between the power and resources at the centre and the interest and ambitions of the periphery'. ACE in its ambitions to celebrate and support the growth of the periphery is still at the centre of arts funding and policy making. Where it does support risk, we might then see, this errs towards the avant-garde, as one might well expect in the hegemonic desires of late-capitalism. In this scenario, Barker is neither central through usefulness nor peripheral through novelty. By remaining a beleaguered outsider behind protective frontiers, as others in theatre are workhorses of economic utility, he may continue to have both redemption and breakthroughs in theatre-making on his own terms.

21 for 21

- **Aberystwyth**, Wales
  A Wounded Knife
- **Belgrade**, Serbia
  Judith: a parting from the body
- **Boston**, MA, USA
  The Europeans
- **Burnaby**, BC, Canada
  Gertrude – The Cry
- **Canterbury**, England
  The Possibilities
- **Cape Town**, South Africa
  Death, the One, and the Art of Theatre
- **Cape Town**, South Africa
  Judith: A Parting From the Body
- **Exeter**, England
  13 Objects
- **Exeter**, England
  Judith: A Parting From the Body
- **Glasgow**, Scotland
  (Uncle) Vanya
- **Guanajuato**, Mexico
  The Dying of Today
- **Kranj**, Slovenia
  Victory
- **Lisbon**, Portugal
  Gertrude – The Cry
- **Lisbon**, Portugal
  Fragments, essays and poems, included in *Arguments for a Theatre*
- **London**, England
  Crimes in Hot Countries
- **London**, England
  Deep Wives / Shallow Animals
- **London**, England
  He Stumbled
- **London**, England (The Wrestling School)
  Hurts Given and Received
- **London**, England
  Seven Lears
- **London**, England
  The Road, The House, The Road
- **Los Angeles**, California, USA
  A Hard Heart
- **Lyon**, France
  A Literary Salon

- **Lyon**, France
  Und
- **Melton Mowbray**, UK
  13 Objects
- **Murdoch**, Western Australia
  Wounds to the Face
- **New York**, USA
  Gertrude – The Cry
- **New York**, USA
  Judith: A Parting From the Body
- **New York**, USA
  Pity in History
- **Newcastle**, England
  The Castle
- **Newport**, South Wales
  Lullabies for the Impatient & The Europeans
- **North Vancouver**, BC, Canada
  A Hard Heart
- **Paris**, France
  Deep Wives / Shallow Animals
- **Paris/Perpignan**, France
  Various excerpts
- **Perth**, Australia
  Gertrude – The Cry
- **Portland**, Oregon, USA
  Ursula
- **Reykjavik**, Iceland
  Knowledge and a Girl
- **St Helier**, Jersey
  Claw
- **Seattle**, USA
  Brutopia
- **Second Life®**
  13 Objects
- **Sheffield**, England
  The Castle
- **Tel Aviv**, Israel
  Gertrude – The Cry
- **Toronto**, Canada
  (Uncle) Vanya
- **Vancouver**, Canada
  The Dying of Today
- **Victoria**, Canada
  The Castle
- **Vienna**, Austria
  Deep Wives / Shallow Animals

Acknowledgements: With sincere thanks to all those who 'lit fires at the same hour' and saw that they 'could both *move* and *speak* in the light, and be beautiful …'[21]

Notes

1   H. Barker, *The Forty (Few Words)*, unpublished.
2   For details see http://spa.exeter.ac.uk/drama/projects/21421/index.shtml. Accessed 25 March 2013.
3   H. Barker, 'The Olympics Killed my Theatre Company', *Guardian Theatre Blog*, 5 June 2007. www.guardian.co.uk/stage/theatreblog/2007/jun/05/theolympicskilled mytheatre. Accessed 15 October 2012.
4   Rabey offers an opening salvo in D.I. Rabey, 'Chasing the Ellipses: Staging Howard Barker's *The Forty (Few Words)*', *Studies in Theatre and Performance* 32, 3 (2012), 286–7.
5   D. Spencer, 'International Howard Barker Day', *Daily Telegraph*, 21 October 2009.
6   Barker, 'The Olympics Killed my Theatre Company'.
7   For an articulate exploration of this see M. Robinson, *Making Adaptive Resilience Real* (London: The Arts Council, 2010). Available online www.artscouncil.org.uk/publi-cation_archive/making-adaptive-resilience-real/. Accessed 15 October 2012.
8   H. Barker, a poem for participants in *21 for 21*, unpublished (original emphasis, Brighton, 21 October 2009).
9   J. Surowiecki, *The Wisdom of Crowds: Why the Many Are Smarter Than the Few* (London: Abacus, 2004), pp. 41–65.
10 The author and Mick Mangan were directors of the fund.
11 For details see www.arts-archives.org/index.htm. Accessed 7 February 2013.
12 S. Goldingay and M. Mangan (eds), *Studies in Theatre and Performance* 32, 3 (2012).
13 Barker, 'The Olympics Killed my Theatre Company'.
14 Silbert, R. (Dir.), *The Castle The Royal Shakespeare Company*, Theatre Royal, Newcastle, 21 October 2009.
15 C. Cochrane, 'The Pervasiveness of the Commonplace: The Historian and Amateur Theatre', *Theatre Research International* 26, 3 (2001), 233.
16 In 1933 Edward Chamberlain proposed the idea of product differentiation which is now a key approach that organisations use in their marketing strategies to set themselves apart from their competitors and better aim their product at particular groups of customers.
17 R. Shaughnessy, 'Howard Barker, The Wrestling School, and the Cult of the Author', *New Theatre Quarterly* 5 (1989), 264–71.
18 C. Cochrane, 'The Pervasiveness of the Commonplace', p. 233.
19 M. Costa, 'Howard Barker: "I don't care if you listen or not"', *Guardian*, 1 October 2012, www.guardian.co.uk/stage/2012/oct/01/howard-barker-scenes-execution. Accessed 15 October 2012.
20 National Assembly of State Arts Agencies (2010) 'Why Should Government Support the Arts', NASAA available at www.nasaa-arts.org/Advocacy/Advocacy-Tools/Why-Government-Support/WhyGovSupport.pdf. Accessed 25 March 2013.
21 H. Barker, a poem for participants in *21 for 21*.

12

I Saw Myself:
artist and critic meet in the mirror

Mary Karen Dahl

My tapestry is true if you want history weave another one (*OP4*, 56)

There is a scandal at the heart of making theatre and it is this: artists don't stand aside but always are implicated in the messy, typically bloody, weaving of the day-to-day events that become history.[1] Art and artist do not hold up a mirror to nature: they make the world. Barker's play *I Saw Myself* (staged 2008) is his most elegantly developed probe into ways that creative acts and actors go to work. Part of my immediate attachment to the text derives from its depiction of the desiring, desired, aging female subject (and the temporarily objectified male). Here, however, I am focused on the effects the play's dramaturgy has on my conviction that thinking is doing and doing, thinking.[2] More, playwright and audience are tightly coupled, locked in a mutually reflective embrace. This text calls me to attend to my own practice as a creative responder, sometimes called 'critic'. If artists are implicated in the making of the world, in the writing of history, and if artist and audience reflect each other, see one another, how then am I as a critic implicated in the world-making that the artist practises?[3] The commentary that follows traces my effort to enter into conversation with the text and derives from the proposition that this play, like others, produces complex meanings that become available through the audience's interaction with the performed text.[4] Unlike many others, however, this play text insists that readers (and eventually spectators) confront the activity of meaning-making as the fundamental 'doing' that constitutes making art. *I Saw Myself* uses an extended staged metaphor of weaving to embody the artist's creative process – a process that requires confrontation, negotiation, self-scrutiny and sacrifice to determine not just what story to tell, but who will tell it – who will literally *take* centre stage. Although the struggles creation entails lie concealed within the finished narratives, they shape history and its political consequences. The play represents history-making as subjective, personally invested and power laden.

The situation the play presents is simple: it is set in thirteenth-century Europe; able-bodied men have followed their noble lord to war; that lord has been killed, and the play's action takes place in the widow's household. The widow – Sleev – and her serving women are weaving a tapestry that will depict the heroic tale of how the men left their homes, fought and died. According to convention, the finished product would have three subjects or 'streams': warriors take central focus supported by lesser images of faithful women and natural resources signifying the prosperity that motivates their sacrifice (*OP4*, 20). This activity, weaving, shapes the through-line of the play. As the action onstage unfolds, decades pass, the enemy approaches. The women of the household flee the chaos, taking the tapestry with them, leaving Sleev behind – alone.

The play opens on the widow and her three serving women weaving. Sleev's first action is to stand abruptly, saying 'Again I cannot do the face'. Moments later she goes to a wardrobe standing in the room, '*examine*[s] *herself*' in the mirror on the door, opens the door, regards '*with a pained detachment*' a naked man standing mutely there, and closes the door (*OP4*, 11). The play spins out threads of the argument her actions introduce.

I On seeing

The first of these threads twists together self-consciousness and self-scrutiny with desire and gendered power and ties them to a founding myth in the western tradition (13–15, 34, 36–7, 49–50, etc.). In her first of several interpretations of Eve's story, Sleev claims that, in the beginning, there were no mirrors. She speculates that Eve was 'self-conscious' but her 'self-consciousness … could never be relieved by scrutiny'; Eve could see herself reflected in Adam's eyes, but 'the terrible eyes of Adam revealed not Eve, but the effect of Eve on him'. As Sleev says, 'this was not mirroring' (*OP4*, 13). Her efforts at seeing herself would be obscured by his response, whether desire or disgust. Following that train of thought, moments later she argues 'It was Adam's gaze that forced on Eve the agony of self-consciousness'; it was Eve's own awakening desire that made the mirror necessary, but it 'only served to deepen the anxiety desire inevitably creates' (*OP4*, 14). She approaches the mirrored wardrobe and consults her image, 'Eve now suffered the dread that she was insufficiently beautiful' (*OP4*, 15). Sleev reads Eve through her own anxiety, which in the opening scenes repeatedly drives her to the mirrored wardrobe as if to confirm her beauty as sufficient. Targeting a succession of male characters, she repeatedly tests her sexual potency, exercising her ability to awaken desire. Repeatedly she provokes their desire then denies its release, its fulfillment. In Sleev's reading, desire gives rise to potentially unequal, gendered dynamics wherein Eve depends on another's 'terrible eyes' for confirmation of her very existence; Adam's gaze produces her self-consciousness, which then requires self-scrutiny. The action of the play will reconfigure those terms.

Sleev's interactions with Modicum, the man in the wardrobe, demonstrate just such differential power relations. While his is a consciousness whose response she seeks in affirmation of her beauty, understood as a sign of her agency as a (sexual) being, here the terrible eyes would seem to be Sleev's. The door opens, she looks. He submits to her gaze ('*His head hangs in the usual way*,' *OP4*, 40). He obeys Sleev's rules: he must neither speak nor intervene in her life (*OP4*, 27). Gradually, however, it appears that the arrangement is sustained by Modicum's willing capitulation to Sleev's dominance. He is free to come and go (*OP4*, 22). Finally, shamed as a 'USELESS \ MALE' by Sleev's servant Ladder (*OP4*, 40), Modicum vacates the wardrobe; the army conscripts him (*OP4*, 51). He returns years later, filled with violent authority as a 'king' and exacts revenge on the old woman Sleev has become. He forces Sleev to fellate him and beats her (*OP4*, 69–75), and in doing so realises the abusive potential of interdependent, but unequal gendered relations.

II On representation and truth

Sleev's inability to represent what we learn is her dead husband's face captures complex ideas in a single gesture. She argues that widows – on account of their emotional involvement with the subject – are least able to 'describe' husbands (*OP4*, 11). Her son-in-law, Guardaloop, picks up this thread, asking whether wives see their husbands after 'long years of intimacy' and if that (not) seeing affects 'Representation' (*OP4*, 16). Relationships and their attendant emotions shape acts of description and infect the process of depiction. As a consequence, the activity, representation, creates hotly contested sights/sites of meaning.

While the widow draws back from describing, much less actually depicting her husband, the text calls attention to representation of another sort: a daughter's ability to stand in for her father (*OP4*, 12). Sleev says her daughter Sheeth can serve as a model for the husband's face in the tapestry. We learn, too, that as a child Sheeth witnessed her mother's sexual transgressions (*OP4*, 56–7). Here emotion works to different effect. Sheeth honours patriarchal rules: she looks through the father's eyes and through her the Father who authorises history sees and judges.

These instances, linking seeing to representation, trouble the relationship, introducing subjective experience – intimacy, habituation, emotion – into the equation. Then, drawing analogies between the characters' acts of creation and the act of performance, the text invites spectators to interrogate our responses to the embodied images moving before us. It prompts a kind of thinking – what Foucault calls 'the labor performed to know' – that can modify subjectivity.[5]

The play also ties telling and performing (stories) to weaving: they are similar narrative acts. Sleev actualises this linkage. She begins the action at fifty and ends at seventy (*OP4*, 23, 78). Over that time she designs, she sews; she relates her sexual encounters and reinterprets Eve's myth in light of her own experience. She relives her story in the stitching of it. It changes, triggering changes in the narrative the women of the household must weave. As they wrestle with the story to be told we see that the tapestry gathers together, stands in for, and materialises conflicting attitudes towards their shared history. Connections to theatre are easy to find. Making the tapestry calls attention to the invested effort such work requires.

Theatre, too, demands intense negotiations over intended meanings, selection of imagery for spectators to read, and scrutiny of the narrative depicted to ensure its communicative power. Sleev causes her story to be made and remade, inviting recognition that any one depiction is just that: one of many incomplete attempts to capture approximations of a truth that escapes always. The through-line, weaving, exposes the labour involved in rendering the text before our eyes. The character Sleev, who authors and performs the subject the weaving represents, parallels the actor who authors and performs the character. Sleev's continual reworking of her past and focus on the means of representing that material not only captures the actor's process shaping the character, but engages spectators in parallel work that takes account of our interpretive shifts, complicates what we know, truths closely held.

III On weaving history

Ladder 'says weaving is the truth we must put truth into the tapestry' (*OP4*, 19). The object itself commands respect – the women will risk all to carry it to safety. It is regarded as the authorised source of truth about 'what happened' (*OP4*, 19, 20–1, 22, 56, 66). Consequently, the stakes are high: whose truth will it be? Convention dictates the tapestry should center on men's military feats. Sleev's daughter Sheeth asserts that 'the tapestry is a thing of love' as well as 'Devotion' and 'Piety' (*OP4*, 15–16). Obedient wives preserve their chastity at all costs. They devote their widowhood to embroidering tales of their husbands' valour. Sleev repudiates that role. The plot turns when she fully, truthfully, engages as author of the text. The tapestry's narrative develops through a battle of wills. Her servant, Ladder, the expert seamstress who is her primary antagonist in this matter, insists Sleev's infidelity be shown. She capitulates, but defies convention. She will displace her husband as the 'subject of the Great Stream' (*OP4*, 35–6). She, not he, will anchor the history the tapestry tells. She chooses its truth: the focal panels will show her in the throes of passion; her husband's beheading by the enemy will occupy a lesser stream. In actualising that vision the characters struggle to overcome internalised societal norms. Physical acts of creation require the artist to confront notions of what can be said and to choose instead to depict what must be shown. Such choices articulate politics and make ethics manifest.

Sleev and the weavers redirect traditional iconography to represent the oft-untold, always-feared story of the disobedient woman who is not patient, not subservient. Might such a subject free herself from the reflection in Adam's eye? Perhaps, but the effort requires sacrifice: as Sleev works to make manifest the meanings chosen, she loses her sight. Making truthful art (however subjective) blinds the maker.[6] Upon the tapestry's completion, she marks the event by pricking the finger of each weaver but one, who later mourns the cowardice that caused her to be left out. Their blood stains – is incorporated into – the final ritual stitch (*OP4*, 64–5).

Like this bloody stitch, the play's action translates the artist's ethical imperatives into physical terms. Creating the tapestry manifests an array of attitudes and motives – defiance, confession, atonement, resistance, acceptance – that supplement the dialogue without requiring explicit argumentation. The characters argue over the truth to be told. That *agon* leaves its traces in the tapestry. Changes in its content must be rendered in material form. That materiality has consequences. Frustrated by her failure to create the likeness of her husband, Sleev allocates that task to her women and directs them to unpick twelve of its panels (*OP4*, 12). They will be redone. Immense labour is involved. But because creating the tapestry requires many hands, the process opens up the possibility of incorporating conflicting points of view. Just before the last stitch is set, Sleev discovers that Ladder has interpreted the husband's death to suit her own politics of gender: she has rendered the scarlet blood of his beheading spattered over the faithless wife transported by desire (*OP4*, 63). Sleev rejects the apology the image implies, but when Ladder offers to unpick the offending splash, Sleev refuses. The beauty of the image – 'its scarlet is exquisite on the midnight blue of my canopy' – outweighs Ladder's subversion of her intent, even though this misrepresentation of her story will endure in the tapestry (*OP4*, 64). Indeed, Sleev, who reminds us of Eve's lies (*OP4*, 34, 49–50), knows the tapestry tells less than her own truth: 'I wish I had been more honest' (*OP4*, 65). A version of events only, it exceeds her grasp even as she serves as its primary author and subject. Additionally, in its material form, this telling of his story that has become her story is immense, extending to sixty panels. Sheeth and the serving women strenuously wrestle it off stage (*OP4*, 80–1). The narrative, rendered (reduced and aestheticised) as art, is nearly unmanageable. Once it has left the stage, Sleev utters the simple words, 'I saw myself' (*OP4*, 81).

Contemplating that moment, it is tempting to decide that, unburdened, Sleev finally faces her reflection unmediated by another's consciousness. The gazer concealed behind the mirror whose thoughts she imagined and sought to shape has gone. Her female companions and hopeful lovers have fled. Only the mirror potentially reflects her image. But like the tapestry, the mirror reflects a version, partial only, of the subject. And Sleev speaks in the past tense: She does not see her self. She looks through a glass darkly. Or rather, she sees through a vision darkened (blinded) by her efforts to render the story of her self.

Self-consciousness and its companion, self-scrutiny, exact a price: 'I have gone blind from studying myself' (*OP4*, 70). Perhaps she glimpses her image, but it would seem that the only actual view is in the mind's eye. It is transitory, retrospective, her own.[7] Even so, truth eludes her: she 'no longer know[s] the subject' – herself (*OP4*, 79).

IV The critic in the mirror: unpicking the panels

As Sleev's interactions with Modicum imply, even when we think we are in control (self-possessed), awareness that another watches/sees calls us to tend (and attend to) his or her desires. The pressure lessens only when others are gone for good. In the absence of others, she comes into relationship with the self she authors and performs: self-fulfilled, tragic in the old style. But of course, she is not alone. I remain. What if, as in Eden, like Eve, the artist sees her- or him-self in the distorted reflection of the spectator's eyes, my desiring (self-interested) gaze? The views of others cannot be said to vanish; they continue to infect her self-regard. I am one among others responding to character and artist in the moment. Indeed, we command the gaze with which actor, playwright and director struggle.

The play extends the analogy between Sleev and her companions to the relationship between creator and critic. Within the action, characters repeatedly engage art-making through critical analysis. The weavers select from an established vocabulary of imagery to construct the narrative for others. Daughter and servants carry the tapestry to safer territory where future viewers will honour it as the authorised version of 'what happened' or suppress it for its subversive message.[8] Onstage scenes explicitly lay out the processes such viewings entail: reading, response, interpretation, reaction. Seeing the completed tapestry, Sheeth reacts with shock at the offensive actions it depicts, but overcomes her revulsion and joins in preserving the report of her mother's story (*OP4*, 47–8, 80). Modicum, similarly appalled, denies its value as art, redefines it as 'carpet,' and contemptuously tramples it underfoot (*OP4*, 72–4). Club reads the tapestry's message then rewrites it, vastly exaggerating Sleev's infidelities to embellish his own narrative of heroic achievement (*OP4*, 51–2, 61, 68).

These responses to the tapestry dramatise the dynamic relationship between art and interpretation and the potential traps facing the critic, a term I've rendered as 'creative responder'. Modicum's outraged dismissal of the object and its meanings reminds me to move beyond impulsive judgments to productive contemplation. Club's re-action alerts me to the urge to rewrite art to suit my own purposes. My desire for a dramatic action that satisfies, like Club's need, often succumbs to frustration. Like Ladder and Sheeth, I wrestle to come to terms with, to consciously negotiate the meanings produced by the work before me. And like Ladder, I reserve the right to assert my view of it (to sew my interpretation into it) once I have taken account of what I believe it to say.

To go back to the beginning: like artists, critics do not stand aside but are always implicated in the weaving of the day-to-day events that become history. And if thinking and doing are closely tied, then the ways in which I speak to art become my own means of reworking my self and setting stitches in the fabric of history. Like the characters onstage, I place myself in relationship to the staged depiction of Sleev. Like many other female subjects in history, I too am consti-tuted with reference to cultural norms that construe Sleev's actions in terms of the iconic, eternally desired and desiring Eve. Barker's play deploys wife-mother-whore imagery in complex formulations that both entice through a flattering celebration of womanly power and terrify in their invocation of irresistible, insatiable female sexuality. The depiction cuts close to the bone.

Sleev understands desire in its very nature and operation. She exercises power through that knowledge and in that regard the text creates in her an admiring portrait of mature female sexuality. It also, however, angrily sketches in the temptress who manipulates and frustrates male response. Sleev exercises agency by evoking desire and denying its satisfaction. To counteract that power, men seek to dominate her to guarantee that their desire may be fulfilled and hers controlled and channeled to their liking (*OP4*, 68–71). The societal norms that Ladder urges and eventually incorporates into the tapestry's narrative reinforce that effort. Partway through the action, Sleev puts out a call for 'a fat man' to marry her (OP4, 31–2). Is this her shamed admission that she requires such a man to confine, channel or physically suppress her uncontrollable desiring actions? Has she at last completely internalised societal strictures (as voiced by Sheeth and Ladder in particular)? Or might she long for the complete union with another (Genesis 2:24–5) made impossible by the fall?

The opacity, the undecidability of the character's motivation calls to mind Sleev's initial interpretation of Eve's plight in Genesis. Just as Sleev seems to express frustration at Eve's inability to see her self except as reflected in Adam's desiring eye, so might readers and spectators resent or resist the male author's depiction of Sleev in terms of her preoccupation with her status and behavior as a desiring female subject. On one hand, if Eve cannot see herself without Adam, neither can we see Sleev without recourse to the image reflected in/through the dramatist's eyes. On the other hand, like Barker's Sleev, a feminist critic may well take account of gendered positions, including the position of the artist, as part of clearing the ground. Sleev shows the way. Even as she attends to the gendered consciousness that occupies the wardrobe, she also challenges interpretations of her actions and place in history. In doing so, she summons onlookers to their own productive, perhaps resistant, readings of the dramatic action.

From my own perspective, then, the staging deftly puns on feminist views of patriarchal authority as controlling language and dominating the other since time began. Barker puts a man in a phallus *cum* confessional, nails a mirror to the door, and writes a female protagonist who tells the man to be quiet. Just in case we do not see the immense violation of order this represents, that protagonist invokes Eden and through her actions reminds me of the blame I carry as Eve's daughter for the fall from grace. Then the protagonist transforms his into her story and claims her own actions (her seductions, in fact) as worth recording. But the flush of victory fades as the action unfolds. Sleev at the last is companioned only by the mirrored wardrobe, now emblematically emptied of consciousness. Have we shifted to an image of the aging woman past generating or experiencing desire? Or have we entered another territory and come face to face with the fall in its fundamental effects: mortality, separation, solitude? 'Void the body,' Sleev says. 'A VOID ME' (*OP4*, 80).

If I consider the playwright's position as analogous to Modicum's, both as the consciousness in the wardrobe/phallus/confessional and in his subsequent actions to abject Sleev, it exposes the writer's ambivalent relationship to the characters he creates/controls. As writer, he determines speech and defines character; as director, he actively shapes the actors' actions onstage; as onlooker, he indulges his desire to watch, to consume the view, without risk of reciprocation. The character Modicum points to Barker's own culturally potent, gendered position. At the same time, from that place of privilege he designs a female protagonist filled with agency who (like himself?) takes pleasure in acts of transgression who (like himself?) deliberately elicits yet frustrates the desire to come into a fully knowing relationship with the self or its creations. He self-reflexively writes himself into Sleev's generation of self through art.

Barker authors Sleev's desire. In defining the character's agency through her desiring subjectivity, he risks limiting the character. He creates a character of tragic stature who strives to write herself into history, yet in doing so, he participates in (and potentially reinscribes) narratives that blame Eve – who is said to have succumbed to temptation – for the loss of Eden, after which Adam was condemned 'to till the ground from which he was taken' (Genesis 3:23). Barker goes to the centre of the attack on female agency – the scandal of her desire – and creates a character who takes on that tradition and struggles to interpret it in light of her own experience and to reconcile her needs with its demands. Her failures are the failures of that tradition. Her success is in her hunger to make sense of tradition in relation to her self. So, what initially seems to constitute Sleev in terms dominated by her relationship to sexual desire emerges as part of a larger narrative complex that (over)determines her unresolved agon with Eve's story. That narrative complex deforms her search for a new husband who, she specifies, must not only be large, but must be able to debate the meaning of Genesis with her (*OP4*, 31). Sleev's quest for meaning structures her actions as a character throughout the play. In my own reading of Genesis, Eve's desire for knowledge fuels her action (Genesis 3:6). Here, rather than delineating a simple temptress, Barker writes a character marked by sexual desire, but driven by a greater urgency, a desire to become wise, even at the cost of knowing (her own) good and evil.

I recognise in Barker's protagonist the image in which others have sought to create women. At the same time I recognise in that protagonist and her architect the pursuit of a self-reflexive creativity that I seek in enacting critical thought as I write and speak it. In this the play keeps me company as I strive to enact an ethics of criticism. The best example of reader/critic/interpreter is Sleev herself, who wrestles with Genesis and its tale of fallen beings and recounts stories of her own sexual temptation and fulfillment. As a stand-in for Eve she materialises an ethic of fallen knowledge: an unending striving towards understanding, a desire always in motion that cannot achieve satisfaction.

In the play, Sleev tells stories of arousal and seduction: how she gave in to and acted on desire (*OP4*, 17–18, 30, 54–6). She uses these tellings to intervene in and shape what others will know of her. She deploys them to seduce (spectators along with the characters onstage); they titillate, arouse, repel, and embarrass, depending on the hearer. In the telling, she makes and remakes memories of actions that comprise her past and, in these acts of narration, she constitutes a shifting never finished self in continual process of articulation, always only able to name partial truths, glimpses of the self in motion, in the making.

Like Sleev, I find myself engaging the work before me as she engages the story of Genesis, reading and rereading it in order to come closer to the truth of her (my) own desiring narrative. The character prompts me likewise to constitute my self in motion as I unpick the character. Just as Ladder, Club, Modicum, and Sheeth struggle to come to terms with the tapestry, I wrestle with an other's creation, invent narratives that account for (1) what I see, (2) the meanings I make, (3) what I bring to the process and (4) the actions I will take as a consequence of these acts of interpretation. Circulating among, endlessly redoing, acts of interpretation recalls me to the fact that I view the subject through eyes dimmed, speak in language obscured by, the effort to express my experience of it. The subject tempts, but always eludes my completed, satisfied knowing. Like Sleev, the text elicits the desire to know, to come into ever closer relationship to it, then sustains that tantalising desire by refusing catharsis, the release that (momentarily?) satisfies.

Notes

1 Barker's texts regularly force questions about the creative act and events that overtake the creator: *No End of Blame, Scenes from an Execution* and *Terrible Mouth* come to mind. I say 'creator' because, whether cartoonist, painter, or engineer like Krak in *The Castle*, what binds these characters is the act of making, doing. Here lies the connection with me as creative responder, sometimes called critic. How might my creative action, my criticism, go to work in the world?

2 My overly tidy distillation of a proposition developed elsewhere, rooted in Foucault's distinction between *connaissance* ('the process that permits the multiplication of knowable objects') and *savoir* ('the process through which the subject finds himself modified by what he knows, or rather by the labor performed in order to know. It is what permits the modification of the subject and the construction of the object.'). See 'The Subject, Knowledge, and the "History of Truth"' in *Remarks on Marx:*

Conversations with Duccio Trombadori (translated by R. J. Goldstein and J. Cascaito. New York: Semiotext(e), 1991), pp. 69–70. Foucault makes it possible to see more clearly (1) making theatre as a labour we perform in order to know and (2) responding to art as work that constructs an object and in that process modifies subjectivity.

3 I am indebted to Aaron C. Thomas for this formulation. His careful notes added much to this essay. Thanks also to David Ian Rabey for his insightful comments.

4 One could productively use this play with its mirrored wardrobe to interrogate Lacanian theories of subject formation and desire. Here my project is somewhat different. Consistent with the proposition that doing – specifically theatrical doing – is thinking, I encounter the play as embodied theory.

5 In the terms identified in Note 2, above.

6 Sleev describes a monk who went blind illuminating manuscripts. On her last visit he was in the Abbey courtyard surrounded by white sheets to focus the light as he worked (*OP4*, 16). The image recalls Barker's paintings, the opening of *A Style and Its Origins* by Barker writing as Eduardo Houth ('Beginning with the white sheet …', *ASIO*, 13–15), and his 2003 play *The Moving and the Still*.

7 Barker directed the premiere of *I Saw Myself* performed by The Wrestling School at the Jerwood Vanbrugh Theatre in London, April 2008. After hearing my initial rather humanistic reading of the scene, he described his staging: the mirrored door opened slowly and passed by Sleev; the character did not directly confront the image.

8 Similarly the play will be received as telling a true tale or rejected for the truths it lays open to view. In the course of the action, Sleev comes to another understanding of truth based in scrutiny of the self: 'My tapestry is true if you want history weave another one' (*OP4*, 56).

13

'His niece or his sister': genealogical uncertainties and literary filiation in Barker's *Gertrude – The Cry*

Vanasay Khamphommala

Hamlet's father comes in a 'questionable shape'[1] in more ways than one, as Shakespeare's questionable use of the word 'questionable' itself underlines. He not only raises the spiritual question of the afterlife, the excruciating problem of our relation to our forefathers or the theatrical *cul-de-sac* of the representation of the spectral. Hamlet's doubts about his father also apply metaphorically to his literary father, Shakespeare, who is also believed to be the first performer of the part of the ghost. *Hamlet* can thus be read as a play in which the question of authority is translated into an encounter with the ghost of the father, and speculation about Shakespeare – as the various sources for *Hamlet* have all tended to obfuscate the origins of the play and in doing so, have participated in its transformation into a myth.

Such a dilution of authority necessarily affects any intertextual undertaking, and Howard Barker's *Gertrude – The Cry* (2002), first performed in 2002 in Elsinore, is no exception to the rule. But stretching the concept of authorship has been part of Barker's aesthetics from his first plays onwards, and far from being Barker's first foray into the territories of intertextuality, *Gertrude* prolongs the experiments he carried out in such plays as *Henry V in Two Parts* (1973), *Women Beware Women* (1986), *Seven Lears* (1989) and *(Uncle) Vanya* (1996). Barker extends this questioning of the figure of the author by creating characters who are themselves authorial, and often authoritative figures, from the painter Galactia to the weaver Sleev through the poet Sleen or the painter Poussin. Moreover, Barker has tended to blur the line between fiction and reality by attributing some of his work, on stage, but also in publication, to fictitious alter egos (such as the biographer 'Eduardo Houth', and the scenographers 'Billie Kaiser', 'Tomas Leipzig', 'Caroline Shentang' and 'Paula Sezno').

Gertrude, however, does take the question of the link between intertextuality and authorship one step further by literally focusing on Hamlet's matrix, his point of origin, his mother Gertrude. By giving Gertrude a 'tragic daughter' (*OP2*, 147) with Claudius, Barker metaphorises his own literary enterprise, which consists in giving *Hamlet* a sister-play, in deriving a new dramatic text from pre-existent material. But far from elucidating the relationship between both tragedies, this genealogical metaphor on the contrary complicates their link by flaunting a mode of interpretation that is, in turn, questionable, both as a hermeneutical tool to attain certainty and as a valid trope to represent intertextuality. This chapter will examine how does Barker metaphorise intertextual ambiguity as genealogical uncertainty in *Gertrude – The Cry*? And, what are the aesthetic consequences of this conflation? In order to try and answer these questions, I will first examine how Barker creates, within the plot of *Gertrude*, a systematic ambiguity surrounding the questions of genealogical relations. I will then move on to analyse Barker's poetics of intertextuality and how they apply to the relation between his play and Shakespeare's. Finally, I will try to define how Barker's refusal of recognition creates a specific aesthetic framework for those who venture into his work.

'I am perhaps her brother' – unsettling genealogy (*OP2*, 149)

Barker's *Gertrude* can in many ways be considered as *Hamlet*'s offspring. Yet by choosing to name his tragedy after the mother of Hamlet, Barker seems to contradict this literary lineage and announce the genealogical confusion that will infiltrate his own play. The choice of Shakespeare's source text, to be sure, offers its share of such ambiguities for Barker to seize, as illustrated in Hamlet's famous first two lines:

> CLAUDIUS: But now, my cousin Hamlet, and my son—
>
> HAMLET: A little more than kin, and less than kind.
>
> CLAUDIUS: How is it that the clouds still hang on you?
>
> HAMLET: Not so, my lord, I am too much i'th'sun.[2]

But Hamlet's uncertainties are not solely restricted to his relation to his uncle. His suspicions, on the contrary, seem to contaminate his perception of the bonds of family in general, and lead him to question, among others, how his father and Claudius, 'Hyperion to a satyr',[3] could be brothers in spite of their physical dissimilarity. Moreover, Claudius's relation to his mother, that Hamlet somewhat surprisingly describes as 'incestuous',[4] brings further confusion to a traditional, clear-cut conception of family patterns, already eroded by the homonymy that links Hamlet to his own father and thus threatens to cancel out differences between generations.

   In *Gertrude*, the birth of the queen's daughter Jane in scene sixteen brings this confusion to a high point, so much so that the word 'born' itself seems to become unpronounceable to Hamlet:

Are they not the inheritors of the earth and all our labour is it not directed to the
enhancement of existence for the newly and the as yet un
THE NEWLY AND THE AS YET UN?   (*OP2*, 149)

This confusion however is best expressed in Claudius's telling hesitation: 'Show
him [Hamlet] his niece or his sister is it let him see the function's functioning'
(*OP2*, 145). Claudius's epanorthosis contributes to an obscurity that characterises
the entire line, whose binary structure – hinging on two synonymous imperatives and the final polyptoton – all seem to point towards a tautological repetition that attempts to circumvent the inexpressible status of the newborn child.
Language, indeed seems inadequate to describe Hamlet's relation to Jane, who is
only partially his sister (they do not have the same father) and not at all his niece,
which would require for Hamlet to be the brother of either his mother or his
uncle.

Jane's birth throws off the fragile balance of genealogical order by provoking
a series of reversals and upheavals underlined by the text. Her very conception is
described by Hamlet as a challenge to natural order: 'Is forty-three and by the
laws of nature if nature were not so contaminated with disease should have shed
her last egg whole easters and christmases ago this faded and' (*OP2*, 144). In fact,
Gertrude's pregnancy appears as a provocation for the younger generation of
women expected to procreate, and Gertrude's revelation of her condition to
Ragusa in scene five is meant as 'a way of slapping [her]' (*OP2*, 103).[5] This
inversion of natural order is prolonged by Gertrude's behaviour after the birth of
her daughter. As Claudius notices before sucking on Gertrude's breasts and
depriving his daughter of her milk, mother and daughter already seem to have
traded places: 'SHE CRIES / Not the child the mother' (*OP2*, 145).

The striking image of Claudius drinking his lover's milk contributes to the
play's assault on traditional representation of parenthood, which in turn
problematises heredity and genealogy. Even Ragusa's supposed interest in what
she pompously calls 'the welfare of the child' (*OP2*, 154), and that prompts her
to bring a lawsuit against Gertrude, does not prevent her from later drowning the
baby. Barker's parents refuse to conform to their duties, not even to that of
naming the child. Gertrude and Claudius literally refuse to recognise their child,
to give her a name, and hence an identity and a place in the order of the family.
When asked about the name of his daughter, Claudius merely shrugs and leaves
it to Cascan to pick one (*OP2*, 147–8). Two scenes later, when Ragusa removes
Jane from the arms of her mother, Gertrude, apparently unmoved, simply
remarks: 'Her name is Jane / But that was in her first life' (*OP2*, 147).

Leaving the choice of a name to Cascan may seem ill-advised, seeing as he
considers that the first use of a name is to identify graves (*OP2*, 147), and since
his own name is so hateful to him that he refuses to disclose it ('My mother gave
me such a foolish name I have never dared reveal it … No one knows it now'
(*OP2*, 148)). Moreover, the name he chooses, Jane, is mainly remarkable for

being absolutely unremarkable, even more so in the context of the names of the other characters in the play. By choosing Jane, one of the most generic and nondescript first names in the English language, Cascan denies the baby what the very process of naming was supposed to give her: an identity.

The vagueness of Jane's name, however, is only the most explicit symptom of a malaise that has much deeper roots. Indeed, in spite of Gertrude's protestations that Claudius is the father of her child, the suspicions regularly raised by other characters about Gertrude's prolific sexuality are not easily dismissed when it comes to ascertaining Claudius's paternity. Gertrude asserts that '[she] know[s] the day [she] know[s] the place' (*OP2*, 103) when the baby was conceived, and touching her pregnant belly, tells Claudius that unlike her baby, Hamlet is 'not [their] child' (*OP2*, 135). But Hamlet's repeated allusions to his mother's promiscuity, his suggestion that she has slept with Cascan (*OP2*, 110), his calling the baby 'the howling product of her delinquencies' (*OP2*, 144) cannot but undermine our readiness to believe her. Paternity in the play becomes unverifiable as a result of the very nature of female sexuality, uniformly described as literally uncontrollable, ungovernable. If marriage, and the vow of fidelity that comes with it, is one of the fragile means that is supposed to uphold the legitimacy of a lineage, it is one that the women of the play seem to circumvent easily: Gertrude's betrayal of her husband in the first scene only upgrades the example set by Isola in scene four, and of which she was a witness. Similarly, in scene eleven, Claudius questions the true identity of his brother's father:

> She was a whore in her own time
> MOTHER
> A whore in her own time yes
> MOTHER
> My brother for example
> NAME HIS DAD
> (*Pause.*)
> MOTHER
> (*He is distraught.*)   (*OP2*, 128)

Gertrude — The Cry therefore appears as a play in which matters of heredity are constantly questioned, opening up large areas of uncertainty surrounding the problem of origin. In a play that is so explicity intertextual, this obsession about the undecidability of paternity cannot but acquire a meta-dramatic aspect, and this is all the more so if one takes into account Barker's idiosyncratic take on intertextuality.

Exploring the interstices of the intertext

Barker's recurrent resort to 'what — depending on your point of view — is the charnel house or the pantheon of European drama' (*AT*, 154) as a basis for his own plays has prompted him to express himself in two major essays on the question of intertextuality: 'Love in the Museum: The Modern Author and the Antique Text' (*AT*, 171–8), and even more importantly, 'Murders and Conversations: The Classic Text and a Contemporary Writer' (*AT*, 153–7). A striking rhetorical feature of both essays is the way in which intertextual relationships are compared to and metaphorised as interpersonal relationships, more often than not of a transgressive kind, culminating in the concept of 'literary necrophilia' (*AT*, 153). This comparison, based on a personification of the text, leads Barker to a strange realigning of text, character, and author:

> And how much broken will attaches not only to the characters of these plays [Lear and Vanya], but to their creators? There is no answer to this question, but I raise it to suggest the intimacy that conditions the first conversations between a living and a dead artist, conversations which, as they unfold, might reveal not only the desire felt by one for another, but also the potential lethality of it, for there's no passion where the spectre of murder does not haunt the room. (*AT*, 157).

If conversations are the starting point of Barker's intertextual enterprises, they develop into complex relationships of an illegitimate nature, bringing together desire and destruction, in a manner that is reminiscent of the agonised love affairs that Barker stages in the plays themselves. In fact, it is this parallel between literary creation and sexual desire that Barker's more recent philosophical work *Death, the One and the Art of Theatre* (2005) ceaselessly explores.

By comparing his confrontations with other texts to 'the early stages of a love affair' (*AT*, 175)., by placing them under the sign of passion and illegitimacy, Barker forbids a coolly intellectual or conventional approach of intertextuality. In fact, his insistence on the illegitimacy of this practice, its obscurity and even sacrilegious nature withdraws his plays from the frame within which intertextuality is usually assessed, and claims for them an ambiguous and original status analogous to that of adulterous children. Rather than rewritings, as they are often called for reasons of convenience, Barker's intertextual plays therefore appear as renegotiations of a new kind that eschew traditional categories. *Hamlet* and *Gertrude*, as plays, are without a doubt related, but the nature of their relation remains to be defined. How much do they look alike? How do they differ? *Gertrude*'s plot swerves too much from *Hamlet*'s for Barker's play to be defined as a parody or a burlesque in any conventional sense, all the more so since these types of intertextuality pertain for the most part to comedy, when Barker insists on the tragic nature of his writing. As for their stylistic features, both plays have too little in common for *Gertrude* to be considered as a pastiche. In fact, Barker seems careful not to quote Shakespeare explicitly, as he had done in *Henry V in Two Parts*.[6] When he does so, as with the expression 'Gertrude, do not drink',[7] it is for words that are so banal that attributing them to Shakespeare at all becomes doubtful (should one choose however to consider them as a direct quote, Barker's prosodic treatment of the phrase, that he breaks up into four lines, immediately challenges the continuity thus created between both plays).

By refusing to abide by a conventional definition of intertextuality, Barker throws off our usual landmarks and invites the reader or audience to question from scratch such basic questions as: how does intertextuality manifest itself? How is literary influence to be defined and grasped? The paradox of *Gertrude*, in respect to *Hamlet*, is that it seems to flaunt its reference to Shakespeare's play as a red herring, a means to set the audience on a wild goose chase the better to frustrate them, because *Gertrude* resembles *Hamlet* just enough for their differences to be all the more noticeable. This can be felt as early as in the *dramatis personae*, in which Barker makes a peculiar use of the indefinite article, whose usual function consists in introducing a new referent into a discourse, in contradistinction to the definite article that refers to a referent already familiar to both speaker and addressee. By writing 'GERTRUDE, a Queen', or 'HAMLET, an Heir' (*OP2*, 81), Barker blurs referentiality and introduces known referents as if they were unknown, and entirely new to us. Moreover, the use of generic nouns (queen, heir) strips the characters of their defining traits to reduce them to archetypes: Gertrude is no longer, as in Shakespeare's first Folio, 'GERTRUDE, Queen of Denmark', but 'GERTRUDE, a queen', and perhaps any queen. This explicit attempt to defamiliarise, to introduce something long familiar as something strange, participates precisely in what Freud has defined as the aesthetic of *das Unheimliche* (the uncanny) that is so pervasive in Barker's theatre.

References to *Hamlet* in the play as a whole operate very much in the same manner, playing on confusion between familiar motifs and deliberate innovations. They remind the audience of *Hamlet* but only under the form of doubt: identification is suggested only to be put into question. This is particularly the case with the characters created by Barker, and especially Ragusa and Mecklenburg, whom audiences and critics alike attempt, irresistibly, but necessarily indemonstrably, to fit onto Shakespeare's original. Mecklenburg, for instance, first introduced as Hamlet's friend (*OP2*, 111), does bring to mind Shakespeare's Horatio, before posting his army on the frontier (*OP2*, 167) and turning into a new figure of Fortinbras. But what is most striking about these traits shared with Shakespeare's characters is their unassignability, and how they do not suffice to account for Barker's creation. As for Ragusa, as the sole young woman of the cast, and involved as she is in a torturous relationship to Hamlet, she appears as an obvious candidate for the part of Ophelia. But Barker seems to frustrate our desire to identify both young women by leaving out most of Ophelia's distinctive features and thus refuses the audience the satisfaction of an explicit recognition.

Barker's poetics of the intertextual thus seems to focus mainly on the interstitial, on this space of uncertainty that belongs neither to one work nor to the other, but is both a point of contact and a breaking point between the two. Such is the power and the paradox of the allusion, that it keeps the right distance between affirmation and denial of a link that relies on the audience's speculation.

It is on this speculative participation of the audience that I would like to focus to conclude this essay.

Unrecognisability as aesthetic paradigm

This strategy of deliberate refusal of recognition is not solely to be found in *Gertrude – The Cry* but pertains to Barker's aesthetics as a whole. In a painting exhibited in Caen in 2008, entitled *Elsinore, Home for Incurables*, Barker applies to the canvas an aesthetic that is highly reminiscent of his way with the stage. The thirty-six-inch square painting represents two characters in the centre of a landscape with three trees in the background and a red flag. One, apparently a man, is seated; the other stands on the right, a woman hiding her face behind her arm. Not that one could recognise her if she revealed her face: as is so often the case in Barker's pictorial work, faces are absent, so that characters are constructed as structurally unidentifiable and remain a secret that cannot be elucidated. Their bodies gesture towards an identity of which they are finally deprived by the absence of a face. This functioning applies not only to the characters in the painting, but also to the situation in which they are set, that suggests a relationship between both characters that remains ultimately unverifiable: are they relatives, lovers? Does the distance between them signify estrangement, desire? We find here again the problematic interstice of allusion that allows for speculation but not for verification.

Speculation is of course encouraged by the presence of a title that cannot but move the spectator to try to identify the characters and the scene represented in the painting. Are these Gertrude and Claudius? Hamlet and Ophelia? Is this an episode of *Hamlet*? And if so, which one? It could be of course that the answers to these questions are disseminated in the frame and only require for the spectator to lean forward and have a closer look. But what if these answers were simply not there? What if the picture were simply the thing wherein Barker catches the conscience of his audience? What if the title's reference to Elsinore, which one easily implies to refer metonymically to *Hamlet*, were in fact no reference to it at all? This may or may not be the case, but even if certainty could be attained, one cannot but notice how Barker seems to discourage us from trying to find it at all, by generally favouring confusion and doubt over distinction and clarity. As a matter of fact, indistinction appears as a major motif both in his paintings and in his plays. In *Elsinore, Home for Incurables*, this indistinction can be found on several levels. Within the picture itself, beside the sketch-like quality of the drawing that combines a feeling of urgency to that of imprecision, the restricted palette, consisting mainly of shades of grey and brown except for the red flag, drowns out single, specific details in an organic continuity between landscapes and characters. But even within Barker's collection of paintings, the refusal of identification appears as a governing principle. It seems indeed that nothing distinguishes this painting from others in the series, whether in format, in style or in chromatic choices. Whether in his paintings or in his plays, the dominant impression created by Barker's work is not one of difference but of sameness and repetition.

Barker has eloquently rejected recognition as aesthetic paralysis in *Arguments for a Theatre*, instead of which he seems to promote unrecognisability as aesthetic paradigm. The impossibility to recognise, sometimes even to see, becomes the condition for that instability of meaning, that speculation that is at the heart of Barker's poetics. It is therefore arresting that *Gertrude – The Cry* should open on a scene which apparently resolves and clarifies what Shakespeare, in *Hamlet*, refuses to represent directly, thus giving his hero so much ground for speculation, a scene which is apparently explicitly intertextual, yet reproduces a scene that is precisely absent from the original. But for all its apparent explicitness, *Gertrude's* first scene, rather than disclosing meaning, reveals on the contrary the futility and even the desperation that attaches to its pursuit. This scene problematises rather than yields meaning, because, as the stage direction suggests, the 'music of extremes'[8] uttered by the characters hints at allegory and points towards an excess of meaning that the image can only suggest but not show. This double movement (suggesting meaning but refusing its revelation) is buttressed in the scene by the obsessive use of the lexical field of vision, understood as a means to achieve certainty and rationality:

CLAUDIUS: Let me see the reason I am killing
GERTRUDE: (*Tearing off her clothes.*) Yes
    Yes
CLAUDIUS: And if he stirs
    If his eyes open in his agony
    Show him the reason he is dying
    Let him see what I have stolen
    What was his
    And now belongs to me
    THE THING
    THE THING   (*OP2*, 84)

But paradoxically, Claudius's thirst for an 'ocular proof', literally embodied in Gertrude's nakedness, does not enable him to reach clarity, but leads him on the contrary to an ever-growing confusion betrayed by the growing imprecision of his language, ending in paraphrase, repetition and lexical indistinctness. Showing or seeing reason thus become oxymoronic expressions that uncover not the continuity but the incompatibility of the paradigm of vision and of the paradigm of reason.

In this first scene, primal in every sense of the word, Gertrude is thus already constructed as the ungraspable sign of a meaning to which she simultaneously points and bars access. This scene, however, does not only read as an exposition of what Cascan terms the 'ever-receding quality' (*OP2*, 84), if not of ecstasy, at least of meaning, nor does it solely serve the clarification of intertextuality by representing a scene at which Shakespeare's original only hints. *Gertrude's* first scene, in several ways, appears as a scene of conception in which the beginning of an adulterous love affair is also made to represent metaphorically the beginning of Barker's liaison with Shakespeare's *Hamlet*, which will result, dramatically, in the birth of Jane, and metadramatically, in the completion of Barker's play.

In conclusion

Finally, I would like to comment on one of the most striking differences between *Hamlet* and *Gertrude – The Cry*: the disappearance of the ghost of Hamlet's father. This removal, however, does not prevent spectrality from pervading Barker's play – on the contrary: once Barker does away, and quite explicitly so in the beginning of scene three, with Shakespeare's main source of doubt, uncertainty comes back kicking and infiltrates every aspect of the text. It is not surprising, from a psychoanalytical point of view, that this absence of the father should thus trigger suspicion and scepticism to take over the stage. Lacan, using Shakespeare as a case in point, thus describes paternity as necessarily speculative when he defines what he calls 'paternal undecidability':

> … the fact, so often commented on in Shakespeare's plays, that the father is always a suppositional father, a father by imputation, rather than by unimpeachable biological proof. […] This doubt, on which paternity, legitimacy, inheritance, primogeniture, and succession all depend, is the anxiety at the root of the *cultural* failure of the paternal metaphor – that is, its failure because of its status as metaphor, its nontranslatability into the realm of proof. (*OP2*, 83–4)

This metaphor, however flawed, is at the core of Barker's *Gertrude*, in which he exploits the polysemy of paternity to the fullest, both to create dramatic tension and to problematise the question of literary authorship that necessarily affects a play that relies so intensively on intertextuality. Paternity, as a paradigm of the unknowable, thus becomes both a thematic crucible and as a structuring principle of the play.

Notes

1 W. Shakespeare, *Hamlet* I, iv, ll 672.
2 *Ibid.*, I, ii, ll 266–9.
3 *Ibid.*, I, ii, 333.
4 *Ibid.*, I, ii, 361.
5 *Ibid.*, p. 103. This idea is forcefully expressed in Barker's play *Knowledge and a Girl* (2003), where Snow White, unlike the queen, is unable to become pregnant.
6 Broadcast in 1971 (unpublished).
7 W. Shakespeare, *Hamlet* 5, ii, ll 3942 / H. Barker, *Howard Barker: Plays Two* (London: Oberon, 2006), p. 157.
8 *Ibid.*, p. 84.

14

History in the age of fracture: catastrophic time in Barker's *The Bite of the Night*

Jay Gipson-King

What are the politics of time? Can ruptures in time be used to affect the viewing experience? Can temporal shape be used to repoliticise myth? And can form alone, without reference to topical politics, create a subversive political system? Howard Barker proves that the answers to all of these questions is 'yes'. In addition to the many theatrical conventions that Barker explodes in his Theatre of Catastrophe, Barker manipulates *time* at multiple levels of the theatrical experience in order to upset conventional habits of viewing and attack the political-moral system embedded within linear realism. I will begin by suggesting how time might be considered politically – as opposed to philosophically or scientifically – and introduce a framework for examining time on stage. Next, I will explore how Barker manipulates narrative time, audience time, and dramatic time using *The Bite of the Night* as my primary example. A close reading of the text combined with critical reactions to the performance reveal how Barker's use of temporal shape allows him to fulfill many of the goals stated in *Arguments for a Theatre*. Finally, I will discuss how Barker's use of time defamiliarises the myths of his plays, thus reactivating their political potential, while simultaneously attacking what Mary Karen Dahl calls the 'deep structure of things'.[1] Barker's unconventional depictions of time do nothing less than create a theatrical-political system that empowers its spectators.

First, what are the politics of time? Can time even have a politics? Great thinkers from Kant to Einstein and disciplines from physics to anthropology have grappled with time, bringing to the problem their own sets of questions and methods of investigation. The combination of these approaches suggests that the day-to-day experience of time is the result of multiple layers of functionality. At its most basic level, time is a fundamental aspect of the universe, as essential as space and inseparable from it. The physics of time are then refracted through human biology: the brain, the body, the breath, and even the circadian rhythms of individual cells. The physical experience of time is refracted again through language – the means by which we express and think of time. The mental perception of time is further modified on an individual level by personality and mental health, and such circumstantial factors as mood, situation and even weather. A myriad of factors contribute to the experience of any particular moment of time.

On top of all of these factors, human perceptions of time are shaped by culture, and as such are subject to the forces of human agency. For example, Robert Levine's cross-cultural survey of the *pace* of life indicates that 'people are prone to move faster in places with vital economies, a high degree of industrial-isation, larger populations, cooler climates, and a cultural orientation toward individualism'.[2] Technology also influences our perceptions of time. Levine notes that the word 'punctual' did not enter the English language until 1700, because before then clocks were not accurate enough for the concept of punctuality to exist. Even the simple question, 'what time is it?' has little to do with the position of the sun relative to our current longitude, and much more to do with economic and governmental decisions made just over 150 years ago, as commu-nities switched from local time to global time zones at the prompting of railroads and government agencies.[3] Time, then, is a political entity.

Moreover, perceptions of time reflect and influence perceptions of the world at large. Western cultures tend to perceive time as *directional, irreversible* and *contin-uous* – in other words, as *linear*.[4] This model is tied up with Christian cosmology, which moves in a straight line from creation to Armageddon,[5] and with the Industrial Revolution, which segmented time into discrete, linear units in order to increase productivity in the factory.[6]

Given all of these factors, how does time work on stage? As in real life, time in the theatre is a multifaceted phenomenon that operates on both a collective and an individual basis. An analysis of theatrical time must take into account the reality of the auditorium, the fiction taking place on stage, and the interaction between them. Therefore, I would like to introduce a framework of Audience Time, Dramatic Time and Narrative Time in order to break down and analyse temporal experience in the theatre.

Audience time, as I define it, is time as experienced by a spectator sitting in the house. This includes the duration of the performance, the number and spacing of intermissions and each spectator's personal absorption or boredom with the performance, as the case may be. *Dramatic time* refers to the progression of the plot or dramatic action. Does the story proceed from beginning to middle to end in Aristotelian fashion? Does the action move backwards from the climax to the inciting incident, as in Harold Pinter's *Betrayal*? Or is the dramatic action more diffuse, as in the repetitions and revisions of Suzan-Lori Parks? Lastly, *narrative time* is the fictional time experienced by the *characters* within the story. In some cases narrative time can be synchronous with real time, as in Molière's *The Impromptu at Versailles*, or it can also stretch over days, months or years as in Shakespeare. Combined, these three types of time create what I call a play's temporal shape, or form. Phenomenologically speaking, form is the *container* that holds the content of the actual story. Like all containers, its *shape* alters the observer's perception of the object contained.[7] Temporal shape, therefore, becomes a vital part of the overall experience and meaning of any play.

Howard Barker deliberately manipulates time as part of his Theatre of Catastrophe, or in more current terms, the Art of Theatre. Barker's theory and practice are widely known, but I would like to call attention to one particular passage from *Arguments for a Theatre* that illustrates his use of time. The audience, he writes:

> must be liberated from its fear of obscurity and encouraged to welcome its moments of loss. These moments of loss involve the breaking of the narrative thread, the sudden suspension of the story, the interruption of the obliquely related interlude, and a number of devices designed to complicate and to overwhelm the audience's habitual method of seeing. (*AT*, 53)

This passage, originally published in the *Guardian* as a means of preparing audiences to face *The Bite of the Night*,[8] describes a fractured temporal shape and begins to indicate how ruptures in time can be used to disrupt the viewing experience. *The Bite of the Night* serves as an excellent demonstration of this practice, as it makes use of audience time, dramatic time, and narrative time to striking effect.

Originally written in 1985, *The Bite of the Night* was produced in 1988, directed by Danny Boyle at the Barbican Pit for the Royal Shakespeare Company.[9] As Barker himself describes the plot, 'a classics teacher at a defunct university [Savage], having driven his father to suicide and his son into vagrancy, takes his favoured pupil Hogbin on a reluctant tour of the Eleven Troys of antiquity, engaging with Helen in a succession of political systems each of which reduces her physically until she is no more than a voice in a chair' (*AT*, 83), a summary that belies the complexity of Barker's most ambitious work to that date.

One of the play's most distinctive elements is its use of audience time as a means of altering the typical theatrical experience. Barker wrote in his program notes, '*The Bite of the Night* is not contemporary, nor satirical, neither is it short. It is mythical, tragic and very long' (*AT*, 38). With a total playing time of four hours and twenty minute, 'not short' is something of an understatement. Although the curtain went up at 7:00 pm, the play did not end until 11:30, *after* London public transportation had stopped running, making the trip home both inconvenient and expensive. Several critics left after the *second* intermission. However, audiences were given fair warning. As Barker reports with some chagrin, 'at five hours long, this was deemed such an affront to human tolerance that the RSC box office were given instructions to dissuade potential customers by prefacing all ticket sales with details of its length and obscenity. Some nevertheless found the courage to defy this health warning' (*AT*, 101).

It is easy to say that the play was merely *long*, but in point of fact, the physical time of the performance altered the entire theatre-going experience. In the first place, the proliferation of warnings limited the audience to a group of self-selecting volunteers who were prepared (or who should have been prepared) for the length of the performance. Second, the extended duration would have made the performance physically challenging for anyone to sit through, with any discomfort leading to an increased perception of duration, thus compounding the effect. 'Bum numbing' was a term brandied about in more than one review. And by all reports, the play was mentally exhausting as well, due substantially to the abundance of violent and disturbing imagery. Michael Ratcliffe of the *Observer* described the event as 'a pugilist's play, fought without rules, to test the receptive attention of audience and actors alike'.[10] The duration of audience time helped to overwhelm spectators physically and mentally, furthering Barker's stated aim of breaking down traditional methods of viewing.

Barker compounded the unsettling effect of audience time with his use of dramatic time – that is, the progression of the dramatic action. In some respects, the dramatic time of *The Bite of the Night* is outright Aristotelian. By virtue of the two act breaks, the play had a clearly demarked beginning, middle and end. Additionally, Savage goes through a perceptible character arc, ultimately gaining some of the self-knowledge he sought from the outset. However, aside from these basic organising principals, the action of the play is incredibly diffuse, with no discernible rising and falling action or predictability. The characters wax and wane with power at an alarming rate of speed as Troy progresses through its various forms of government. Characters couple and uncouple as dictated by the chaotic and irresistible forces of desire, making romantic relationships equally unstable. The dramatic action meanders, proceeding not in linear progression but haphazardly. Moreover, simply a massive amount of events take place – a feat made possible due to the length of the play – violating Aristotle's rule that spectators should be able to hold the complete shape of the play in their heads at once. Like audience time, dramatic time threatens to confuse and overwhelm.

Barker disrupts dramatic time even further with the use of two interludes that punctuate the ends of the first and second acts. In the first interlude, taking place in what Barker scholar David Ian Rabey calls 'a different historical plane',[11] two Muslim cartographers set up a picnic with the aid of a 'European servant' (*CP4*, 49). The scene *seems* to take place some hundreds of years after the main action, as Islam did not even exist at the time of the original Troy. It is a severe anachronism, then, when Helen's daughter enters with a group of soldiers and has the cartographers executed 'because what [they] tell me I don't wish to know' (*CP4*, 53). The second interlude depicts Heinrich Schliemann, the real-life archeologist who may have discovered the actual city of Troy in the 1870s, excavating artifacts that were used by Helen and Savage in the previous scene.

Structurally, the interludes serve as bookends to the prologues that begin each act. The prologues and interludes serve a similar function for Barker, who explains that they 'encourage [the audience] to suspend its urge to organise the material until the conclusion of the performance' (*AT*, 83–4). Temporally, the prologues and interludes interrupt the flow of dramatic time, changing the shape of the play into something fractured and jagged.

Finally, narrative time – time as experienced by the characters within the world of the play – is one of the piece's most complex elements. The fictional story is filled with disorienting anachronisms as the temporal setting of the play remains unfixed. Barker describes the play as if Savage and his student travel backwards in time to classical Troy (*AT*, 101). However, the play begins with Savage's modern university town having been sacked by rampaging Greeks, and the inhabitants of the ancient city discuss all manner of modern technologies, from plastic surgery to nuclear fall-out. So it is less that Savage has traveled through time than that the two historical periods have somehow collided. In the RSC production, the soldiers sported a historical cross-section of armor and weapons, from swords to rifles and grenades.[12] Homer himself makes an appearance, breaking through boundaries both temporal and literary. Barker writes that 'the ahistoricity of this journey is obvious, the collapsing of time and narrative signaling to the audience that it must forsake its conventional expectations of meaning' (*AT*, 83). Indeed, the anachronisms here are so pervasive that nothing could be said to be truly *out of time*, because there is no stable frame of reference from whence one can depart. Rather than shock or intrude (as, for example, the jets do at the end of Barker's play *The Castle*), these anachronisms disorient, as they deny a fixed time and place on which the audience can ground itself. Spectators must either accept Barker's suggestion to 'experience the play moment by moment', or fight for coherency, with the likely frustrations that would ensue. Reviewers of the production had both reactions, with far more expressing frustration than acceptance.[13]

Barker uses the entire temporal shape of *The Bite of the Night* – audience time, dramatic time, and narrative time – to disrupt the viewing experience and overwhelm his audiences. In this he was clearly successful given the report of so many critics who felt angry or discomfited. While Barker manipulated time at all levels of the performance, the play's length in particular (i.e., audience time) provoked an inordinate amount of anger from reviewers. Sheridan Morley complained bitterly in *Punch* that:

> four and a half hours in the Barbican Pit seems to me careless and arrogant in the extreme. Not only does a close-by-midnight final curtain show a willful disregard for audiences with public-transport problems from an already inaccessible Barbican, it also assumes Mr. Barker has a right to occupy more time than *King Lear*.[14]

Clive Hirschhorn (*Sunday Express*), Milton Shulman (*Evening Standard*), and Jack Tinker (*Daily Mail*) echoed Morley's sentiments almost exactly, even down to comparisons with Shakespeare.[15] However, given that Barker writes in the programme notes about restoring dignity to the audience, there is a discrepancy here between intention and reception, behind which lie assumptions about the use and value of time.

As always with Barker, there are several things going on at once. The classical works referenced by the critics, such as *Lear* and *Hamlet*, which are presumably 'allowed' to be long, possess a cultural cachet that Barker lacks. As Jim Hiley wrote in *The Listener*, Barker 'committed the sin of ambition – acceptable in dead playwrights, less often so in living ones'.[16] Furthermore, as a catastrophic play, there is no redemption, no 'lesson,' no kernel of truth. Nothing rewards the expenditure of time and effort for critics looking for a traditional payoff; consequently, they felt their viewership was a *waste* of time. However, what Barker really did was break the temporal expectations of his time and place – the cultural assumptions surrounding the theatrical event. In fact, Barker flaunts these expectations. In birthing such a 'monster of the stage', in Ratcliffe's words,[17] he is making a statement against conventional theatre and its trappings. Tony Dunn wrote in *The Tribune* that 'plays of this length, making these intellectual demands on the audience, are very unusual in these days of flash consumption. The only way to appreciate them is to experience them'.[18] The temporal shape of the play – the very act of staging it in its entirety – becomes an affront to the theatrical system of flash consumption and easy meaning that surrounds and seeks to contain it.

Additionally, Barker's use of time opens up into greater areas of political significance in relation to history and myth, topics Barker and others would consider synonymous. As British historian Malcolm Smith explains, it is not that history is 'a load of lies to be uncovered', but that it is 'a widely held view of the past which has helped to shape and to explain the present'.[19] In other words, history is what we *believe* about the past. But if history is myth, there is a danger here. Literary theorist Roland Barthes defines myth as *depoliticised* speech, speech that creates a sense of inevitability by erasing the evidence of its own construction, thereby denying alternative courses of action.[20] To Barthes, myths perpetuate the status quo. *The Bite of the Night* is based on a literal myth (Helen of Troy) that might also be history (the city of Troy), that also constitutes a foundational literary trope (*The Illiad*). However, instead of simply retelling a familiar tale, Barker takes the received narrative of the fall of Troy and rewrites it within his own moral and theatrical framework. Furthermore, Barker's disruption of time alters the entire experience of the myth, making it unfamiliar, strange, even upsetting. The anachronisms that permeate *narrative time* deny a stable landscape where spectators can ground the action. The anachronisms, the interludes, and the diffusion of events deny the cohesion of a linear *dramatic time* or the predictability of rising and falling action. The proliferation of disturbing imagery, combined with the excessive length of the play, create an *audience time* that overwhelms traditional methods of viewing and that shatters theatrical conventions. By defamiliarising not just the content, but the entire experience of the historio-literary myth, Barker exposes its method of construction; in other words, he reveals the myth *as* myth – something invented and therefore open to change – and so reactivates its political potential.

What then are the politics of Barker's particular use of time? Rabey writes that, 'Barker opposes History – the impositions of ideological and moral narrative form – with Anti-History – the disruptive fragmentation of this form by the testimony and performance of individual pain'.[21] Barker's manipulation of time is essential to this fragmentation. Furthermore, Mary Karen Dahl argues that Barker 'undermine[s] current institutionalised power relations by creating disturbances at the deepest, most individual and private levels'.[22] Time, like Michel Foucault's disciplines, stretches from institutions of power that regulate public time down into the nooks and crannies of individuated experience.[23] If perceptions of time reflect worldview, then depicting time *differently* can challenge that worldview and potentially challenge the institutions that perpetuate and profit from the dominant temporal paradigm. Howard Barker's timeplay – as expressed not only in *The Bite of the Night*, but in the multitude of plays produced over his career and by The Wrestling School in particular – does nothing less than create a theatrical-political system in opposition to linear realism, and the 'moral imperatives of gross simplicity' (*AT*, 48) that, in Barker's view, are embedded within such systems.

Notes

1 Dahl, in personal correspondence with the author.
2 R. Levine, *A Geography of Time* (New York: Harper Collins, 1997), p. 9.
3 *Ibid.*, p. 65; I.R. Bartky, *Selling the True Time: Nineteenth-Century Timekeeping in America* (Stanford: Stanford University Press, 2000), p. 2.
4 G. Lakoff and M. Johnson, *Philosophy in the Flesh: The Embodied Mind and Its Challenge to Western Thought* (New York: Basic Books, 1999), p. 138.
5 G. Agamben, *Infancy and History: The Destruction of Experience*, translated by L. Heron (New York: Verso, 1978), p. 94.
6 E.T. Hall and M.R. Hall, *Understanding Cultural Differences* (Yarmouth, ME: Intercultural Press, 1990), p. 14.
7 Donald Schawang, 'A Vision of Substance', dissertation, University of Kansas, 2001, p. 52.
8 Barker, 'The Triumph in Defeat', *Guardian* 22 August 1988.
9 The Royal Shakespeare Company production remains the only professional staging of the play. To the best of my knowledge, the only revival of any kind took place at the Royal Scottish Academy of Music and Dance in 2004, under the direction of Hugh Hodgart. Special thanks to Mark Brown for pointing out this production.
10 M. Ratcliffe, review of *The Bite of the Night*, *Observer*, 11 September 1988.
11 D.I. Rabey, *Howard Barker: Politics and Desire An Expository Study of his Drama and Poetry*, second edition (London: Macmillan [1989] 2009), p. 221.
12 *The Bite of the Night*, Royal Shakespeare Company, Shakespeare Centre library video, 1988.
13 Jane Edwards found the performance 'an enormously frustrating experience, a

desperate attempt to make sense of its contradictions, which rarely succeeds in Barker's avowed aim of freeing the imagination' (*Time Out*, 14 September 1988). Jim Hiley, on the other hand, described it as 'lucid, fast-moving and even funny' (*The Listener*, 15 September 1988).

14   S. Morley, review of *The Bite of the Night*, *Punch*, 23 September 1988.

15   Milton Shulman: 'There is something impertinent in Mr. Barker's assumption that his views on evil, knowledge or sexuality [...] need occupy us almost an hour more than Shakespeare's *Hamlet*' (*Evening Standard,* 6 September 1988). Clive Hirschhorn: 'his play has less to do with art than an arrogant contempt for his public' (Sunday Express 11 September 1988). Jack Tinker: 'I was infuriated that the RSC should encourage his growing delusion than an audience should be required to invest so much time, stomach and money for so little enlightenment or reward' (*Daily Mail*, 15 September 1988).

16   J. Hiley, review of *The Bite of the Night*, *The Listener*, 15 September 1988.

17   Ratcliffe, *Observer*.

18   T. Dunn, review of *The Bite of the Night*, *The Tribune*, 16 September 1988.

19   M. Smith, *Britain and 1940: History, Myth and Popular Memory* (London: Routledge, 2000), p. 2.

20   R. Barthes, *Mythologies*, translated by A. Lavers (New York: Hill and Wang, 1957, 1972), p. 143.

21   Rabey, in K. Gritzner and D.I. Rabey (eds), *Theatre of Catastrophe: New Essays on Howard Barker* (London: Oberon, 2006), p. 18.

22   Dahl, in *ibid.*, p. 95.

23   M. Foucault, *Discipline & Punish*, translated by A. Sheridan (New York: Random House, 1975, 1995), p. 137.

15

The Dying of Today and the meta-stases of language: from history to tale to play to *mise-en-scène*

Elizabeth Sakellaridou

Barker's recent play *The Dying of Today*, which received its London première in October 2008, is a fascinating cat-and-mouse situation between a Mephis-tophelian character called Dneister, who is trying to establish his complete domination over his interlocutor, and a common man, a barber, who struggles to keep up his human dignity and integrity and to avoid his victimisation. Such tensions are reminiscent of other, earlier Barker duets such as Judith and Holophernes in *Judith* and Und and her invisible lover in *Und*. Similarly to these plays, in *The Dying of Today* the theatrical paradigm becomes a strong hermeneutic metaphor. The surface storyline can be summed up, in theatrical terms, in a simple comprehensive schema, in which Dneister is the omnipotent stage director, in full charge of spatial arrangements, viewing angles and mirrors and the Barber is the obedient actor pushed into an asphyxiating role in a complete, pre-fixed performance text. Beckett's short play *Catastrophe* (1982) is perhaps an even more appropriate comparison here since it highlights most pointedly the precarious position of the director as total controller of the *mise-en-scène* and, furthermore, the possibility of power reversal in the actual performance – a risk and an anxiety also acted out in Barker's play. The austere dyadic structure of the latter – a notable exception in the Barker canon of excess – intensifies even more the instability of power distribution.

However, Barker, as always, aims at even greater complexity than this surface theatrical scheme. In its deep structure the play is about historical narration – more precisely the recounting of world calamities, the reporting of worldwide bad news – and its modes of mediation, which in a contemporary post-structuralist context are 'multi-disciplinary' and treat narrative as 'mediated enunciation,' including also non-linguistic parameters as offered by the performing and iconic media: drama and film.[1] With more specific reference to the currently developing new morphologies of the dramatic text, Jean-Pierre Ryngaert observes:

> A general tendency for dramatic dialogue to be contaminated by narrative features … The dramatis personae thus come to include all manners of narrators, reciters, monologists, storytellers, and reporters – all manner of mediators between the fiction and the public.[2]

The Dying of Today is an exemplary play regarding the deployment of specific dramatic strategies pertinent to the genre, for the mediation of narrative through pure narration, dialogue, commentary, role-playing, visible and invisible narrators.[3] The play is also about intertextual narrative discourses and cross-genre renarrativisation since behind Barker's story lie two ancient complementary stories: the account of the Athenian catastrophe in Sicily during the Peloponnesian War of fifth century BC and the reception of the disastrous event in the city of Athens. The first part of the story, the actual destruction of the Athenian fleet and army, the macro-history, is covered by Thucydides' extraordinary dramatic account of the event in Book VII of his *Histories*. The second part, which refers to the first, unofficial breaking of the bad news to the Athenians in a barber's shop in Piraeus by a complete stranger, is provided by Plutarch in the form of a travelling oral story, a fabulised micro-history: a tail-story to the undisputed 'real event' supplied by Thucydides. Starting from this dual, classical source narrative (behind which one must detect various other layers of earlier oral and possibly written accounts), Barker, on a first level, renarrativises Plutarch's unstable 'tale' (whose authenticity Plutarch has already questioned himself[4]) by transforming it into the backbone of his own dramatic story. On a second level, he buttonholes and relativises Thucydides' official history by staging the hidden narrative strategies of the sanctioned historical discourse. It is important to note here that Thucydides himself was writing history by proxy (memory, hearsay, lateral experience and fantasy), projecting on the Sicilian military defeat, which he never witnessed in person, his own military involvement and experience as an army general in an earlier, failed Athenian expedition to Amphipolis.

Barker's transformation consists of a masterful conflation of the two stories into a new *fabula*.[5] On one level, Plutarch's anecdotal narration provides the *dramatis personae* (the barber and his customer) and the psychological and ethical frame of the new play (the impact of the bad news on the populace and the responsibility of the storyteller). On another level, Thucydides' minute description of the catastrophic events is remediated via an interminably shifting narrative voice and model, which also question their own efficiency and thus ensure the dramatic tension of the play through their dialogical and dialectical nature:

> [BARBER]: Perhaps the pleasure you take in delivering bad news is matched only by the terrible sense the news is welcome?

(*DNEISTER lets him continue.*)

As if there was an ache in all of us a void which even in the midst of laughter yawned and only the terrible could fill it?

(*Pause.*)

Otherwise to tell bad news to make the telling of bad news a work for life as you do AND I DO NOT LIKE YOU VERY MUCH

DNEISTER: It's all right

BARBER: I DO NOT

DNEISTER: It is perfectly all right to dislike me

(*The BARBER frowns, bites his lip.*)

BARBER: Would be

(*He struggles.*)

Would be

(*He articulates.*)

THE VOCATION OF A SADIST

DNEISTER: Which I am not

BARBER: Which you are not no not a sadist are you?

(*Pause.*)

And this ache this void this thing the bad news fills which was empty and which now has a dead boy in it a dead boy in the quarry the soon-to-be so famous quarry this

(*He struggles again. There is horror in him.*)   (*OP4*, 107)

Obviously the focus is on the stylistics and the performance of narration – particularly that of an atrocious nature – and the affective implication of both storyteller and listener in the process of mediation. How far the godlike Dneister, the initiator and then the prompter of this narrative of catastrophe, is himself affected by its theatricalisation becomes clear in his long monologue towards the end of the play, where he comes to admit his own partial disintegration:

DNEISTER: [...] I should have liked to have seen your face the crisis of indecision *as for me oh dear I have broken the first rule never to be animated* and the second always catch the first boat out *I'm not myself* the bad news was too bad even for me I should be miles from here in a deckchair the stiff sail flapping in the breeze and this faint frothing of doomed people fainter and fainter as I strained my ears *too bad too late* too everything

(*Pause. The city hums in its crisis.*)   (*OP4*, 113: emphasis added)

According to narrative theory 'telling a story demands a certain kind of context and in itself establishes a particular interactive reality'.[6] In the narrative context created in Barker's play both characters are equally important contributors but their quantitative and qualitative contributions to the narrative are in a reverse relationship to each other. Given that in our postmodern experience the primary, original understanding of narrative's location in literature and discourse has been broadened to include also popular culture, the media and everyday life, the function of the narrator is accordingly seen as a series of more amplified, relaxed and flexible possibilities.[7] *The Dying of Today* offers the full spectrum of such possibilities that ranges from a professional narrator, an artist, a stylist and an aesthete – in other words a real 'connoisseur,' a master of theory and 'orchestration' (*OP4*, 91) of movement in time and a poseur – to an experiential narrator, an amateur performer of 'spontaneity' (*OP4*, 91) – that is, one who acts out a genuine narrative of pain and passion. In this bipolar conception of narrative poetics, initially, it is Dneister who holds the pole of the fictional/artistic narrator and the Barber that of the experiential or factual storyteller. Dneister's introductory monologue is a real tour-de-force of narrative expertise and sophistication:

> DNEISTER: (*At last.*) Do you like bad news I do I'll give you bad news if you want it why do you prefer bad news I ask myself do you like grief do you like chaos not at all only I think men are more beautiful flung down than standing up say if you want my news
>
> (*The BARBER cuts.*)
>
> And another thing that justifies my preference for bad news over good is the way bad news is heard the fascination of the audience their bulging eyes their hanging mouths the clenching and unclenching of their fists they cling to every word I am heeded with a gratifying intensity
>
> ....
>
> Say if you want it this very bad news
>
> (*An interval of scissors ...*)
>
> You prefer to hear this news from someone else ... I don't protest you are entitled to hear it in any form you wish I will say to you however that this someone else is unlikely to possess my talent for telling it nor I daresay my infinite capacity for detail for example I resolutely forbid myself the slightest embellishment of the facts and believe me that is not easy with news so extraordinary as this one is seduced by the rapt attention of the audience whose appetite for horror is insatiable ...   (*OP4*, 87)

Starting with a seemingly innocent question to his speechless interlocutor ('Do you like bad news?', *OP4*, 87), he moves on to an imperative ('I have to tell you', *OP4*, 88), then to psychological pressure (through an inverted threat and a false diagnosis of malaise in his chosen victim, *OP4*, 88–9), then to ordering the Barber to do certain things ('shut the shop', 'turn the sign around', 'sit in the chair', *OP4*, 89). Obviously Dneister feels at ease and even enjoys performing all necessary rituals of preparation for a successful narrative to begin. In parallel, he theorises on his methodology: 'a little coercion', 'strategies of rhetoric', 'deliberately delaying', 'timing', starting with an outline and a context ('first I will outline the situation in which the bad news occurred', *OP4*, 90, 91). In the meantime he has also openly advertised his unique 'talent for telling', his 'infinite capacity for detail' and his commitment to precision ('I resolutely forbid myself the slightest embellishment of the facts', *OP4*, 87) – all three being virtues traditionally attributed to Thucydides as the first model historian of the Western world.

Through such eloquent histrionics, Dneister poses as Thucydides here, assuming the role of the uncontested, official historical voice but also displaying the major narrative skills of historical account: feigning spontaneity ('such spontaneity if spontaneity it ever was', *OP4*, 91) and fabricating a gripping tragic story out of historical accident ('the ways in which the accident might be recounted for the benefit of others', *OP4*, 92). He thus ironises and relativises his authority as a historian, in a very Nietzschean fashion, by proving this role fake and artificial: Dneister is a poseur – a fictional character and a performer – from beginning to end. By the time he has concluded his fourth sweeping monologue on his aesthetic principles, the Barber, who had so far reacted only with a diffident, monosyllabic 'yes', at last senses the falsity of Dneister's narrative charms and exclaims impatiently 'you are not telling me' (*OP4*, 92) – a statement he repeats three times before deciding to step in and grasp the narrative in his own hands with a firm '*I'll* tell you' (*OP4*, 93, emphasis added). A stage direction notes at this point that '*he is altered*' (*OP4*, 93) and, indeed, the Barber's own monologue, segmented by pauses, marks his passage from a mood of mere observation and a pragmatic account of the situation to that of personal involvement, of guessing and imagining things. The Barber is obviously now becoming the subjective historian/narrator/fabulist and he stands up to emphasise through movement his rising position in the play's dramatic economy. As a result of his domineering gesture, Dneister's role now shrinks to almost monosyllabic intervention, placing the latter in a secondary position, although this seeming reversal of roles between the two protagonists is neither actual nor final. Narrative theory cautions us that a narrator often simply 'recedes into the background', does not disappear from the story after introducing the characters.[8]

In the meantime, the newly appointed narrator, the Barber, agonises in the midst of a variety of sources and styles, oscillating between personal history (the loss of his soldier son) and national history (the destruction of the Athenian army and navy), between factuality and fictionality. His narrative is fuelled by latent experience ('I was at Amphipolis I saw death', *OP4*, 95) and affective reaction to the suspected loss of his son and the city ('*He sobs and laughs*', *OP4*, 93); and his opening diction is certainly marked by physical and affective language:[9]

> BARBER: You are not telling me
>
> (*Pause.*)
>
> I have shut the shop I have sat down exactly as you asked me to and still you are not telling me

(*Pause.*)

Perhaps you cannot bring yourself to tell me?

(*Pause.*)

Having ascertained I am the father of a son and as the father of a son specially susceptible to what you might have told me you have perhaps been overcome by pity you said you liked my face

(*Pause.*)

Or knowing just how bad this very bad news is you are afraid I'd kill you such things have happened and we are alone in here with razors utterly alone that was your decision not mine

(*Pause.*)

Then again you might be mad oh yes that occurred to me as soon as you walked through the door mad and with nothing at all to tell nothing whatsoever I have a son I also have a business and in the time I have been sitting here three individuals have come and gone away again two of these were regulars of mine they seemed perplexed to see me sitting in a chair I never sit in as for being closed on Tuesday it's unprecedented a barber is dependent on his regulars wholly dependent now there's another one that's four probably they think a crime is being committed and I look shocked I look peculiar possibly they have gone directly to the police is that the police that might be the police now is that them?

(*Pause. He is altered.*)   (*OP4*, 92–3)

At the same time he tries hard to disengage his thought from the insignificance of his personal situation and to anchor himself in the vastness of History, changing the micro-narrative of 'my boy is dead'[10] into a macro-narrative, in which he speaks 'from the general the social the cultural point of view' (*OP4*, 93). In doing so and by asserting his determination to go on with this grander narrative, he boldly claims the status of the official historian Thucydides, stealing the role from Dneister – a major gesture of appropriation, to which the latter pretends he is only too happy to concede:

BARBER: ... I MUST STAND UP SORRY SORRY I MUST STAND

(*He does so.*)

I'm standing up that helps it's natural to me a barber stands he might have aching knees still he prefers the upright posture one dead boy what's that oh I can see you share my opinion of the value of a solitary boy I'll go on now never mind the boy forget the boy the boy what's he already he has vanished down the corridors of history [...] I am going on now

DNEISTER: *Yes*

BARBER: I know perfectly well the bottomless oblivion in which my boy belongs I do know so

(*Pause. He recovers.*)

So

(*Pause.*)

The fleet of seven hundred vessels I saw some of them [...] and they are all dead are they all dead yes all dead I'm telling you the bad news they are all dead *shall I describe the water or shall you?*

(*Pause.*)

DNEISTER: I think you

(*Pause.*)   (*OP4*, 94, emphasis added)

However, the Barber's identification with Thucydides – although he speaks actual lines from Thucydides' historical text – is in no sense any more whole than Dneister's. The Barber's own storytelling contains also a critical meta-narrative, which proves the historical aspect of his narration inauthentic and his role as a historian that of a poseur. His authenticating strategies (for example, references to his boy and witnessing the preparing fleet in the harbour and especially his four emphatic references to his participation in the Athenian expedition to Amphipolis – actually an element borrowed from Thucydides' own biography) are undermined by an equally systematic set of narrativising techniques very much like those in Dneister's discourse, which blend the factual and the fictional aspects of history, the imaginary and the affective, in line with various postmodern concepts of historiography.[11] His dramatic split between the arrogant, godlike Thucydidean voice of 'I AM THE TRUTHTELLER' (*OP4*, 102), and the humble admission 'I am a barber not a speaker' (*OP4*, 97), is already discerned in his earlier troubled appeal to Dneister 'TRUE OR FALSE I SAID' (*OP4*, 95). This is a pivotal moment of relativisation and ambiguity, which sets up a dialectical narrative form and a mood of ambivalence for the rest of the play. Right after this dramatic statement of doubt on the part of the Barber the play enters a new phase of vivid narrative interaction: a modern variant of the classical 'stichomythia', between the two protagonists.

Dneister is reintroduced as the artist/aesthete/commentator par excellence and his function in the play is re-established as the major, most articulate meta-narrative contributor, who also controls and shapes the narration from the wings.[12] During this phase of interactive narration the Barber produces a narrative of pain and suffering that transcends into ecstatic vision and Dneister provides his expertise on aesthetic theory and artistic form and prompts the Barber to further action:

DNEISTER: [...] Stand by your door you beautiful and devastated barber and when the enemy swarms ashore wild with vengeance be still as wood your dead boy like another rib in you of course they will do terrible things to you a clean apron would be nice

(*Pause.*)

BARBER: Yes

DNEISTER: You'll do that for me?

BARBER: Yes

DNEISTER: Others will defend the city

BARBER: If the city is defended at all   (*OP4*, 116)

Through this synergic activity the narrative reaches its tragic peak, with the Barber acting out the apotheosis of catastrophe while Dneister lingers back in order to enjoy the ecstatic pleasure of witnessing its full manifestation at the risk of his own life.[13] Both characters are in a unique state of divine euphoria, the Dionysian and the Apollonian respectively. In his delirium of pain and epiphany,[14] the Barber even mixes Plutarch's ethical concern about causing panic to the people,[15] by an asthmatic enactment of infectious agony: 'He tells she wails she runs she tells they wail they run they tell it's a it's a' – an arresting verbal performance, to which Dneister contributes the crucial missing word 'Contagion?' that frames this extraordinary narrative of panic (*OP4*, 108).

Within this Nietzschean dialectical scheme that gives balance and solidity to the dramatic structure of the play, there is an equally important element of progressive movement and vitality which saves the play from a theatrically static verbocentricity. This inner dynamic is best manifested in the gradual transformation of the Barber from an insignificant nonentity of limited potential to a tragic hero of superhuman dimensions, whose changing physical image is successively seen as 'animated', 'inspired', 'radiant with hopelessness', 'beautiful and devastated' (*OP4*, 100, 101, 104, 116) – much to the approval of his intoxicated prompter Dneister. The latter has now arguably become elided by association with the figure of the dramatist, as a consistent creator and theorist of a tragedy of catastrophe.[16] However, from the successive transformations of the two characters the Barber's is certainly the major, externally dramatised metamorphosis because Dneister's subtler psychic changes still leave him on the side of the master of plots and the prompter of action (even though a melancholic, internally agonising, cracked one).[17] Ostensibly, it is the Barber that traverses all the ground from unaffected natural narrative and performance to the structuring principles of narrativity and narrative control. Towards the end of the play he emerges as a sophisticated connoisseur and an articulate thinker (albeit an unstable and ephemeral one), turning Dneister, the 'professional', to 'dilettante' by the latter's own half-mocking admission (*OP4*, 104). By this time the thematic focus has already imperceptibly shifted from issues of history and narration to Barker's more intimate preoccupation with the definition and the achievement of the tragic. Accordingly, the two protagonists are left to negotiate their own position in a tragic vision of history that Barker has textured around them. The last '*agon*' between the two equal opponents – the naïve, extrovert Barber and his brooding, self-contained, scheming customer Dneister – is who will pull the final strings of the narrative and so fix the other to the pose of the complete loser, the despair of utter catastrophe: to turn the other into a monumental construct of tragedy.

Dneister verbalises this statuesque tragic vision as he delivers his last dramatic appeal, which has already been quoted in full ('Stand by your door you beautiful and devastated barber'), and he claims the unique privilege of witnessing such indescribable greatness.[18] But soon after, the Barber looks at catastrophe from the other side of the mirror and claims the privilege for himself, using an equally lofty language:

> Forgive me [...] I have been ungracious I have been sarcastic I have attempted to belittle you when despite the terrible character of your visit it was now I can judge it more objectively a privilege and a profound compensation for my loss no others can be brought so beautifully to know as I have been the awful things they are destined to know and your advice is exquisite I shall stand at my shop door exactly as you indicated
>
> (*Pause. DNEISTER is puzzled.*)
>
> Hide now
>
> (*DNEISTER hesitates.*)
>
> Hide
>
> (*He dithers.*)   (*OP4*, 116)

The question of victory and defeat remains unresolved but the play has managed, through its subtle, labyrinthine narrative pathways to infect the audience with the same anxiety and despair of accidental historical existence and its equally frail, transient and ephemeral theatrical transformation into fleeting tragic grandeur: the same existential-*cum*-artistic dilemma that has tormented the dramatic characters throughout the play.

Like the Artaudian metaphor of the plague, conceived as a simultaneously destructive and healing force in his 'theatre of cruelty', Barker's respective Theatre of Catastrophe is of a similarly dubious infectious nature. *The Dying of Today* itself creates this contradictory (fascinating and terrifying) metaphor of a lethal but purifying disease when it wonders 'what oceanic transformations [the narrative of bad news] brings with it it is medicine it is disease' (*OP4*, 98); elsewhere it defines this sense of sickness as 'contagion' (*OP4*, 108). With these associations in mind I am borrowing the medical term 'metastasis' (which is the transformation and reappearance of a disease, particularly cancer, in another organ of the body[19]) in order to describe metaphorically the unlimited, unpredictable transformations in perspective, modality and temporality that narrative takes in Barker's play and its incessant translocation from one – often ventriloquist – speaking mouth to another (including Thucydides, the historian; Plutarch, the biographer; Barker, the contemporary fabulist; the two Barkerian (re)fabulised and fabulising characters; and all present and future directors and actors that may transfer the play to the stage).[20]

Barker is very fond of the word 'ecstasy' (in Greek '*ecstasis*'), which in its philosophical use (*ec-stase*) means moving off the normal position: a *dislocation* that also brings in a new vision of the world. My own borrowed term, 'meta-stasis', additionally means a *relocation*, a reappearance, which also bears the notion of surprise – beyond the ambiguity it creates with its nosological references. I, therefore, consider it as a more apt term to describe the insidious ways in which Barker's narrative changes content or form, and pops up in the mouth of invisible, crypto- or pseudo-narrators: spectral presences impersonated by the two visible, on-stage characters, themselves also struggling to eclipse each other from view or from the narrative. Phrases like 'I am going' (*OP4*, 103), 'You should go now' (*OP4*, 112), 'I can't stay I have to leave' (*OP4*, 115) and 'Goodbye I said' (*OP4*, 117) are typical and very central speech acts in the relentless stage game to which the two characters are committed. It is this fascinating network of linguistic and extra-linguistic *meta-stases* of the narrative that turns *The Dying of Today* into what Fredric Jameson has called a 'synthetic vision', one that encompasses various cognitive activities in culture, including historical thinking, philosophical contemplation, psychological analysis and art theory.[21] All these are major concerns in Barker's writing and they combine masterfully in his postmodern narrative system, which incessantly cuts across genres and modes of mediation. If it is a new grand narrative, as Angel-Perez has contested,[22] because of its all-encompassing and consistent mythopoetic potential, it still remains a very mobile, *meta-static* one in texture, form and audience appeal: surprising, threatening and infectious.

Notes

1 S. Onega and J.A. Garcia Landa (eds), *Narratology: An Introduction* (London and New York: Longman, 1996), pp. 1–2.

2 Quoted in D. Mounsef and J. Féral (eds), *The Transparency of the Text: Contemporary Writing for the Stage* (Yale French Studies, no. 112; New Haven, CT: Yale University Press, 2007) p. 19.

3 Arthur Asa Berger, *Narratives in Popular Culture, Media, and Everyday Life* (Thousand Oaks, CA: Sage, 1997), pp. 7–8.

4 Plutarch's vocabulary is full of words of doubt, which undermine the authenticity of the story: φασί (they say), ὡς ἔοικεν (it would seem), λόγους ἐποιεῖτο (made words), σαφές οὐδέν εἶχε φράζειν (he had nothing concrete to say), λογοποιός (story-maker): Plutarch, 'Nicias', in *Lives III* (edited by E.H. Warmington, translated by Bernadotte Perrin, Cambridge, MA: Harvard University Press, 1967), pp. 207–311 (308–11).

5 In an interview to the writer on the occasion of the Greek production of the play Barker explained the imaginative freedom he takes with existing myths, referring also to Shakespeare's similar method. Interview published in the book/programme of the Nea Skini production: *Howard Barker, To Istato Simera (The Dying of Today)* (Athens: Nea Skini, 2009), pp. 69–76 (76).

6 U.M. Quasthoff and T. Becker (eds), *Narrative Interaction* (Amsterdam and Philadelphia, PA: John Benjamins, 2004) p. 1.

7 Berger, *Narratives in Popular Culture*, pp. 7–8.

8 *Ibid.*, p 8.

9   Narrative theory notes the spatiotemporal shift of telling a story from the here and now to past events. It also underlines the narrative's function as communicating emotions and attitudes. See Quasthoff and Becker, *Narrative Interaction*, p. 1.

10   For Gerald Prince even statements such as 'the king died' or 'the boy came' constitute a narrative according to its 'minimal definition': 'Remarks on Narrativity', in Claes Wahlin (ed.), *Perspectives on Narratology* (Frankfurt am Main: Peter Lang, 1996), pp. 95–105 (95).

11   See Christopher Nash (ed.), *Narrative in Culture* (London: Routledge, 1990), p. xiv; also Wahlin, *Perspectives on Narratology*, p. 97.

12   In this sense he is reminiscent of the invisible, demoniacal lover in an earlier Barker play, *Und*.

13   As Barker suggests: 'like the gnawing of an irrepressible sexual hunger, the need to imagine death steals over us, and in the form of a *fascination* (what cannot be done must be done / what cannot be said must be said / what cannot be entered must be entered). This fascination is falsely described as *morbid* …' (*DOAT*, pp. 30–1).

14   A comparison can be made here to other Barker plays such as *Judith, Und, Ursula*, and *The Europeans*; see Zimmermann's comprehensive article 'Images of Death in Howard Barker's Theatre' in K. Gritzner and D.I. Rabey (eds), *Theatre of Catastrophe: New Essays on Howard Barker* (London: Oberon, 2006), pp. 211–30.

15   Plutarch's account also includes the unfair punishment of the poor barber by the city magistrates, who wrongly assumed that he was spreading false news and so was unduly upsetting the citizens.

16   Barker himself did not conceal his preference for and fascination with Dneister as a character to identify with; 'interview to the writer', *To Istato Simera*, pp. 71–2.

17   This type of figure is a major preoccupation in many of Barker's plays and has drawn the attention of scholars such as Charles Lamb (*The Theatre of Howard Barker* (London and New York: Routledge, 2005)) and David Ian Rabey (*Howard Barker: Ecstasy and Death. An Expository Study of his Drama, Theory and Production Work, 1988–2008* (Basingstoke and New York: Palgrave Macmillan, 2009)). Half-messianic and half-daemonic this dark male figure often betrays his sense of strain and fracture: examples would be Starhemberg in *The Europeans*, Lvov in *The Last Supper* and Lucas in *Ursula*.

18   'John was a god and I beheld him' (*OP4*, 115).

19   The *OED* gives the following definitions for 'metastasis': '*rhet*. A rapid transition from one point to another; *phys*. and *path*. The transference of a bodily function, of a pain or a disease, of morbific matter, etc. from one part or organ to another'.

20   At this point I should attempt a cursory comparison in style between the British premiere production by The Wrestling School (at the Arcola Theatre in London in October 2008, directed by Gerrard McArthur) and the Greek Nea Skini production (at the Cycladon Theatre in Athens in November 2009, directed by Lefteris Voyatzis) simply to indicate how the initial complex textual narrative has been translated in physical terms in two pointedly different synaesthetic narratives of the stage. The set in the British production was sparse and tended to abstraction, while the acting favoured austerity and stylisation. The Greek production, on the other hand, generated a stronger surrealistic feeling by juxtaposing a highly selective artistic naturalism with the play's mythological dimension.

21   See Foreword in Nash, *Narrative in Culture*, especially p. xi.

22   E. Angel-Perez, 'Reinventing 'Grand Narratives: Barker's Challenge to Postmodernism': keynote speech delivered at the 'Howard Barker's Art of Theatre' Conference in Aberystwyth, Wales (10–12 July 2009), and published in this volume (pp. 38–50).

16

'The substrata of experience': Barker's poetry, 1988–2008

David Ian Rabey

Barker's first three volumes of poetry – *Don't Exaggerate (desire and abuse)* (1985), *The Breath of the Crowd* (1986) and *Gary the Thief/Gary Upright* (1987) – featured extended poems, monologues intended for theatrical performance by Ian McDiarmid, Maggie Steed and Gary Oldman (though the *Gary* poems remain unperformed by Oldman; McDiarmid performed *Don't Exaggerate* in London, 1984, Cheltenham, 1986 and Brussels, 1998, and on BBC Radio 3 in 1990; Steed performed *Breath* in Cheltenham, 1986, and London, 1988).

Barker's fourth volume of poetry, *Lullabies for the Impatient*, was published in 1988. Unlike its predecessors, this collection features no extended piece intended for performance by an actor; it is suffused with a more meditative atmosphere, which is itself consciously dramatised, even interrogated. The notes on the cover invite the reader to question the stance and conclusions involved in a series of conscious and deliberate disengagements from the norms and dictates of a myopically, merely contemporary perspective: 'The poems assert the individual's right to selfhood in a time of moral disarray and populist stagnation, but their ironic tone also sounds a warning – at what point does our insistence on our own identity threaten its corruption?' This sets a new keynote for Barker's succeeding volumes: *The Ascent of Monte Grappa* (1991), *The Tortmann Diaries* (1996) and *Sheer Detachment* (2009). In these collections, a poetic persona emerges: a wryly reflective observer who strives to maintain the emotional distance which might permit a peculiarly Barkerian sense of 'divine comedy': a response to the ironic reversals of history, which mock any sense of natural justice or discernible theory. Instead, the poems offer a series of observations, and perceptual variations, which might more consistently be associated with the grotesque tragicomedy of endurance, and of enduring (but constantly refocused) passion. Indeed: this persona knows his own (and everyone's) equilibrium of detachment to be permanently threatened by passion: by the pain of wanting; by the inextricable irrationalities of fixation upon the specifics of a particular woman; and by the frustrations and indignities of one's own inevitable confinement to a specific historical and social juncture, and the limitations of its dominant received opinions.

On the one hand, the striving for a perspective which is not limited to the characteristic prejudices of a specific era of self-confident 'modernity' aims, like numerous examples of Barker's drama, to challenge the permission to look at others as subhuman. On the other hand, the speaker also knows that he, like others, is not inescapably immune to the instable provisionalities inherent in any position of judgment: in the words of a draft copy of the 2006 Barker play *The Road, The House, The Road* (but cut from the broadcast and published versions of the text), 'we proceed by error and the correction of error of course the correction might be error too'.

Time, decay and beauty: *Lullabies for the Impatient*

Time
How silly time is
What is time anyway?
Only decay
And beauty

The Swing at Night (SN, 15)

Lullabies for the Impatient opens with the extended poem, 'Chelmno', in which an imaginary nineteenth-century English watercolourist Arthur Taylor proclaims the eponymous Polish castle 'an unrewarding / Subject until / Some history happens here' (*LI*, 8). Patronising in his search for patronage, Taylor considers the castle and its impoverished owner ('in debt to the Jew'); his perspective is spared the future's awareness of the location as a site of massacre of 400,000 Jews during the Second World War. Thus, minor resentments between Taylor and his patron are projected, in the geometric sense, into an ominous sense of the history that will happen.

The poem, 'The Early Hours of a Reviled Man', imagines the French writer Louis-Ferdinand Céline awaiting the atmosphere of illegality associated with the night: the time and juncture when he regularly ceases his daytime practice of medicine, and applies himself to write in mockery of 'the catastrophe of cultures / Wishing it was over' (*LI*, 12), like a gargoyle on the edifice of post-war Europe. He burns to escape the damnation of continued life, and mocks the corruption in the surrounding 'violent symmetry' of reconstruction and reconciliation (this position is paralleled elsewhere in the collection in the poem 'Caxais', in which the Portuguese revolutionary Carvalho becomes captive in a prison he had formerly liberated, as part of the ironic reversals of history).

The historically telescopic perspective of 'Chemlno' is reversed in the poem 'The Hapsburg Barracks, Prague', which ironically expresses contemporary ideological superiority and its requirement to belittle, with self-congratulatory hindsight, the postures of the past: 'Oh, the misplaced loyalty of cadets! / If only they possessed our tools / Of social analysis!'. The faith and confidence of the troops, laughing and swaggering, is viewed as poignantly (rather than ludicrously) misplaced, but the enlightenment view of history as a linear progression is also ironised: asking, how much more secure can we be, in our contemporary historical and national faiths and confidences, if we conclude 'Oh, the comic pathos of other men's convictions! / And we so opulent with means / To separate the slogan from the valid!' (*LI*, 16). In this respect, Barker articulates, more searchingly and discomfitingly, the insight expressed in Arnold Wesker's 1970 play *The Friends*, that, whilst the rebel hates the past, the revolutionary perspective sees the past as too rich with human suffering and achievement to be dismissed; rather, the past represents the responsibility of an accumulation of centuries of endeavour, experience and sensibility (crucially, this premise opposes all effects which ultimately confirm contemporary moral superiority over an earlier age or different ideological regime; effects frequently offered by the drama of Tom Stoppard).

The complacency and apparent inertia of contemporary Britain is characterised elsewhere in *Lullabies for the Impatient* as 'Another Transitional State' by the poem of that title: the narrator deduces 'Obviously we are waiting for something', even as he settles the mask of his face into the 'necessary features' of bliss for 'the perfect evening prior to a war' (*LI*, 15). A sense of degeneration is identified: both in terms of emotional relationships (in nuances and discriminations which nevertheless constitute 'Five Proofs of Existence'), and of national artistry, where the poem 'On the Sickness of Art Forms' notes the predominant contraction of theatre, from being 'a platform / Against which those who had no power / Of description might cling / Empowered and emboldened by surprise', into

A
    Laughing
        Box
            Descending
                The
                    Stairs   (*LI*, 24)

'The Tide's Advice' and 'The Moon's Advice' reinvent the complementary polarity of Milton's 'Il Penseroso' and 'L'Allegro', dramatising the attractions of contrasting impulses: in this case, of stealthy resilience and fierce intransigence, as ways of opposing one's lived moment of cultural history. This conscious sense of both inhabiting and resisting a cultural moment is the focus of the title sequence of poems, 'Lullabies for the Impatient', which note both 'the decay of ideals' ('where passion was prized / The idol of accumulation stands' (*LI*, 68) and 'Things dignified by the implacable / Hostility of states' (*LI*, 59); including 'the pagan attitude of endurance'); if 'It is only a matter of waiting' for theorists to expire (in both life and authority) (*LI*, 59), those who currently succeed them are moral infants, who vengefully 'affirm everything / In their tantrums' (*LI*, 62). The narrative voice proposes heretical, Célinian wisdom, rather than naïvely self-defeating outrage:'You think we are governed by thieves? / Not for the first time … Peace might be worse than war / Harmony worse than dissonance' (*LI*, 62). The strategic likening of self to a stray mongrel which 'lives only for itself' may cultivate corruption, that of the thin-skinned individual who barricades himself in a preposterous (and self-defeating) autonomy. The counsel in the face of predatory populism, 'Learn the art of walking slowly / In the street' (*LI*, 67), offers a minor but decisive form of purposeful disengagement from civic pressures, in order to prove unusually (perhaps even charismatically) perceptive. Finally, 'History Poem' recognises how all forms of labour, from agricultural restoration to intellectual fulmination, have to be bounded by a sleep, and not judged on the progress of a single day: an apt conclusion for a collection which acknowledges loss, dispiriting decay and the combustions of frustration, but places its faith in the informed effort of a historically informed and cumulative perspective.

The degeneration of truth: *The Ascent of Monte Grappa*

Barker's fifth volume of poetry, *The Ascent of Monte Grappa* (1991), develops further some of the themes explored in *Lullabies for the Impatient*: notably the ironies of time, the decay of ideals, the dialectic of emotion and calculation, and the discovery of an implacable dignity in refusing assent to the comprehensive reductivities of the merely contemporary vantage point. The title poem considers religious, political and sexual associations of the Italian mountain: the siting of a monument by Pope Pius X in 1901; the Italian army's battles against the combined German and Austrian armies in 1917 (including the Twelfth Battle of the Isonzo, which would suggest a title for Barker's subsequent play) and 1918; and the pilgrimage of two contemporary lovers, mindful of the fragility of their own conciliations, to which the mountain might offer a rebuke ('Perhaps this time we shall not arrive / At a conclusion', *AMG*, 4). They require, in contrast to the ironically silent mountain, to find, if not agreement, then at least shared terms of meaning: ('Being what we are / We must give this discomfort form', *AMG*, 7). The narrative voice of the male lover discovers a perspective, beyond shame at the 'undamaged life' which he and his companion ('late products of calamity' from the viewpoint of the dead) personify: he recognises, 'We … are living the requirements of a time / No less than these shelved fragments' (*AMG*, 13); the couple's union, formed by 'passionate strife', will begin its dissolution with the 'weighing of advantages', in the wake of having achieved its breathless summit; with the substitution of calculation for hunger, 'Making texts of absences / And rituals of dissimulation' (*AMG*, 17). In distinguishing his own perspective from the lures of either 'piety' or 'mutiny', the narrator (who might, to an unusual degree, be associated with Barker himself) determines to borrow the mountain's 'contempt for laws' whilst avoiding its ironies and posture of omniscience; rather he will 'be a chemist of unstable elements' (*AMG*, 19).

The peculiar promise of 'unstable elements' (including the isolated and singular personal testimony) provides a keynote for the collection as a whole. The Roman emperor Valerian reflects on his subjugation by the Persians, rehearsing '*Time's mockery of potentates / The knife behind the courtier's smile / The comedy of disease*' ('On Being a Despot's Foot Stool', *AMG*, 20); whilst in 'Madman's Jug', a contemporary ranter seeks, through his curses, to pursue and shatter the composure of the (never identified, and possibly random) agent of his marginalisation, 'The One Responsible / Who banned him from all intimacy' (*AMG*, 24). 'The Character of the Actor' is also defined in terms of the (poignantly brief) power to unlock the packaging and labelling of the world in terms which would diminish it to a familiar and manageable surface; the actor flings 'his life's conclusions in the air', dividing 'common assessments', and annihilating shame, even as he 'Weeps with anticipation of inevitable silences' (*AMG*, 27).

The narrator of 'The English in Lapland' casts a cold eye on the self-conscious performances of both natives and foreigners, and discovers 'The mark of truth is in degeneration' (*AMG*, 34); a premise which is projected to its most personal terminus of death, and the terms of its admittance (or even choice) in 'Let Us Marry'. This poem reprises and pursues from 'The Ascent' the sense of erosion within personal accommodation: the narrator bids his lover entertain her new paramour noisily, when his own death is imminent, all the better to accomplish a perfect exhaustion of the will ('I should die better then / Delivered of reluctance / And impatient to be gone', *AMG*, 40), so that he might become, himself, a significant exclusion.

The focus widens for '1989', described on the collection's cover as a 'simultaneously apprehensive and celebratory' poem, which presents a 'cacophany' reflecting the tumultuous upheavals in European revolutions and identities of that year. This poem is notable is various respects: its textual arrangement, which represents both competing simultaneity and formal symmetry; the vertical use of incomplete 'headlines', reflecting the excitement of social scientists, theorising feverishly to regulate upheaval, ominously utopian in their non-specificity ('A RENAISSANCE IS PREDICTED IN THE RUINS OF COLLECTIVITY THE PROFESSOR OF CULTURAL STUDIES PROVIDED ECONOMIC'; 'THE FIRST NECESSITY IS FOR MEDIA TO GENERATE THE THING WE CALL PUBLIC OPINION SAYS A SPECIALIST IN COMMUNICATION', *AMG*, 54–5, 56–7). This poem is poised in the fine balance of exhilaration, at catastrophe's power to confound 'sentimentalists and determinists both', and of wariness, towards the political form of any restored authority ('Look, they are carrying the cabinets of the secret police to other quarters'), which might extend to the narrator's article of faith: a secret 'cave in roaring England', where the reader might be welcomed in a future refuge against British totalitarianism ('TO THE DISMAY OF ENGLISH EDUCATORS THE TRIBE PERSISTS', *AMG*, 59).

The final sequence, 'Mates of Wrath', provides pithy, resonant images of urban decay and the persistent emotional resilience which springs up in its cracks, defying the security of the ideologue who fetishises poverty, his 'arrogant bid of impossible closure' where totalitarian impulses masquerade as charity. The prevalent degeneration and aggression visible and palpable in a seaside town (resembling Barker's native Brighton) are at least enlivened by a febrile and convulsive energy borne of 'NEVER / GIVING / YOUR / ASSENT', where the degraded passions of 'MONOTONOUS HOSTILITY' are at least preferable to the anaesthetic torpor and smugness of 'MONOTONOUS LOVE' (*AMG*, 77). The image of the ultimately ungovernable straying dog finally returns: the poet summons his art 'As a man whistles his lingering mongrel' (*AMG*, 80), recalling Kristeva's image of the significantly excluded deject in a catastrophic landscape, who tirelessly situates himself in, and demarcates, a catastrophic landscape without belonging to it, 'on a journey, during the night, the end of which keeps receding'.[2]

Distinction in disintegration: *The Tortmann Diaries*

Barker's sixth collection of poetry, *The Tortmann Diaries* (1996), demonstrates fierce developments: both in the principal theme, as described by the cover: 'the intimate confessions and aspirations of a solitary and diabolical figure, an ecstatic roamer of cities and later self-imposed exile, who from his rock of misanthropy subjects himself and his world to an unflinching critique'; and also in the form of the poems, the lines of which frequently lengthen so that a plethora of unbroken details and meanings extend surprisingly across a line; or even, as in the last poem 'Ceasing to Assume', cascade over line-endings without a punctuational stop, producing an effect of syntactic torsion and reeling senses which might well be termed ecstatic, in its rushing complexity and unremitting semi-surrealism. The theme of the collection partly develops from the 'Mates of Wrath' sequence (in *The Ascent of Monte Grappa*), in detailing the perambulations and ragings of an existentially murderous *flâneur* who unleashes his relish and scorn upon an increasingly feverish urban landscape characterised (again like Brighton) by the squalor and resentment of a merely petty criminality. 'Love's a Pause' deduces how 'Dispersal is the law' of the city rather than permanence, and how 'Things breathe' and transform in the 'poverty of night' ('more precious than day's yellow money', *TD*, 1). 'Tortmann's Meditations on the Deluge' wilfully extends this principle of burgeoning chaos to visit a surging cataclysm on London: the narrator identifies with the forces of chance and loss, and hymns the inventiveness and transfiguration briefly possible in the collapse of authority. Unflinching scrutiny characterises several poetic studies: of the dissolution of a corpse ('A Girl Salvaged'), of a poor model ('Tortmann at the Life Class') and of the satisfactions of murderous retribution ('On a Girl Abducted, Tortured, Raped and Burned to Death, December 1994'). This theme, and imaginatively remorseless discipline, extends into 'Tortmann and a Bomb Outrage', in which the title character discovers the corpse of a woman known to him, sundered by a terrorist's 'Vanity of Temper'. The bomber excuses himself, declaring his victims' 'hours were already arbitrary and what's my will / But accelerated time?' (*TD*, 12). Tortmann in his own strangely ecstatic way overturns this dismissiveness and vanity; in the later poem, 'Tortmann in the Wilderness', he will assert 'The disciplines of beauty abhor casualness'. Accordingly, Tortmann subjects the corpse to reverence, study, temper and a final strewing in the park; he subsequently awakens to a 'dazzling hour of blue hope'. In 'Tortmann and a Victim Chosen Not Quite at Random', he plots the murder of a maddening neighbour (perhaps the one in the poem 'Local Injuries'), but cannot bring himself to 'The inevitable smothering of all distinction' against which names serve as talismanic defences. The acute sense of distinction, even in disintegration, characterises the analyses of emotional dissociation in 'Staring and Stirring', 'Labels' and 'Dead Driver's Day'. 'For Those Who Must Live Longer' is an additional Lullaby for the Impatient, advice for survival in a meanly conformist society, hostile to individual purpose.

These features and themes come together most powerfully in 'Tortmann in the Wilderness', in which the title character has exiled himself on a rock, where he claims to build 'the immortal church / of repudiation', amidst forts distinguished by 'angles of deception which an unwary / Love might stumble in', hoarding his 'crafted feelings' in defence against their 'repetition or decay' (*TD*, 35). Tortmann has driven away his lover, in his 'ardour for antithesis', and personifies and punishes his clock and books, to prevent 'worse mutilations', even as he seeks 'a better death than dying': 'To cease participating / As a gambler walks from a room / To cut his losses' (*TD*, 38). He conducts symposia and conclave with flotsam, wilfully construing the passing air and sea traffic as tribute and exhortation; however, his refined expertise in evasion is challenged by his 'appetite / For punishment' which drives him to return to the subject of his mistress, concluding 'How perfectly uneducated by experience I am' (*TD*, 41). Rather than yield to common sense, law or the defence of passion, he rules his surroundings 'according to the moonlight's / Passage on the stair' and the tidal surges of the blood in his brain. Tortmann's volatile senses of interrogation and wonder reflect the recognitions and active seizure of 'alternatives' to the limitations of mortality, as identified in the major poem, 'Infinite Resentment': namely, 'The infinite reversibility of things / The seduction of opposites / And how to part the colours of the night' (*TD*, 69). This theme reaches its culmination in 'Ceasing to Assume', in which the narrator (Tortmann?) sees all things as open to strenuous imaginative harrowing: 'The night's material is not so stiff it can't be torn' (*TD*, 77); indeed, desecration seems a raging universal principle here, with all defence, belief, hope and faith torn and stripped out by forces both treacherous and invasive; whilst within, 'The undead child of rage' runs wildly in the cellars, unsubdued by the 'furious embroidery' of soporific lies: a daemon of cacophonous and unenviable vitality.

An eye for the cracks: *Sheer Detachment*

The collection *Sheer Detachment* (2009) begins with the poem 'Called In', which compares the scenes of two parks, across decades: one from which a boy is called in by his father; one in which a figure, perhaps the boy grown to manhood, roams, with 'no one calling him in'; provoking the double-edged *aperçu*, recognising a (possibly ominous and unenviable, but defiantly purposeful) freedom in isolation: 'The unkind leave us unconfined'. The fragmenting upheavals and chaotic reversals of revolution, detailed in the poem 'Old Regime', are immediately contrasted by the succeeding 'Impending 1 and 2', which depict the details of 'warless wait / Percussion of hiatus' which would generally serve to 'Push mortality a laughing pace away'; however, 'Impending 2' suggests how, in such times of languorous heat, things also swell to friction and burstings: train wheels, hot bottles, a hanged man's impatience with his life. The sense of deadly inertia reappears later in the collection, with 'Hiatus': 'Foetuses studied their fingernails neither dying nor / Developing nothing had a term and the cervix closed' (*SD*, 11).

'29 December' offers a further contrast, reflections of, and on, five women whose vivifying erotic disarray countered, for the narrator, the surrounding 'slopped gallons of monotony'; women whose middle age offers something infinitely more enticing than innocence ('I do not ask for cleanliness or that you / Berate your husbands only let me lift you high'), a resurgence flourished by 'your mouth a red sun / Painted and painted again over the rage cracks' (*SD*, 7). Similarly, 'In the Dark' rejoices in private disconnection from conversations and goodwill, a murderous intimacy which mocks municipal populism: 'Wife of agility her thigh goes / Higher than advertisements.' 'Old Mad Still' also studies a woman who 'In the habit of the eye' has 'not parted / From that self who cleaner than she is now / Made men loud or sullen for her nakedness', notwithstanding a futile haste which increasingly beckons the ominous spectres of 'the gathering women of old fields' with their 'stiff legs'. However, despite this woman's sartorial 'distress' and clutter of 'nothingness', the narrator acknowledges 'a greater obligation diminishes disgust', overturning the gravity of decay, as he imagines himself with her 'in her rotting room', 'Sculpted from consolation her thigh lifted / And a tremor in our single belly' (*SD*, 13). This progression through an appreciation of (sometimes potential) contraries provides a tidal rhythm for much of the collection. Whilst '72' offers a dispassionate, but almost pitying, observation of mundane but implacable male desperation in a coupling, 'The Rumour She Gardens Naked' discovers an admiration for the naturist whose hardened frankness is invulnerably oblivious to the 'spoiling savagery' of voyeurs, who are imaginatively penned in a world of vulgar constraint, whilst she 'pisses standing', 'one earthed hand spread on her wood hard belly'. 'Are Your Hands Wet' gathers this appreciation of paradoxical contraries into a single poem/subject, as the observer wonders at his mistress's simultaneous moist liquidity and 'pear wood' hardness.

Sheer Detachment also yields the seeds and residues of several Barker plays: most obviously, 'Found in the Ground', but also 'The Loveless Move', observing the doomed odyssey of Johannes Aventinus, imaginatively developed and detailed in *The Road, The House, The Road*; 'Second 13th February', which alights on the moonstruck nakedness of a consciously transgressive wife who jettisons domestic familiarity for a tryst with thieves, and who seems to be Mrs Williams, protagonist of the most memorable playlet in Barker's compendium *Five Names* (written 2002); 'Old War Somewhere Here' recalls the memory of a wartime coupling such as that at the heart of the opera libretto *Stalingrad* (written 2000, staged 2002, Denmark); 'Darling the Word' distinguishes the ultimatum of that endearment from the word 'dear', in terms which recall the darkling realisations of *Gertrude – The Cry*: how the utterance of the word 'darling' is ambivalent in its resentment of the power of the beloved, and the dependency it breeds; the word re-presents a fearful investment in a 'cry' which

> Hangs on desire's flanks and is its hound
> Treading long nights on the boards
> And mewing under doors for that cold clear
> Before your breath covered him.   (*SD*, 27)

'16th June' is a particularly urgent self-addressed 'lullaby for the impatient' in which the eyes of stone lions advise the observer to 'adopt their / Lassitude' or court death amidst hurtful limitations; conceding to a pause, the narrator refines his self-performance ('I would not capitulate to generosity / I declined to be wise … I nursed my criminality') so slyly that his surroundings themselves are lulled and disarmed: 'birds drowsed' in his presence, and the warm wall becomes complicit, 'kinder even than that woman love that / Asks only for your eyes to close' (*SD*, 10).

'A Slave Receives Instructions' depicts a king directing an assassin in how to dispatch his queen with the required combination of lethal desecration ('Spoil everything') and detached solemnity (her head is to be carried back 'severed but unkissed'), so as to permit the king a crucially immoral fastidiousness. By contrast, 'The Great Servants' proclaim themselves less 'encroaching' than the objects and relations which they deferentially maintain as 'true inhabitants' of a space and time; their professed lightness aims for minimal impact beyond some complicity in inevitable and natural erosion. To others, the laws of disintegration are writ more startlingly: the narrator of 'The Losses' notes 'The way the impenetrable comes apart / Invisible faults / And undermining':

The acts go first
As if memory trod one deck
Clean-heeled above unspeakable cargoes   (*SD*, 17)

Disintegration yields beauty for he who can recognise and 'know the perfection in the remnants', 'value the rag for its losses / And the stark hall for its cold' ('June 19th'); it also withers (or intensifies?) a couple's relationship to 'siege' and 'Scrupulous/Uncritical' accommodation ('The Still'), and challenges the capacities of those who do not will or bid its manifestations, the mockery of their emotional investments. The familiar objects in a house often serve as witnesses, mutely reflecting back indices of former presence which surround the occupant dialogically, and sometimes offer unsettling intimations: these include bedsheets indelibly inscribed by the body of the departed, which the dissociative owner nonetheless declares he will not read ('I Fling You'); cooking pots, clothes and books which sometimes offer sounds and textures for personal confirmation (in the absence of rewards, ambition and arguments) but also suggest forebodings of an inescapable traction: 'the bird of aching days / Calling in the mirror-hall' and 'the doors of fallen homes / Still slamming in the clouds' ('Only', *SD*, 34). 'Powerless' draws a further explicit parallel between human lives and the persistence of objects, 'sediment', 'But uncollected', 'Learning what need never be learned'. Mirrors are of course the most apparently confrontational witnesses, and in a poem of that title, an occupant considers a lifetime of argument and sacrifice, in which mirrors offer a salutary objectivity amidst mutiny and restoration, 'They do not clamour for improved reflections yet'. Conversely, the subject of 'Prodigal' is a man who returns to die in the house of his childhood, only to find an absence of odour, heat or graves ('Missing parents had betrayed their oaths to wait'), in a disappointing scene as diminished as his senses. The narrator of '8th February' is more fortunate; if he now sees the cemetery gates 'walking to me open-armed / Like loving uncles freed from wars', he also discovers a pity for those desperate to paint 'new orders better orders' on signboards rinsed by rain of 'every fear and all advice' (*SD*, 41). In accordance with, and development of, this disengagement from merely contemporary and conventional value, '5th March' proclaims a voracious yet patient appetite for that which bespeaks the relief and yielding of decay: 'rinds and husks' rather than 'great green flourishes', 'shame and apologies / Never the bold claims': exercised not in acts of dispossession, but in surprising and disemburdening acceptance of what a culture would conceal as embarrassing. Surprisingly, in the poem 'Casanova', the words etched in a window glass, 'You will forget me too', attain longevity beyond the inscriber or subject, and thereby suggest both apprehension and transcendence. 'The Route' discovers a wry humour of accordance in startling clarities: the city as an apt landscape for the narrator's treachery and (self-)deceptions, its dark roads drawing adjacent lovers together and apart through 'transference' and 'calculation', as when a builder 'with a lover's touch' ponders his brick 'affectionately / Before splitting it' (*SD*, 56).

A further series of poems considers the way that passion can absorb, or forcibly exclude, the self. 'Her Arse' discovers an almost comic speed and degree of exultation in sexual longing, as if an unrestrainable animal 'shot from / Under him' to the 'Drumtrap of her stride', renouncing all other cultivations: 'His brain drowned gratefully ...' (*SD*, 45). 'Some Language' rejoices in the narrator's power to bestow, as well as receive, the ecstatic dissolution of the self, with an artfulness recalling that of John Donne:

> I am educated in this nothingness
> And teach nothingness
> That is the verdict of your going eyes
> As the floors of you rise   (*SD*, 60)

Such escape from the self is deferred from the strategic observer of '23rd November', who watches and calibrates the detail of strategy with which a husband is deceived, the search of him 'dying in your dark / And dawn-shed'. '23rd January' contemplates the hastening extinction of a self which may, or may not, be resisted ('I won't be long-lived if she delivers me / One child or three / I shan't be long-lived'). '25th February' expresses a wry commentary on endeavouring to implement dissociation, 'Intentionally / To dismantle the effective parts', whereby the narrator finds himself 'pitying my / Becoming this / Resenting my own coercion'. '12th May' imagines paradoxical reversibilities: the estranged lover returned 'To laugh out the volume of our separation'; the narrator calling down to his patrolling self in encouragement:

> How well you balance those chandeliers on
> A thin rod
> They dip like crystal ships in the night air   (*SD*, 63)

This links with further developments on the theme of persistence (artful, unenviable, or both) broached earlier in '16th June', and moving the poetic vistas into more surrealistically feverish landscapes. 'Arrival An Anxiety' presages the opening (and potential closures) of a new phase of life, to be negotiated 'As if certain it must have its perimeter / As grief does', requiring 'A going without compasses / Even love's compass'; still the narrator achieves an acceptance ('Let it be so'), an openness ('Make the heart a quartered fruit') and an expressiveness:

> I am leaf-dry and singing
> To the bone flute of my torso
> Singing of the nothing-to-hold   (*SD*, 55)

'I Asked' testifies to a grim resourcefulness in asseverating the disintegratory anatomisation of a relationship, moving through the recalcitrances of Poetry

('But she was nerves only') and the Moon, to the discovery of a 'stagnant sun' and Laughter, which provide aids to forcing the unracking of a memory ('You went from your shape') with the dispassionately precise itemisation of a butcher. 'A Rage Came In' imagines rage incarnated as a mercurial feminine, who enters, provocatively tearing the night, but who should rightly be permitted to 'stay truthless / And simply holy'. The title poem of the collection 'Sheer Detachment' is the one I find the most haunting in the collection: it describes an encounter with a man 'who sat naked in tall weeds childless and godless', perfectly alone ('He caused nothing any more and what he had / Caused did not trouble him'; 'He drove nothing away nor did he say kind things'). This man resembles the dead ('He stank of things before my time') yet occupies a place preferable to the coercive reiterations of 'Where the rebels marched with their three words'. Like the dead, he has ceased 'the valuing of values' , and his repetition of the narrator's name 'as if he / Might clean it with his spit and sell it on as new' makes the nameless man's 'sheer detachment' seem almost generous in its solvent relief from the specifics of a given time and place (*SD*, 71).[4] In the final poem of the collection, 'In Bowls and Stains', women, at the juncture of catastrophe, rediscover the ancient tactic of displaying menstrual blood to enemy forces in order to discourage rape: manifestations which re-present 'A learning old and blind but / Swiftly remembered' amongst the (profoundly human) disintegration. This reappearance, by instinct, of the old habits which modern society only *appears* to have rendered unnecessary indicates 'the secret world, never really abolished'[5] which Barker has made the territory of his poetry. The last line of 'In Bowls and Stains' describes the sound of the armoured vehicles of the enemy advancing down the suburban street, 'the fate of all peoples' at some juncture, at which apparent compliance and artful accord may render some individuals 'likely students of survival'.[6] Here and in the title poem of *Sheer Detachment* we encounter 'the substrata of experience' in forms and ways which link with Barker's theatre: the underlying culture of Europe, excavated and made explicit; and the interpersonal, generally imperceptible redefinitions which occur, in 'the un-transparent depths of instinct and memory',[7] which may call into question the so-called 'actual', and which, at a later date if not immediately, prove significant.

Barker reflects resonantly, on the eruptive cultural pressures which inform both the characters' exclamations in the landscapes of his plays, and the expressive fissures of his poems:

> The emphasis on experiences such as flight, invasion, seemingly-arbitrary movements of people, death from the skies, mass execution, the extermination of books and faiths, and so on, are deeply embedded in the European psyche – and not only from this last century. That such mayhem occurred within a culture of extreme sophistication naturally makes this shock the greater. I have said elsewhere that the European (hardly the English, I have to say) experience is one of intensification unknown elsewhere. One has to see the endless struggle between reason and instinct (not

culture and barbarity) in this light. See *The Road, The House, The Road* perhaps, for some antecedents …[8]

Notes

1 Barker/Houth identifies 'The Ascent of Monte Grappa' as a testament to Barker's love for Marcia Pointon during the 1980s and 90s: H. Barker/E. Houth, *A Style and Its Origins* (London: Oberon, 2007), p. 69.

2 J. Kristeva, *Powers of Horror*, translated by L.S. Roudiez (New York: Columbia University Press, 1982), p. 8.

3 H. Barker, *Death, The One and The Art of Theatre* (Abingdon: Routledge, 2005), p.21.

4 'Death renders irrelevant all that was relevant. Whilst this injures the still-living (the still-loving) might this not be one of death's *generosities*?' – Barker, *ibid.*, p. 37.

5 Barker, letter to the author, 20 April 2009.

6 *Ibid.*

7 *Ibid.*

8 Barker, letter to the author, 15 September 2010.

17

Reading Howard Barker's pictorial art

Charles Lamb

(*Editors' note*: This paper was given at the 2009 'Howard Barker's Art of Theatre' conference in Aberystwyth, Wales, at which an exhibition of Barker's oil paintings formed a backdrop for the plenary lecture space, and for a perform-ance; and the author provided further illustrations of Barker's drawings and paintings, with powerpoint projection. The prohibitive costs of colour printing means that images from the drawings and paintings cannot appear to accompany this essay. We are grateful to the author for recasting his essay so that it is not dependent on illustrations; and we hope that his observations inspire the reader to seek out one of the increasing number of exhibitions of Barker's pictorial art.)

Currently, Barker's fine artwork falls into two distinctly different categories. There are the books and there are the oil paintings. The former contain drawings executed in coloured inks and pastels which relate directly to the play he is working on at the time. Barker describes these books as 'notes to the plays' and 'entirely within the context of daily writing'.[1] The drawings, then, would appear to be an important part of the creative process – a practice that brings to mind Brecht's creative dialogue with Caspar Neher, his most renowned designer. This involved Neher sitting in on blocking rehearsals and supplying Brecht with a constant stream of drawings to assist him in the construction of his stage pictures. Neher, in effect, designed both settings and the action. Barker's variant of this process, obviously, unites the two roles of director and designer in one person – necessarily so if the aim is for the work to represent the product of a single consciousness. The drawings in these sketchbooks are executed in coloured inks and oil pastels on hand-made watercolour paper. These, then, are created to be both working sketches with a 'practical' use and high quality works of art. The status of both formats is demonstrated through this investment of the best of materials.

This tension between use and aesthetic is evident in their content. On the face of it, these look like fairly rough sketches which have been executed quickly at the expense of 'finish'. However, the quality Barker claims to be seeking is precisely this. As he puts it:

> The paradox of drawing is that its urgency – and frequently, the inaccuracy of representation – serves to create a sense of vigour that too great study would diminish.[2]

These notebooks are quite small – less than A4 size and more square in shape. In addition to this format, Barker clearly wanted to work on a larger scale. Initially, this took the form of using oil pastel on paper; some drawings illustrated scenes from the plays, but most, while reflecting their grotesque, anti-realist spirit, pursue an independent agenda. Eventually, Barker abandoned these materials in favour of oil on board and seems to have arrived at a creative form and method which, judging by the quantity of his output, is highly congenial to him. Barker himself has stated that when he is engaged in oil painting he feels relieved of the responsibilities and obligations which he sees as incumbent upon him as a writer.[3]

In the respect of 'oil series', there are two major formal elements which apply to all of the paintings. First the boards measure 91.5 x 91.5cm or thereabouts. That is to say, when fitted into a frame (usually black) the whole amounts to a metre square. As Barker points out, square pictures are comparatively rare compared with rectangles:

> I like the square. I think because it gives a lot of opportunity for suggesting solitude in the landscape. When you're in a landscape, say the Downs, there's an awful lot above you, which is what makes you look lonely. And if you use a rectangle, you don't get that sense of weight coming from above. I think distributing figures around the square is now to me vastly more interesting than distributing figures around a rectangle.[4]

This uniformity of style can be quite striking – particularly when a number of paintings are hung together, as happened at the Caen Exhibition in 2008. Barker has also indicated how his role as a director has influenced his painting in that his customary viewpoint on the action is from the centre front of the circle – looking down on the performers and the stage: because of the restricted sightlines this leads to the disappearance of the sky and a focus not on the normal panoramic rectangle but on the acting ensemble centre stage.[5] In addition to Barker's complex perception and representation of proxemics on canvas and on the stage, his perception and use of colour in his productions is also symbiotic with his painting.

The second main characteristic of the 'oil series' is its restricted palette. Initially having made use of a wider range of colours, Barker has cut these down to combinations of four paints – raw sienna, yellow ochre, black and white. This is sometimes described as monochrome, a term which may perhaps be applied to the finished impression but clearly isn't strictly accurate. (This is an important point because the stage sets of The Wrestling School are generally monochrome – being restricted to black and white.) The effect of this palette on backgrounds (and therefore on the general atmosphere of the paintings) is pronounced: landscapes appear barren – whether one is contemplating desert or tundra. Skies are leaden gray. Parks, whether of the gentrified or civic style, are similarly dull-coloured with strangely shaped trees which look as if they might conceal lurking criminal gangs. It would not be going too far to suggest that these vistas with their yellow miasmata foster an authentically catastrophic feeling such as one might expect from the originator of the Theatre of Catastrophe.

It is quite rare, for instance, for Barker's paintings to make out a face with any degree of clarity. Barker's comment on this:

> … they're not really required because all the emotional energy is meant to go into the body, so the face is a mask.[6]

In fact, light in Barker's paintings is generally quite pale and cold. What is interesting is how much of Barker's artwork feeds back into his theatre. This is the case in particular with his interest in gesture – finding new gestures to replace the cliché – recycling stylised and period gestures. Then there comes what the painters refer to as 'composition' and the theatre calls 'blocking': the positioning to maximum effect of figures within the frame. These influences on practice are not confined to the notebooks but include aspects of the work done in oils.

Notes

1   H. Barker and C. Lamb, Unpublished interview, 11 May 2009, p. 1.
2   H. Barker, *Exhibition Catalogue* (Caen, France: Musée Des Beaux-Arts, 2008).
3   Barker and Lamb, Unpublished interview, p. 1.
4   *Ibid.*, p. 1.
5   *Ibid.*, p. 2.
6   *Ibid.*, p. 1.

18

Howard Barker's paintings, poems and plays: 'in the deed itself', or the triple excavation of the unchangeable

Michel Morel

Always the knowledge kills / […] You will starve of their scholarship[1]

My argument here is that painting, poetry and theatre being three generic means that make one see – painting shows, poetry lays bare and theatre does both through re-presentation on the stage – Barker's triple creation operates a centripetal triangulation. I will take advantage of this fact to show how the paintings and the poems may allow one to read the plays more effectively, not in terms of what they say, but of what they, too, actually and repeatedly do 'in the deed itself',[2] the least disruptive critical approach being, according to me, to keep track of the artist's procedures, to try and 'have [as good] an eye for the cracks'[3] as him, and to learn 'how to watch'[4] what he actually does.

Making us see 1 – the 'arrogance' of painting[5]

My starting point is Barker's exhibition of thirty-five pictures (36 x 36 inch oil paintings) shown in Caen in 2008, supplemented by the catalogue of *Landscape with Cries* (1996–2006), for his 2005 Paris exhibition.

What immediately struck me as I stepped into the square room of Caen's gallery was the prevalence of one colour: 'A painter of yellow shades' in the words of Barker's poem 'Detritus' (*SD*, 32): an ambivalent yellow touched with brown, on which silvery grey white figures stand out, all of this suggesting denied or subverted mimesis.[6]

A second, more belated, impression concerned the similarity in the chrono-tope, or space-time coordinates: the simple iteration of the digging, again and again, into a common fund of vision, the same characteristic applying to the poems, and the plays despite the variety in their subject matters. As is shown by *The Hospital*,[7] one of the most striking pictures in the exhibition, the sense of place is deterritorialised. Vision is shaped by an oneiric idea of space rather than by topographic representation, the high and vaguely tangible horizon suggesting both a low-angle vision and seeing from above, with two persons standing on a white plinth overlooking a surface littered with corpses protruding under white shrouds, the last one, up right, seeming to float away on what looks like ground, but could be water.

And so it is with *A Sacred Place,* picturing a high horizon again, pale traces on the ground converging towards an empty whitish centre that might seem to represent a blurred face; left centre, stands a noncommittal spectator facing a threateningly exposed Stonehenge-like desolation, a distant row of thin stakes prompting the visual association; while love-making is taking place downstage on the left, the standing lovers apparently profaning a legendary place, but in reality making it 'safe from violation'.[8]

In *Darling I Love You*, one notes the absence of any receding viewpoint, along with a kind of temporal collage, as in Medieval paintings whose continuous narration juxtaposes successive episodes in the life of a saint: above, the headboard of a bed with strewn pieces of white and black feminine underwear; below, a naked couple, the woman (seen from the back, down on the right) bringing flowers to the seemingly surprised man (seen in quasi-profile, more upstage on the left); on the whole, the same vision from both above and under, and consequently the same contradiction between feelings of power and oppression.

Dead You Said adds a time dimension to a rather abrupt incline causing a kind of vertigo: oblique parallel lines of lighter orange-yellow smudges dot the ground half-way up and mostly on the left, slanting up from left to right in the direction of a hidden horizon; one is made to view the scene both from on high and from very near (with a very large 'plate', down centre), a man hauling a naked body by its feet in the direction of a woman, slightly bent in the foreground and facing him, who has just thrown down her minimal white underwear. The whole sets up an elusive 'moment' scene, not suggesting any story though with a before and an after, but concentrating the two into a suspended present, a visual rendering of the stilled eternal return of catastrophe.

A third constituent cutting across the whole series is the fact that all these scenes are 'possibilities' taking the form of challenging *exempla* – originally, instant cautionary stories – or allegories (both remaining cryptic, a contradiction in itself). *The Punishment of the Judges* seemed to be the central piece of the Caen exhibition, its apparent clarity amounting to a denial of understanding, the scene possibly echoing the line in Barker's poem 'Impending 2': 'The hanged man sack-still in blue woods' (*SD*, 4). A quick comparison with Jacques Callot's 1633 naturalistic engraving, *L'Arbre aux pendus*[9] with the wide horizontal branches of a central tree close-packed with hanged men, or with Goya's 1814 *A Heroic Feat! With Dead Men!*[10] where three naked corpses are exposed on a dead tree, the severed head and arms of the one on the right tied to a branch next to his upside down mutilated corpse, makes the difference immediately manifest. In Barker's picture, the ominous overhead mass of trees – 'oak dumb' (*SD*, 2) – darkly overloading the upper half of the tableau, the three dead bodies, in black nondescript mantles, hanging from thread-like ropes that reach up out of sight, and the silvery mouse-coloured flesh of the 'judges' dancing or lolling around a refreshment table below them, both illustrate and bedim the apparent clarity of a legend focussed on the discomposing ambivalence of the word 'judgement'; the spectator is left hovering between voyeurism and malaise.

A fourth component concerns what T. S. Eliot calls 'objective correlatives', objects that regularly come back as puzzling *leitmotifs*. A particularly striking example is the frequent recurrence of empty, possibly cracked white crockery. In the *Study of an Actress with an Unloved Child*, the picture features an enormous pivotal tree looming over a woman and a child placed down left, to the right of the broken row of wide empty vessels whose dwindling shapes meander irregularly in the direction of the distant horizon, in a kind of diagonal path from low left to top right. Elsewhere, in other pictures, cracked basins, plates, or even toilet bowls (a scandalous equivalence between eating and defecating). Trees, too, as the massive one in the *Study of an Actress with an Unloved Child* (with the ominous orientation of light coming from the right), massive oxymoronic emblems of life and obscure power, threat, solitude, and ultimately death as in *The Punishment of the Judges*. Sketchy fences, mostly decayed (a denial of the concept itself), implying a threatened centre, as the line of uneven and skeletal stumps on the foreground of *Mental Asylum: Poor State of the Perimeter Fence*, on the marshy immediate limits of a vague mound with two figures on it, one as it were crucified on the ground, the other turned towards the first in the posture of authority. The most cryptic objective correlative that repeatedly comes back is white surfaces: shrouds in *The Hospital*, hanging material on three unevenly placed parallel washing lines in *The Threadbare Flags of Surrender*,[11] three white paper screens with outlined profiles on the two lower ones, making a triangle with a well at its centre (*The Well and its Creator – Women Fighting with Buckets*), a tilted table next to an irregular scar of blackened ground in *A Shrine (Bombed Picnic)*, white altar-like plinths (*My Aunt's Pleasure in my Nakedness*, *The Hospital*), leaning tombstones on the edge of what looks like a deep black crack in the ground in *Tobit Blinded by Sparrows*, each of these diverse objects suggesting the complex but somehow convergent symbolism attached to white in its contrast with the brownish yellow earthy surface.

At all levels, ambivalence prevails, an inbuilt contradiction amounting to visual oxymora: oxymoron being the figure of distance in itself. One eloquent example might be *Killers Denying It* with its three picture-sized figures standing on stump-like legs, receding in a diagonal from right to left, against a rare black sky above the grey brown somehow shelving ground. All three seem to be shouting, at least exclaiming: neither a photographic effect as in Eisenstein's still of the howling wounded nurse from *The Battleship Potemkin* (1921), nor deconstructed as the Pope's gaping mouth in Francis Bacon's *Head VI* of 1948 (from *Innocent X* by DiegoVelasquez); perhaps closer to Edvard Munch's *The Scream* (1893); a kind of stupefaction, with the silent shout, the jolt of surprise and suspended retreating or disclaiming, and the disquieting suggestion of a deviant crucifixion. These and the open arms of the two figures at the back, the metallic robotic hands of the one on the right, the tottering bodies against the black backdrop, take on another meaning when compared with Huỳnh Công Út's now exemplar photograph of the open-mouthed children fleeing napalm bombing at Trang Bang (8 June 1972).[12] One may note strange correspondences between the two images especially in the general forms and their economy: the diagonal placing of the children, the central naked girl following on the steps of a crying boy seen on the left forward, with another two children trailing her on the right, all terrified by the murky sky in the distance, their exposed white bodies standing out against the same sombre background as in the picture, three soldiers closing up the march. Viewed in the context of the photograph, the picture seems to evince the prescience of a scandalous intimacy between victim and torturer. The placing is similar but inverted, the diagonal going from right to left in the picture, for left to right in the photograph. Here too, the postural gestures conjoin violence and helplessness, reversing the photograph's similar ambivalence: the central feminine figure spreads her arms out in the same gesture of appeal, helplessness and acceptance of the incontrovertible, as the little girl's. The epicene person, on the right, starts back in a show of innocence, an innocence turned upside down by the caption: 'Killers Denying It'.[13] Barker's visual fusion of brutality with frailty, in itself a kind of double-bind equivalent to the staggering amputation of the pleading hand in *The Possibilities*,[14] makes it appallingly clear what the 'it' in the title stands for: the scandalous abyss and impasse of the unsolvable in man.

The result, here and elsewhere, is a clinical excavation[15] of the unbearable, provoking a dislocating bipolar identification. Such impassable contradiction, at this and other levels, generates a disquieting distance; in actual words, distance in, and through, the deed itself.[16] The body and its gestures, their mapping out of violence, are shown here to be *the* objective correlative for the unchangeable in man.

Making us see 2 – poetry as 'excavation'

Four main points could be made concerning Howard Barker's poems (here mostly on the basis of his 2009 collection *Sheer Detachment*):

First, to project a kind of sickening humanism on such texts would certainly be ill-advised and completely off the point. Each one seems to be analogous in its condensation to a demanding, provocative *exemplum*, demurring and testing even more than the paintings.

Second, one notes a frequent tendency in *Sheer Detachment* and in other poems to an *ars poetica* of self-distance: 'I am not to be followed and I will not be followed' ('Character', *SD*, 57); 'I am educated in this nothingness / And teach nothingness' ('Some Language', *SD*, 60); 'I take things listen I take / But the rinds and the husks / Never the flesh' ('5th March', *SD*, 42); 'He walks away with our embarrassments smiling' ('5th March', *SD*, 42).

Third, here too, in scenes of all kinds, either contemporary or situated in the past, a series of objective correlatives keep surfacing, 'transitional' states or objects, in the terms of Barker's *Lullabies for the Impatient*,[17] or 'things' in those of *Sheer Detachment* (*SD*, 42), often corresponding to similar elements in the paintings, and in the plays, as the following examples from *Sheer Detachment* demonstrate: breaks and clefts keep returning: 'faults' (17), 'gaps' (23), 'crevices' (39), 'fissures' (56), and above all the 'hiatus' (3); which reminds one of the question: 'Have you an eye for the cracks?' (9), calling up in turn the dark chasm splitting the ground in the painting *These Sad Places: Why Must You Visit Them!*. The poems of *Sheer Detachment* often evoke depth: 'To go into the ground' (6); 'as if memory trod one deck / Clean-heeled above unspeakable cargoes' (17); 'undermining' (17), 'excavations / Where the buried contradict their death' (35). Other artifacts are fraught with a sense of dereliction: 'Car doors caught distantly' (18); 'A car door flops like a dead man's limb' (20); 'It is time for the doors to slam / On the fingers of the preachers' (57); the last two images threading together the idea of an opening and the terminal closing down of death, be it physical or spiritual, a death indirectly connoted by the frequent reference to bones: 'a small bone from the ear: / [...] And underfoot it shatters' (26); 'My song is the breaking of bone' (39); 'Girl of carved bone' (37); 'He lay on boards / A board of ribs' (52); 'Implement / Saddlery / Jaw' (66). Elsewhere, one also finds white cloth and sheets: 'Lying night white cloth' (2) and fences: 'fencing the sky" (12); 'a pen of knees' (20).

Fourth, one often comes across figures of speech putting equivalence or balance in jeopardy, like distorted chiasmus or indirect and direct oxymoron: 'I take things listen I take' (42); 'Learning what need never be learned' (57) (with the comforting reciprocations of a symmetry immediately counteracted by the maze-like situations). If *Sheer Detachment* takes the shape of a random log-book, titles in the form of dates returning without any clear logic except to suggest things never change in spite of their everyday mutability, what emerges from the volume is the ingrained inconsistency and contradictoriness called life. Hence the insistent return of the oxymoron in all forms, from the linguistic to the metaphoric. On the linguistic or grammatical side one may quote: 'The bird is boiled who renounced its predatory / Habit [...]' (31), in which 'who' and 'it' command two opposite but equally imperative linguistic universes; the same for 'Kill I / Kill I / My breath is a torrent of rats / Kill I / Kill I' (39), where the absence of the question mark seems to contradict the interrogative form, thus equating two irreducibly antagonistic meanings, the whole under the aegis of an imperative symmetry of form. One encounters the metaphors: 'Lying night blazing / Lying night white cloth behind her grazing' (2); 'The world renews itself in suicides' (49); 'heatless fire' (51). If such metaphorical renderings are somehow less difficult to make distorted sense of, they express a similar situational gridlock.

What the poems illustrate repeatedly and delve into, is this very state of being caught in an unfathomable quandary between opposing issues, all legitimate in their own contrary ways. In its diversity of forms and expressions, the same insistently recurring blockage keeps forcing on us the idea that the condition of the double-bind is ours. This prevailing and constant straining between contending demands could be said to be dialogic, if dialogism is understood as the pitting of meaning against contrary meaning within a single voice: the resulting immanent pressure leading to distance, an agonising distance, at once knowing and strangely undecided. Similarly, in the catalogue of extremes offered by *Lullabies for the Impatient*, the competing contexts at the back of the first poem called 'Chelmno' make for tortured reading between aesthetics, self-conceit, tourism and Nazism (*LI*, 1).

Making us see 3 – in the deed itself

> That corpse you planted last year in your garden,
> Has it begun to sprout? Will it bloom this year?
> Or has the sudden frost disturbed its bed?
> O keep the dog far hence, that's friend to men,
> Or with his nails he'll dig it up again![18]

Howard Barker keeps digging it up again, whatever the 'it' stands for. He has never stopped digging and will never do, because this 'it' – that is not 'meant to be understood', as Galactia says in *Scenes from an Execution* (*OP1*, 282) – will always need excavation; a quest for the unexplainable started very early in the writer's career as Prodo's dubious exclamation evidences in the same play: 'Digging out my –' (that is, the mobile bolt skewering his open skull, *OP1*, 228). Such a long and risky exploration is the expression of a 'total aesthetic'[19] making the theatrical approximate to the poetic, and conversely the poetic (and the pictorial) to the theatrical.

If this is not to be 'understood' by us, the only possible approach is to experience and accompany the act of excavation through both heedful and distanced identification. As Goya is made to suggest, we must emulate the artist 'in the deed itself'. Not to remain spectators, as with Edward Bond or even Antonin Artaud (if I understand their aims well), but to be initiated into the entanglements: the unexplainable borderline which individual thought and behaviour are heir to. The deed is not so much to be looked for in actual doings as in the enlightening darkness these bring to the fore, an exposure making us start back at what we surmise. Such a practice might bring to mind the terror inherent in sublimity, in

Edmond Burke's interpretation, sublimity of the abyss rather than of heights. The deep kinship that connects the paintings, poems and plays is due to their parallel exploration of human 'possibilities', whatever the extremes at stake; this on the basis of something very close to a Hobbesian version of life. Desire, our first and only truthful spring,[20] leads to violence, a compulsive violence whose avatars *The Ecstatic Bible* strings out in their persistent resurgence, generation after generation. Such is the unchangeable in man: the heroism of looking into it, at all.

To come back to the few objective correlatives I have pointed out, the conflicted logic which underlies them suggests that the strength of the catastrophic deed does not lie in the effect but in the affect: not in the derivative effect, but in the causal affect. The shock of scandal or catastrophe overwhelming us precedes emotional reactions that, in themselves, are only the spurious end product of the cortex. It plunges us into the abrupt and ruthless truth of the reptilian brain, the fount of preconscious psychic shocks that set us going like puppets, in the image of the denying killers of the picture. Referring back to Barker's pictorial universe: a simple illustration of a process more felt than understood might be found in the emptiness of the teeming basins, that causes a deep and unaccountable uneasiness in us, a discomfort made clear in reverse by the subconscious *jouissance* we take, after Virginia Woolf, in imagining the perfect central dish of fruit enthroned in the middle of the festive table in *To the Lighthouse*,[21] on the occasion of the last meal before Mrs Ramsay's death.

Hence the frequent impression of coming upon what D.H. Lawrence sneeringly calls Pisgah-sights,[22] or inverted Pisgah-sights; here no Promised Land to hope for, except the territory of contradiction inherent in men and women. What better initiation into this than to steep the reader or spectator into the tensions of scandalously discordant givens: the revulsion of seeing someone eating human ashes (*Found in the Ground*); or again, the dismay at the sight of a pleading woman's hand ruthlessly severed by the sword wielded by another woman's hand, 'the ultimate in pity' (*OP1*, 240). In this lies the forcefulness of such ubiquitous and endlessly returning situations: 'I do these things / Oh how I persist I am at least persistent', affirms the epigraph to *A Style and its Origins*. In their totality, paintings, poems and plays forge a three-faceted construct through mutually supporting artistic means whose undisputable legitimacy originates in distortions coming out of the blue: to quote *A Style and its Origins* again: 'for he always wrote blindly, unknowing' (*ASIO*, 38).

In line with what Howard Barker says in the last sentence of what amounts to an undeclared artistic autobiography: 'he required the past and its remnants nearly as addiction, but drew out of it an absolute modernity' (*ASIO*, 118). I would affirm that his works at their best show Modernism at last come true. The Modernists were the first not just to rebel against what the generation before felt and created, as the Romantics had done, but to look into norms and normativity in themselves: a radical stance, in comparison with the precarious distancing privileged by postmodernist writings; a sheer distance, clinical in its exploration of the dim essentials of life, as they still remain and will ever be. The three arts he conjoins are unified in their capacity for exposing and baring 'the contradiction that was the essence of him'.[23] 'Oxymoron' actually means the exquisiteness ('oxy') of thought belonging to a kind of madness ('moron'). In its most arcane moments, human experience is a compendium of such keen extremes: the deed of Barker's art is that it never ceases engaging their relentlessly demanding brinksmanship.

Notes

1 Howard Barker, 'Mirrors' (*SD*, 37).
2 'They call me a moralist. They call me a satirist. I must warn you I am in the deed itself' says Goya in Barker's opera libretto *Terrible Mouth* (1992); quoted in *Landscape with Cries, Howard Barker Painting 1996–2006* (published by The Wrestling School on the occasion of the exhibition and Shillam Smith 3 Gallery, London, 2006).
3 Howard Barker / Eduardo Houth, *A Style and its Origins* (London: Oberon Books, 2007), p. 116; also *Sheer Detachment*, '12th February': 'Have you an eye for the cracks?', p. 9.
4 'like any good poet, he knew how to watch' (*ASIO*, 91).
5 'The art of painting is an art of arrogance. It is arrogance to describe the world and shove the thing into the world's face. [...] To paint is to boast, and if you don't like boasting you ought not to paint': Galactia in *Scenes from an Execution* (*OP1*, 238).
6 'His imagination expressed itself in many and contradictory forms: in his painting, in his set and costume designs, a severe, monochromatic discipline imposed itself' (*ASIO*, 10).
7 *The Hospital: mother and child with dogs and unburied dead.*
8 *ASIO*, 68: this in reference to the copulation with strangers in *The Fence in its Thousandth Year.*
9 'The Hanging' in *Les Grandes misères de la guerre* (*The Miseries and Misfortunes of War*).
10 *Les Désastres de la guerre* (*The Disasters of War*).
11 'The rectangle of pristine white, the bedsheet or the starched tablecloth, features routinely in his paintings and in his plays ...' (*ASIO*, 14).
12 http://en.wikipedia.org/wiki/File:TrangBang.jpg. Nick Ut/The Associated Press, accessed 11 April 2013.
13 '*Killers Denying It* could be described as 'Goya-esque' not only in account of its heavy black pigment but in the way it draws us into an uneasy complicity in atrocity', Howard Barker, *Landscape with Cries*, p. 14.
14 'The Unforeseen Consequences of a Patriotic Act' (*OP1*, 202–5).
15 'Only the clinical have permission': 'Impending 2' (*SD,* 4); 'Barker called his poems excavations' (*ASIO*, 16).
16 'They call me a moralist. They call me a satirist. I must warn you I am in the deed itself', Goya as character in *Terrible Mouth* (1992; *TM*, 15); quoted in 'Landscape with Cries', p. 14.
17 'Another Transitional State' (*LI*, 13).
18 John Webster and T.S. Eliot, 'The Burial of the Dead', *The Waste Land* in Eliot's *Collected Poems 1909–1962* (London: Faber, 1963), pp. 71–5.
19 'The production of *Judith* represented a massive surge in his personal and artistic confidence [...], that of a total aesthetic for which he alone assumed responsibility ...' (*ASIO*, 41).

20 '[...] Barker sensed that desire was immune to manipulation ...' (*ASIO*, 88).

21 'Her eyes had been going in and out, among the shadows of the fruit, [...] without knowing why she did it, or why, every time she did it, she felt more and more serene; [...]': V. Woolf, *To the Lighthouse* (Harmondsworth: Penguin, 1969), p. 125.

22 D.H. Lawrence, 'Climbing Down Pisgah' in *Selected Essays* (Harmondsworth: Penguin, 1968), pp. 49–54.

23 This being followed by: '[...] because his whole sense of life – which was redeemed by passion rather than love – repudiated the reduction to single meanings that culture demands as due payment for its tolerance ...' (*ASIO*, 10).

19

Memories of paintings in Howard Barker's theatre

Heiner Zimmermann

Le musée imaginaire, the title of André Malraux's essay on the psychology of the fine arts, denotes the body of works that fashion the sensibility of an epoch.[1] In the following I shall speculate on Howard Barker's *musée imaginaire*, or more precisely on some of his memories of paintings that had a part in the making of his plays and on the ways in which they inform his dramatic discourse. In Pablo Picasso's *Poèmes et Lithographies* the editor remarks '*rares sont les exemples où le texte naît de l'image*'.[2] Not so in Barker's dramas. His plays engage not only with a library of books but also with a museum of pictures. Scenes, action, themes, and the conception of character often relate just as much to paintings as to written texts. Barker's theatre appeals as much to the audience's memory of great artworks as it does to their recollection of verbally mediated myth and history. Accordingly, understanding what he does with paintings in his plays is central to their appreciation. Whilst explicit references to specific paintings in the plays are scarce, the author's programme notes and comments repeatedly refer to pictures that influenced their creation.

How much Barker needs both artistic media for his expressive aims is indicated by the fact that he makes books of drawings in preparation for, and accompaniment to, the writing and the staging of his plays. As Jean-Jacques Passera has observed in the catalogue of an exhibition of Barker's paintings at the Musée des Beaux Arts at Caen in 2008/09, these drawings represent suspended action and appear like stills from the respective scenes. However, they are not illustrations of his writing, which usually comes first, but a response to scenes in the narrative he is working on. Barker himself underlines the close relationship between his oil paintings and his dramas in his own preface to the catalogue, where he likens the emotional effect of the gestures and postures of the figures in his compositions on canvas to the physical expression of emotions by actors on the stage. Thus it is only logical that pictorial masterworks constitute an important part of '[the] compost of cultural meanings to which [he] add[s] his own re-workings and interrogations informed by [his] own prejudices', as he wrote to me in a letter (31 December 2003) explaining that he made no distinction between the pictorial and the literary models in the heap of cultural relics from which he takes his material. Coming from someone who is both a writer and a painter, this observation cannot be a denial of the difference in the expressive potential and sensual appeal of the sister arts. It may, however, be related to his opposition to modernism's rejection of the referentiality of pictures, its insistence on the gap between the picture and the word. As he stresses he is convinced that, like his own drawings, '*toute peinture, même la plus abstraite, contient du récit*'.[3] Does he mean by this that every painting or drawing is preceded by thought which necessarily expresses itself via language? In this light it makes little difference whether the author is interrogating a narrative in the form of a text or of a picture.

Not so for his audience. An 'iconotext' (i.e. a text that refers to a picture) requires its recipients to construct its meaning with both verbal and iconic signs. In order to decipher the palimpsests in Barker's theatre that result from his allusions to paintings and his ironic or iconoclastic play with them, the ideal spectator has to adopt a kind of double vision and relate what he hears and sees on the stage to his memory of pictures.

Whilst the names of contemporary composers such as Stockhausen, Ligeti or Berio figure most prominently in the list of those from whose works he quotes in the 'soundscapes' of his productions, his favourite painters are old masters, 'the Germans of the Renaissance, Dürer, Altdorfer and Hans-Baldung Grien ...' (*ASIO*, 54, 97). We may safely add Lucas Cranach, Holbein, Andrea Vicentino, Artemisia Gentileschi, Goya, Poussin and Eakins, since memories of their paintings haunt his theatre. His choice of historical works of art seems to be determined by his adaptations of history and myth in his plays, always anachronistically focussing on the 'trans-historical' constants he finds in them. Scenes of violence – execution, martyrdom or battle – are recurrent motifs in the paintings he relates to, many of them from the canon of Christian iconology. Pictures appear to be just as important a means of access to history for him as chronicles. Repeatedly his interpretations are astonishingly realistic, psychological readings.

The translation of a picture into words is denoted by the rhetorical term *ekphrasis* (φράσειν = to show), which means a re-creation of the pictorial original in another medium, in this case language. The words make a vivid appeal to the visual imagination (ενάργεια: 'distinctness'), fusing narrative description and interpretation and transforming the listener into a viewer. By definition *ekphrasis* is *mimesis* in the second degree.

The presence of a pictorial reminiscence in a play by Barker usually results from his interrogation or contradiction of a painting. Only rarely does *descriptio* play an important role. In an attempt to outline a morphology of Barker's adaptation of paintings in his plays, we can distinguish between three types of *ekphrasis*:

1   **Ekphrasis** as allusion to a painting by weaving its description and interpretation into the theme of a play or the conception of a character.

2   **Ekphrasis** linked with an **iconoclash**[4] representing the contradiction between several pictorial representations of the same motif informing the conflict in a play or a scene.

3   **Ekphrasis** as **iconoclasm**, the negation or displacement of a painting/drawing by its re-interpretation in the theme of a play, a scene or a *tableau vivant*.

1   *Ekphrasis*: characterisation as the reading of a painting

From the pictorial to the theatrical portrait of Goya

Barker's essay 'Goya's Grin', published prior to the premiere of the opera *Terrible Mouth* (1992), illustrates the way in which he reads and adapts pictures in his theatre.[5] The text was first printed together with a presumed self-portrait of Goya. In the argument, Barker makes his interpretation of the painter's facial expression in the picture the basis for the conception of his protagonist's character. His method here is parallel to that of Goya himself, who introduces his *Caprichos* (1799) with a self-portrait on the title page establishing a connection between the artist's picture and his work. The engraving shows him as an enlightened, bourgeois (*ilustrado*).[6]

Barker, however, repudiates the received opinion that the Spaniard was an enlightened critic who denounced the horrors of war[7] and exposed the vanities and cruelties of his society. In his eyes, Goya's wide grin in the self-portrait expresses sardonic irony and an affinity with cruelty and malice. He believes that the artist was not only repelled but also fascinated by the scenes of gore and horror that he painted. Barker sees him both as a critic **and** a voyeur, an opinion which by the way is shared by a number of influential experts.[8] It appears that Goya shared this dual view of himself, as we can infer from a self-portrait (around 1800) in which his face is divided into two halves, one cast in light and the other one in shadow, suggesting the coexistence of reason and irrationality.

The operatic figure of Goya in *Terrible Mouth* acts out the character traits Barker discerns in the self-portrait, fusing biographical facts with fiction. His physiognomy seduces and repels his mistress, the Duchess of Alba, who calls him 'terrible mouth'. The protagonist confirms this criticism, explaining to her: 'They call me a moralist. They call me a satirist. I must warn you I am in the deed itself' (*TM*, 15). The remark is corroborated by the historical Goya's practice of inserting himself as an observer in a number of plates such as No. 27 ('Caridad') of *Los Desastres*, or No. 21 of *La Tauromaquia* (1816). When he paints the dead and mutilated victims of war, Barker's Goya emblematically wields a scalpel instead of a brush. His imagination is haunted by images of maimed bodies and amputated limbs, and his contemplation of his mistress's beautiful body drifts off into musings about her bowels, lungs and kidneys (*TM*, 5). Even when she is being tormented and raped, the fascinated artist gazes at the scene and draws it.[9]

It is not of course a negative criticism that Barker expresses when he finds that in the self-portrait Goya displays a 'collusive glance' that makes him 'untrust-worthy'. Sceptical about reason and 'disloyal to conscience', the artist lets himself be seduced by his own subconscious. This makes him Barker's brother in spirit, a man whose works belong to the amoral 'art of catastrophe'.

The surprising thing about the article 'The Truth behind Goya's Grin', however, seems to be the suggestion that like a conventional historical play *Terrible Mouth* aims at historical verisimilitude based on historical evidence, in this case a painting. The Spanish portrait of 1798 is, however, not signed and art historians deny that it is by Goya.[10] Barker must have known this because he says: 'On this preposterous image I based my libretto for Nigel Osborne's *Terrible Mouth.*' The painting's authenticity was quite simply unimportant for him. What mattered was artistic, rather than historical truth. Whatever the identity of the Spaniard it represented, the picture provided him with an idea of Goya and his art which convinced him as an artist and served him as a 'pictorial correlative' for his conception.

2   *Ekphrasis* as description, interpretation and parody

The iconoclash behind the conflict in Scenes from an Execution

Barker's best-known iconotext, *Scenes from an Execution* (1984), not only makes a painting the protagonist of a play, but also presents a complex *mise-en-scène* of a work of art. Its action focuses on the creation of a painting of the battle of Lepanto (1572) by Anna Galactia, from its commission by the Republic of Venice and the first sketches to its completion and exhibition.

An iconoclash prefigures the central conflict between the artist and her patrons over the pacifist stance in her depiction of the battle. Most Renaissance artists such as El Greco in 'The Adoration of the Name of Jesus' or Tintoretto extolled the victory. Paolo Veronese, for instance, transformed the triumph of the Holy League into an allegory. He sanctified the leaders of the Christian forces for their bravery in the service of heaven, the place where, high above the battle, they confer with the Virgin Mary.[11] This glorification is, however, contradicted by Andrea Vicentino's monumental representation in the Sala dello Scrutinio of the Doge's palace (1577). Vicentino confronts the beholder with the rage of the combatants, the soldiers wielding their swords and lances, the shooting of arrows, the bodies of the injured, the dead and the drowned floating in a sea tainted with blood. His fresco makes no distinction between the Ottoman warriors and those of the Holy League and shows the suffering of the victims on both sides.[12]

Barker's heroine arouses her patrons' anger by painting the battle in the manner of Vicentino, displaying the combatants' violence, suffering and death as a 'great waterfall' of torn and injured flesh (*OP1*, 261).Their features are distorted by hate, pain, despair and contempt: feelings that are ignored by official historiography. Denouncing the victory as unclean, she opposes the official glorification of the triumph and discredits patriotic self-sacrifice. In her sponsors' eyes, her representation is a revilement of the Republic of Venice.

Barker's play was originally conceived as a radio drama, so the painting, although omnipresent, is never seen.[13] The dramatist, however, deploys a profusion of rhetorical and dramaturgical devices to make the audience see, hear, smell and touch the picture in their imagination. A talking sketchbook parodies the topos *ut pictura poesis* and the cliché describing pictorial art as 'silent art'.[14]

Though often located in the past, Barker's drama never reconstructs history. Anna Galactia is not a portrait of the historical Artemisia Gentileschi (1593–1653), who never painted the battle. The *mise-en-scène* of her painting focuses on its ideological bias and is not merely a translation of Vicentino's fresco into words.

Postscript: a dramatic character as parody of a figure in a painting

By contrast, the improbable character Prodo in the drama is a clear reference to Vicentino. He is a surrealist parody of the man in the foreground of the fresco with a bolt from a crossbow embedded in his bald skull, conceived of by Barker as the exemplary victim. In the play he also has a cleft hand and an open abdominal wound through which the workings of his bowels can be observed. The grotesque exaggeration ironically underpins the artificial nature of this 'quotation' from a picture. It ridicules the victim, who is also a victim of official ideology and its glorification of war, for Prodo derives his self-esteem from his status as a war martyr and makes a living by exhibiting his wounds. He can cope with his physical suffering as long as it seems meaningful to him. Galactia, however, insisting on the absurdity of war and the agonies it causes, reveals to him the tragic truth of his condition.

Ironically, her representation of Prodo in her painting puts him back where he came from. It reminds the audience that, as in his case, many of the details referred to in the descriptions of her canvas are the theatrical reconstitution of a pre-existing pictorial pattern. The reference to a pre-image establishes 'intermediality' as a play on two semiotic systems. It exposes the drama's mimesis of historical reality as a mere semblance. Prodo, moreover, comments on his portrait by Galactia – an instance of meta-dramatic irony. His explanation of the picture to the visitors at the exhibition predictably defies the artist's ironic intention by emphasising that her painting showcases his heroic self-sacrifice for the Republic.

3   *Ekphrasis* as iconoclasm: the Christian iconic tradition and *The Last Supper*

Iconoclasm lies at the heart of Barker's artistic creativity. The destruction of the icons of the past and the creation of new ones from the debris draws art into the historical process of annihilation and renewal. The mason Gaukroger in the screenplay *Pity in History* (1982) offers his mallet to Puritan iconoclasts for their depredations. For him, the idea of an interminably growing museum of icons kept under glass to preserve them from the effect of time is a nightmare. He admires the ecstasy generated by the orgy of destruction and feels inspired by the chaos and the beauty of some of the debris. Old art reduced to a heap of broken images turns into a quarry supplying raw material for new art. As such, it is a visualisation of the creative principle behind Barker's use of paintings in his plays.

In *The Last Supper* (1988) Barker reinvents the crucial event in the *New Testament*, the foundation of the Eucharist. His 'rewriting' of the biblical myth is tantamount to an iconoclastic painting-over of one of the central motifs in Christian iconography at the climax of the play. This is underlined by the dramatist's cover drawing for the first printed edition[15] and the stage direction indicating that the scene is a *tableau vivant*.

In the drama, the Christ figure Lvov has exhausted his resources for impressing his followers and fears his own demystification. Accordingly, he has no choice but to die if he wants to live on as a myth. His disciples, a group of women and men, must kill him and consume his body to ensure that he and his message will live on. The sacramental act of eating the body of God is taken literally. It is not, however, shown on stage. A *tableau vivant* represents the aftermath: the disciples' spiritual and physical exhaustion, their dejected, bewildered, guilt-ridden condition after this act of cannibalism: '*The DISCIPLES ... are stooping, on all fours, or sitting with their knees drawn up, still and silent as in a tableau*' (*OP5*, 90). In Barker's drawing, however, one woman stands upright pointing at another one standing in the centre, probably Judith, who incited them to kill Lvov. The other disciples lie draped across the table or cower beneath it. Wine from an overturned glass spills across the table. They present an image of utter disorder and abandon. This has not been a feast but a traumatic experience.

To discuss Barker's 'painting-over' of the Christian iconic tradition depicting the Eucharist, I have chosen Leonardo da Vinci's fresco 'L' Ultima Cena'[16] as a representative example, not only because it is so well known but also because it does not focus on the harmony of *agape* but on Christ's revelation that one of the apostles will betray him.[17] This provokes alarm, outrage and horror. In completely different ways the Renaissance painter and the contemporary dramatist depict treason and the disciples' bewilderment as well as the indictment of Judas/Judith. Both artists place the disciples behind a table facing the observer. Leonardo's gesticulating apostles form four groups of three figures interconnected by looks and gestures. In Barker's drawing the disciples are isolated, exhausted and prostrate. The crucial difference between the earlier picture and

Barker's drawing is, however, the absence of Christ in the latter, as opposed to his central position in the fresco. His pre-eminence in Leonardo's painting is emphasised by his composure and the way this contrasts with the disciples' agitation. Christ is set off from the others by the empty space between him and the groups of apostles on his left and right, who are looking and pointing at him. The dishes in front of him are arranged in a symmetrical order. In Barker's *tableau vivant*, the death of God has entailed a loss of the centre without which hierarchy and order cannot be established. Individualism, heterogeneity and moral pluralism are the consequence. The autonomous subject is entirely responsible for her/himself. The people, the masses have taken over the role of God.

4   The dialogue of a drama with a painting: *Ego in Arcadia*

The enigmatic ego

The reference to Poussin's famous painting 'The Arcadian Shepherds'[18] in the title of *Ego in Arcadia* (1992) can hardly be overlooked. The French artist is also a protagonist in Barker's interrogation of the pastoral tradition in literature and the fine arts, which has little to do with *ekphrasis* but assumes the audience's knowledge of Poussin's picture. The play's title alters the enigmatic inscription 'Et in Arcadia Ego' on the sarcophagus in the centre of Poussin's painting.[19] The subject referred to by the personal pronoun *ego* is in both cases ambiguous. According to Erwin Panofsky and Louis Marin, *ego* in Poussin's picture could stand for a dead shepherd buried under the monument, or for Death (as suggested by the death's-head in the Chatsworth version), or for the artist, who imagines Arcadia and is both present and absent in his work.[20] In the play, *ego* again evokes Death and the present/absent dramatist/narrator, but it also refers to the *dramatis personae*. Like the shepherds in traditional pastorals Barker's characters are not rationally determined individuals. They are driven by their passions, by their *id*.

The fusion of image and writing

Like Barker's drama, Poussin's painting fuses image and text, viewing and reading. With the shepherd kneeling before the monument to decipher the inscription at the picture's vanishing point and the questioning faces of the other shepherds, the picture focuses on the act of reading and interpretation. Similarly, the play rereads and deconstructs the pastoral tradition from a contemporary point of view. The gazes and gestures of the four shepherds in the painting form a closed system of communication, just like a scene on the theatre stage. None of the figures looks at the viewer outside the painting. The observer/interpreter is in the image. The painting does not refer to the world but to an absent ego that is not clearly identified. It evokes a diachronic sequence of actions, just like the *mise-en-scène* of a story.[21] Beside Poussin's interrogation of the pastoral mode's relation to death his composition of a historical painting like a scene on stage must have particularly attracted the eye of the dramatist/painter Barker.

Arcadia, death and beauty

In most of the play's ten eclogues Poussin appears on stage engaged in the act of painting. He creates **his** version of Arcadia on canvas in a play that presents **Barker's** version on stage. Unlike Galactia's painting in *Scenes*, his work is, however, never described in the play, nor is its progress commented on. The other characters' remarks merely indicate that it depicts a pastoral scene, which forms a contrast to the drama's desolate '*landscape of dereliction*' devastated by '*heroic cultures*' and technology (*CP3*, 269) and haunted by the din of eternal war. The peaceful idyll only exists in the characters' nostalgic memories and in Poussin's unidentified painting, which could be 'The Arcadian Shepherds' evoked by the play's title. In this picture a 'wild landscape' or 'desert', as it was called in the seventeenth century, surrounds the classical and partly statuesque figures identified as shepherds by the title and gathered around the sarcophagus in the centre. One of them may personify Mnemosyne, another one Clio.[22] The conception of Barker's characters displays a tendency towards allegory.[23] Frustrated by the master's exclusive dedication to his art, Poussin's model vainly slashes the canvas and stabs the beloved artist. Her name, Verdun, recalls the First World War's most murderous battlefield in the light of which the pastoral idyll must appear like a monstrous lie.

Centring on the tomb of a shepherd who died of unrequited love, Poussin's painting evokes Arcadia through elegy.[24] In the Chatsworth version a death's-head makes the picture a *memento mori*. Here already the unmitigated felicity of the Golden Age has left Arcadia for good and remains only as a memory. In Barker's play, nature and the shepherds have disappeared. It focuses on the irrationality of desire, on the catastrophe of 'the absolute of love'.[25] It is a pandemonium of unrequited love, jealousy, envy and hatred, where murder is common but never triumphs. For in contrast to Poussin's painting, death is banned from Barker's Arcadia. As in Jean-Paul Sartre's *Huis clos* this causes suffering without end. When death, personified by Tocsin, finally intrudes on this exclave from reality, Poussin, unlike the other characters, does not want to die. He kills Tocsin, just as he tries to overcome death with his art. He finally discovers the 'intolerable beauty' (*CP3*, 319) of pain for his art, just as the drama replaces the pastoral idyll by the sublime. At the end of the play Poussin adds the portrait of the dead queen Dover to his painting. This transfer of the image of death from Barker's play to Poussin's picture in the play is emblematic of Barker's transformation of the historical Poussin's painting in his drama.

5   The role of iconoclasm and iconoclash in the reworking of a motif

Judith: *the beheading of Holofernes*

An instance of iconoclash (in this case a dissonance between the Christian iconic tradition and the disregard of that tradition in a picture of martyrdom and execution) influenced both the composition of Barker's painting 'Saint Barbara: Female Apprentice' and the handling of the slaughter of Holofernes in his play *Judith: A Parting from the Body* (published 1989, staged 1995). The painter-dramatist Barker admired Hans Baldung Grien's humane portrayal of the executioner as 'an old man without malice' (*ASIO*, 98) in his ink sketch of the martyrdom of Saint Barbara. This breach with the iconic tradition of vilifying, and thus morally condemning, the decapitator and making the martyr saint the focus of the picture is an essential factor in Barker's analogous reworking of the motif in his iconoclastic picture and its *mise-en-scène*.[27] Like Baldung Grien, Barker eschews a moralising approach. He moreover changes the original distribution of gender roles: a 'female apprentice' is cast in the role of the slayer. Like her victim she is shown naked and exposed as she anxiously takes measure for the blow. The posture of her arms recalls that of Baldung Grien's executioner. Unlike his relaxed pose her bent body suggests tension. She does not touch her victim. Two clothed figures watch her; one of them is identified by the painter as an 'ageing professional, willing her to succeed' (*ASIO*, 98). The idea of making the executioner a woman may have been suggested by the apocryphal motif of the slaying of Holofernes. The tension inherent in Barker's painting of the moment before the act recurs in the staging of the execution scene in *Judith*. The determination of his female killer recalls Judith's grim resolution in Artemisia Gentileschi's depiction of the same scene. But unlike Barker, the Italian painting, with its fountains of spouting blood, highlights the hate and brutal butchery of the act.[28] The dramatist shuns this approach. His play subverts the apocryphal myth by transforming the humanity of Grien's executioner into Judith's love for her heroic enemy and victim. In *Judith*'s bedroom scene, desire intermingles with cruelty, tenderness with the necessity to kill. Holofernes dies willingly in the ecstasy of his love. The active participation of Gentileschi's maid-servant, who holds his head down whilst Judith cuts it off, was probably what suggested to Barker the idea of portraying her as Judith's unflinching, patriotic *alter ego* forcing her to do the deed. For unlike Gentileschi's Judith, who identifies fully with her assignment, Barker's heroine has to be deceived by her servant into performing the task. In Barker's play Judith's self-denying deed shatters her identity and paralyses her. The act of killing her own love is suspended for a long moment in which the raised sword remains immobile in mid-air. The obvious references both to Baldung Grien's drawing and Gentileschi's painting in the deconstruction of the myth stress the 'citational' nature of the characters and underline the fact that the action of the play is another writing-over of the myth from a postmodern perspective. As such, it foregrounds the dramatist's refusal to represent historical reality.[29]

Ursula: *the execution scene*

In the programme for The Wrestling School's production of *Ursula* (1998), Barker refers to Lucas Cranach the elder's painting of the martyrdom of Saint Ursula and the 'massacre of the virgin martyrs' for the altarpiece of St Catherine's church in Dresden (1506) as a key image in the conception of the play.[30] The dramatist's eye is caught by the dominant figure of the prince in the centre panel of the triptych. He has ordered the slaughter of the virgins and is shown 'leaning on his unused sword and observing the massacre with the moral detachment of the SS Officer' (programme note). In Barker's view Cranach scandalously shifts the traditional focus on the victim in Christian iconography to the tyrant, described as 'infinitely cold and beautiful'. The human dignity displayed by the impassive observer of these atrocities is a counterpoint to the moral duplicity of the voyeuristic Goya, whose fascination with what he depicts draws him into the scene. It is redolent of the fusion of humanity and cruelty depicted in the figure of the executioner in Hans Baldung Grien's ink sketch.

Cranach's painting is recalled in the final scene of *Ursula*, where the Mother Superior, Placida, assumes the role of the soldiers in the legend. For in Barker's play the prince can no longer wield his outsize 'sword of execution'; it is consequently offered to Placida, who, in contrast to the nuns, ecstatically gives free rein to her sexuality. In a clinical *mise-en-scène* of mass beheadings Placida helps the virgins to consummate their marriage with Christ in death. Prince Lucas, watching the orgy of blood from upstage, is mesmerised. Unlike his model in Cranach's painting, he is shocked and drops the bottle and the glasses he has brought to celebrate with his lover, the executioner.

6 Iconoclasm highlighting contradiction: *He Stumbled*

He Stumbled (2000) took shape during a period marked by a preoccupation with the body in film, theatre and performance art.[31] This fascination was triggered by a scientific revolution in the concept of the human body, its reification into an object susceptible of alteration. Moreover, Michel Foucault's philosophical analysis exposed the inexorable violation of bodily intimacy caused by science. The long-forgotten fascination (and repulsion) incited by the public anatomy lectures accompanying the first sacrilegious incursions into the interior of the body in the Renaissance reared its head once again.[32] In our day, the anatomist G. v. Hagen's notorious exhibition 'Body Worlds', a display of dissected dead bodies preserved by 'plastination', has attracted huge crowds and also provoked scandals and lawsuits. Barker's critical response in his play to this general preoccupation opens up new perspectives.

In the audience's imagination the historical setting of *He Stumbled* and its focus on anatomy as a central motif recall Rembrandt's famous depictions of anatomy lectures.[33] Barker, however, states that the American Thomas Eakins's painting 'The Gross Clinic' (1875) was the inspiration for the play's leitmotif.[34] This reference blurs the drama's location in history and sharpens the contrast between the celebration of the progress of science in the 'pre-image' and Barker's mystical conception of the anatomist and his art. Both Eakins and Rembrandt focus on an anatomist/surgeon lecturing to a company of colleagues and students, thus enhancing knowledge of the human body and at the same time parading surgical skill deployed in the service of healing. Whereas Rembrandt's anatomist Dr Tulp[35] describes to his audience the details of a perfectly dissected and prepared arm taken from a dead body, Eakins' surgeon Dr Gross operates on the diseased thighbone of a patient who is still alive. As he lectures, he wields a scalpel in his bloodstained right hand. The focus of Eakins's painting is on the surgical incision, which is held open with hooks by Gross's assistants. The rest of the patient's body remains invisible. The scenic imagery of *He Stumbled* centres on an anatomy room with an operating table. Amongst the most important props are surgical instruments of the kind displayed in the foreground of Eakins's painting. The drama shows the dissection and disembowelling of a human body, but it is in no way concerned with the progress of anatomical science or surgery. Unlike Dr Gross, who is portrayed as a hero of medical science practising and passing on his expert skills, the fascination of Barker's anatomist stems as much from his priest-like office (ritually dissecting the sacred body of a king) as from his virtuoso dexterity. His anatomical practice has much the same ritual significance as a religious service. After the excision of the king's heart, the surgeon holds it aloft '*and suspends it in the manner of a priest raising the host*' (*OP3*, 180). The dissection and embalming of the royal organs prior to sealing them in caskets and sending them like relics to the holy cities of Christendom is a parodic reference to the historical records of mediaeval practices. The ritual visualises the dissolution and transformation of the king's body natural into a symbol, the body politic. The anatomist's knowledge of the secrets of the body and his dealings with death make him magically attractive to women. Like all abjection, however, the disembowelling of a putrefying body incites both fascination **and** disgust. The dissection of the body is tantamount to its reification, the desecration of its integrity. It is nothing other than a sacrilege. As if testing the proposition, 'the flesh is not the man' (*OP3*, 178, 252), the master dissector rejects moral scruples and insists on the division of body and soul as professed both by philosophers since Plato and by the Christian Church. The rational distance between his own self and the body is, however, negated by his ecstatic sexual relationship with the queen, which defies rational control. A rotting corpse consequently arouses his disgust. He comes to hate his profession and abandons it. Under the threat of execution, the master anatomist heroically mounts the surgical table and cuts out his own heart, thus both affirming and disproving his dictum on the division between body and soul. In its contradiction of Eakins's painting, Barker's final tableau becomes a *mene tekel* warning us of the self-destructive potential inherent in practical rationalism. Seen in this light, the play's title could be read as a reference to the blind Gloucester's critique of empirical rationalism at the end of *King Lear*, when he confesses: 'I stumbled when I saw' (IV.i.29f).[36]

Unlike the study of intertextual connections, the exploration of intermedial relations between texts and the fine arts is still relatively rare. Barker's comments, however, suggest that the dramatist's creative imagination is closely interwoven with that of the painter/draughtsman. Unlike 'pre-texts', the impact of 'pre-images' on his plays implies a translation from one semiotic system to another. But the differences between them appear to have little relevance for their effect on his drama. To test this impression, we have investigated the manifold and complex ways in which paintings fashion Barker's dramatic discourse, thus outlining a 'rhetoric' of *ekphrasis* in his plays. Our interpretations have elucidated how the imaginary presence of pictures as 'pre-images' and citations that are described, alluded to, interpreted, parodied, interrogated or contradicted in his plays has a bearing on character portrayal (Goya, Prodo), motifs (*He Stumbled*, *Ursula*) and scenes (*The Last Supper*). We have seen how iconoclash prefigures the conflict at the heart of a play (*Scenes*) or informs the reworking of a motif (*Judith*, *Ursula*). Further, we have examined how the 'dialogue' with a painting pervades the structure of a play (*Ego in Arcadia*) and how the iconoclastic negation of a picture establishes a dialectical relationship between painting and play, lending the latter greater depth and giving its meaning greater definition by way of contrast (*The Last Supper, He Stumbled*).

The critique of key icons from the past in Barker's drama broadens the referential scope of his plays to an unusual degree. For Barker, pictures are an important cognitive resource, a means of access to historical and religious myths and philosophical issues. Their presence transcends the mutual interrogation of image and text characteristic of theatrical discourse in general and sets off an oscillation between the spectator's memory of a painting and what is seen on the stage. The dialogue that his plays engage in with pictorial models not only both affirms and rejects them, it also reveals their inscription into the tradition of artistic recreations of central myths, thus stressing the refusal to produce a mimesis of topical reality. The scrutiny of *ekphrasis* in Barker's plays not only sheds light on the meaning fashioned by the intermedial warp and woof of their textual fabric, it also points up the poetological programme behind them. The prominence of pictorial recollection in his plays appears as an emblem of postmodernism, where image and reality become indistinguishable and gel into a form of 'hyper-reality'. Ultimately, the intimate interlacing of verbal and pictorial cognition and imagination in Barker's drama prompts us to overcome the logocentric hermeneutics of the era of the Linguistic Turn[37] in order to look for the intersections between language and picture as proposed by picture theory and the study of visual culture – which, proclaiming a change of paradigm, a Pictorial or an Iconic Turn,[38] focus on the picture as the ubiquitous, most important bearer of meaning in the postmodern world emphasising its immediacy and pungent appeal to the senses in conveying meaning; for any hermeneutic privileging of the word over the image (and vice versa) goes against the genius of Barker's creations in pictorial and dramatic art and thus fails to promote their just appreciation.

Notes

1 A. Malraux, *Le musée imaginaire* (Paris: Skira, 1947).

2 'Rare are the examples of literary texts generated by pictures'; P. Picasso, *Poèmes et lithographies* (Paris: Galerie Louise Leiris, 1954).

3 '[E]very painting, even the most abstract one, contains a narrative': Preface to the catalogue for the exhibition at Caen.

4 I do not use the term in the same sense as Bruno Latour in 'What is Iconoclash? Or is there a World beyond the Image Wars?', catalogue for the exhibition *Iconoclash* at Karlsruhe, 2002, pp. 1–43, who defined it in opposition to iconoclasm as an action of which one does not know whether it is destructive or constructive.

5 Howard Barker, 'The Truth Behind Goya's Grin', *Guardian*, 8 July 1992, p. 18; reprinted as 'Goya's Grin' in *AT*, pp. 141–3. Nigel Osborne's opera *Terrible Mouth*, for which Howard Barker wrote the libretto, had its premiere on 20 July 1992 at the Almeida theatre.

6 This is endorsed by his announcement of the publication in the *Diario de Madrid*, saying that 'censuring human errors and vices although it seems the preserve of oratory and poetry – can also be a worthy object of painting'. His contemporaries interpreted his narrowed eyes, his projecting lower lip and snub nose in the portrait as *satírico* and *maligno*. Alfonso E. Pérez Sánchez, Eleanor A. Sayre (eds), *Goya and the Spirit of Enlightenment*. Exhibition catalogue (Boston: Little & Brown, 1989, pp. 84 f): 'None of Goya's earlier self-portraits show him with this censorious expression.'

7 *Los Desastres de la Guerra* (1810–14).

8 See John J. Ciofalo, *The Self-Portraits of Francisco Goya* (Cambridge: Cambridge University Press, 2001), p. 133. 'Goya seems to have found himself guilty of conspiring, through his art, in what he set out to denounce: the objectification, hence, the violation of women'; see also the chapters on 'Quixotic Dreams of Reason' and 'The Art of Sex and Violence – the Sex and Violence of Art'.

9 In his drawing 'Pygmalion and Galatea' (Album F, 1817–20) Goya depicts himself as artist/rapist when he points his chisel at the statue's genitalia. The 'exposer' becomes the exposed in the drawing 'Conjugal Row' (Album F) in which the painter identifies himself with the cruel husband tormenting his wife.

10 The picture was acquired as a Goya self-portrait from 1798 (?) by the Kunsthistorische Museum at Vienna in 1922 and was moved to the Österreichische Galerie, Belvedere, Vienna in 1987. The 'faun-like smile, the drawn up corners of the mouth' and 'the piercing gaze' of the portrait were commented on by Ernst Buschbeck in 'Die Neuerwerbungen der Gemäldegalerie' in the *Wiener Jahrbuch für Bildende Kunst*, vol. 5 (1922), p. 98.

11 St Peter for the Vatican State, St James for Spain, and Venice between St Mark and Justina.

12 Wolfgang Wolters, ,Der Triumph von Lepanto' in *Der Bilderschmuck des Dogenpalasts* (Wiesbaden: Steiner Verlag, 1983), pp. 213–21; Ernst Gombrich, 'Celebrations in Venice of the Holy League and the Victory of Lepanto' in Michael Kitson (ed.), *Studies in Renaissance and Baroque Art presented to Anthony Blunt* (London: Phaidon, 1967), pp. 62–8.

13 David Fielding's stage set for the first production at the Almeida theatre in London showed the audience only the back of a huge artist's canvas.

14 The strong sensual impact of colours reappears in the weaver's ecstasy at the discovery of a new red when his rug is dyed with human blood in the first episode of *The Possibilities* (1987).

15 Howard Barker, *The Last Supper* (London, John Calder, 1988).

16 For other modern parodies of Leonardo such as the 'Beggars' Banquet' in Luis Bunuel's film *Viridiana*, see Ludwig, H. Heydenreich, *Leonardo: The Last Supper* (London: Penguin: 1974), and Judy Chicago's feminist installation 'The Dinner Party', which inspired Caryl Churchill's *Top Girls*.

17 See Goethe's interpretation in 'Joseph Bossi über Leonards da Vinci Abendmahl zu Mailand' in *Über Kunst und Alterthum*, vol. III (Weimar, 1817).

18 There exist two versions of 'The Arcadian Shepherds', one in the Chatsworth Collection in Devonshire (1630?) and a later one in the Louvre. Barker mainly refers to the second.

19 This is of course also a frequently rehearsed *topos* in Arcadian literature.

20 Erwin Panofsky, 'Et in Arcadia Ego: Poussin and the elegiac tradition' in *Meaning in the Visual Arts* (New York: Doubleday & Company, 1955), pp. 295–320; Louis Marin, 'Toward a Theory of Reading in the Visual Arts: Poussin's The Arcadian Shepherds' in Susan Rubin Suleiman, Inge Crosman (eds), *The Reader in the Text: Essays on Audience and Interpretation* (Princeton: Princeton University Press, 1980), pp. 293–324.

21 Marin, 'Toward a Theory', pp. 296–99.

22 *Ibid.*, 317–19.

23 See names such as Verdun, Tocsin etc.

24 The association of these genres has existed from the very beginning, see for example Daphnis' tomb in Vergil's fifth eclogue.

25 Roland Barthes, *Fragments d'un discours amoureux* (Paris: Editions du Seuil, 1977), 'La catastrophe', p.59f.

26 In a painting of this motif entitled 'Tocsin Hanged' Barker uses some red and blue beside the beige, black and white which generally characterise his pictures.

27 He criticises Dürer's rendering of the same scene for its portrayal of the executioner as a 'posturing lout' (*ASIO*, 98).

28 Critics have interpreted the image as Artemisia Gentileschi's revenge on her rapist teacher Tassi, a friend of her father's. This is particularly plausible in connection with the early version of 1612/13 in the Museo di Capodimonte at Naples, which was painted only a few years after her lawsuit against Tassi. Cf. M. Stocker, *Judith: Sexual Warrior: Women and Power in Western Culture* (New Haven: Yale University Press, 1998).

29 In the last episode of *The Possibilities* (1987) 'Not Him', Barker presents a feminist variation of the myth, associating desire with vengeful ferocity.

30 The picture he refers to is in fact 'The Martyrdom of Saint Catherine' in the centre of the triptych, whereas St Ursula is shown on its left wing in the company of St Barbara and St Margaret.

31 See the films of Q. Tarantino, plays such as S. Kane's *Cleansed*, M. Ravenhill's *Faust is Dead*, N. LaBute's, *The Shape of Things*, the body art of G. Pane and M. Abramovič

and Paul Virilio's philosophical analysis, *Die Eroberung des Körpers* (München: Hanser, 1994).

32 See also the exhibition 'Sensation' at the Royal Academy of Art in 1997.

33 'The Anatomy Lecture of Dr. Tulp' (1632) and 'The Anatomy Lecture of Dr. Deyman' (1656), as Christine Kiehl remarks in 'The Body Turned Inside Out', in K. Gritzner and D.I. Rabey (eds), *Theatre of Catastrophe: New Essays on Howard Barker* (London: Oberon, 2006), pp. 198–210.

34 Mentioned by Barker in a conversation during the 'Howard Barker's Art of Theatre' conference at Aberystwyth, 10–12 July 2009.

35 Rembrandt shows this only in the later painting.

36 R.A. Foakes (ed.), Shakespeare, *King Lear*, The Arden Shakespeare (London, Methuen, 1997). See also Christine Kiehl's interview with Barker quoted in her article.

37 The concept was coined by R. Rorty, *The Linguistc Turn* (1967) positing the hegemony of the logic of language as the only means of cognition, a tenet pervading philosophy in the second part of the twentieth century up to Derrida.

38 The terms were coined in opposition to Rorty by William G.T. Mitchell, *Picture Theory: Essays on Verbal and Visual Representation* (Chicago: University of Chicago Press, 1994) and Gottfried Boehm (ed.), *Was ist ein Bild?* (München: Fink, 1994).

20

The sunless garden of the unconsoled: some destinations beyond catastrophe

Howard Barker

It is scarcely controversial to declare that what we find frustrating in Tragedy is its love of The Law. Given the huge extent of its creative mandate, its contempt for the mimetic rule, its hypnotised fascination with transgression, and the poetry it brings to malice, sadism, and the savage accident, this inevitable capitulation can only be experienced as disappointing. In invoking The Law I am not referring only to the prevailing disciplines of State or Faith, but also to the similarly oscillating and insecure concepts of Kindness and the Human. To admit the material condition of the practice of theatre, the fact it is never active unless authorised, hardly compensates for this sense of lack, which is diminished only if one concedes at the outset that Tragedy has not until now been an exercise in moral speculation, but first and foremost a discipline which raised the spectre of passionate disorder only to abolish it again, thereby making of temptation and obliteration twin aspects of a game played out before an audience in order to validate a status quo. Certainly no one has claimed for Tragedy that it was enlightening, notwithstanding the curious fact that the plot of the antique text was routinely described as 'the argument.'

However, one senses it is not only the circumstances of ideology and censorship that have routinely bent the shape of tragic action into this familiar curve. Poets after all, have their ways with authority. We are the perfect liars of this and every age. This conformity of dramatic authors – and artists in general – to the moral climate of their cultural milieu invites speculation into the psychological origins of creative desire itself.

It is hard to resist the suspicion that the profusion of texts in our time which purport to offer critiques of society whilst simultaneously endorsing its values unwittingly advertises a neurosis, as if by demanding deeper and deeper civility in the culture, the authors sensed the decay of it in themselves. It would perhaps be preposterous for any individual to claim he had acquired sufficient autonomy to articulate appalling propositions on the stage without admitting to the private predilections that initiated them, and in any case the extent of an author's implication in the crimes of his characters never affects the outcome. Some greater discipline imposes its resolution. My life in theatre has to a considerable extent been shaped by this conflict between a desire to speculate freely and widely on what it is to be human and the implacable disciplines of theatrical form.

Whatever rudimentary signs of a tragic instinct exist in earlier works such as *Crimes in Hot Countries* or *Victory*, I have consistently identified *The Europeans* as the first of the Catastrophic plays, not only from its narrative inception in a crisis of order but from the insistence of the protagonist on privileging personal instinct over cultural discipline. Katrin's rage at her violation and maiming might be contained and ameliorated by the doctrine of Christ or the doctrine of Expediency, but her sense that to engage in a programme of reconciliation could only maim her further renders her an outcast, and she is routinely described as mentally ill or inveterately perverse. It is perhaps worth differentiating Katrin's moral independence from the struggle of Widow Bradshaw in *Victory*. Bradshaw's choice is to discard by strenuous intellectual effort her whole moral character, and the success which attends on this enterprise perhaps suggests its superficial claim on her. Katrin's determination is visceral, and requires no education. Her criminal apotheosis is perhaps her decision to give birth in public, making of herself what I have described as 'the screaming exhibit in the Museum of Reconciliation', but her greatest and most triumphant infringement of the law is delayed until she has necessarily developed a natural affection for her child and then to wilfully break the maternal bond and return the infant to the army of the enemy whose soldiers had fathered it upon her. At this point it can safely be said that the protagonist annihilates whatever lingering sympathy an audience accustomed to reconciliation as a social principle might have entertained for her.

To invite speculation as to the consequent life of Katrin and her lover is one of the outcomes of this extremity, and I once spoke of writing a sequel to *The Europeans* if only to insist on the character of her spirituality. Imploring her lover to applaud her outrage for its *superba*, if nothing else, with the cry 'Congratulate me, then …!' might on its own have ensured no actress of the Royal Shakespeare Company would ever play Katrin, for this institution may only utter the reconciliation that is the law, if not I suspect, the instinct, of its Shakespearian heritage.

I'd like to advance my account of the dilemmas and contradictions of tragic writing in a culture of moral totality by examining two later works, one relatively established, *Gertrude – The Cry*, and one recently completed and unperformed, *Wonder and Worship in the Dying Ward*, both of which carry the thesis of Catastrophic Theatre into yet more uncomfortable territory, namely the experience of Sacrifice.

The culture of Liberal-Humanism finds Sacrifice comprehensible only in very constrained circumstances. Unwillingly it palliates the death of soldiers by attaching the word to the memorial, but both the rhetoric and the architecture are copied from Thermopylae and the pagan Spartans, and Christ himself, the most self-conscious of all the sacrificed, knew it as a destiny in his God-character, but a nightmare in the man. His desperate pleading to be excused the very ordeal for which he was created is touchingly human and might be seen as the first expression in Western culture of the individual asserting his reluctance to perish for the collective, in other words, to be a *victim*. Liberal Humanism's obsessive desire to identify and eliminate the *victim* is an inevitable consequence of the doctrine of equality, and indeed might be regarded as its ideological justification. Victims are, of course, abundant in tragedy, and constitute the source of the dismay which initiates it, but unless one were whimsical and dared to suggest that the humiliation and death of Cordelia was a sacrifice to the eventual civilising of King Lear, the category of victim is strictly reserved.

To invoke Sacrifice in contemporary tragedy, as it is invoked in the two texts I have described, is to rupture the contract of mutuality that is critical to the contemporary moral project. Pity here becomes irrelevant and conscience ceases to act upon the public as it ceases to act on the protagonist herself. Katrin's unnatural gesture with her own child is vastly less cruel than Gertrude's with hers, but in both cases the act is presented from the perspective of an individual driven to assert her independence not only of social obligation but of the maternal bond, a defiance of biology as well as sentiment. We are familiar with the fact that in the confined spaces of public permission, the making of one self is frustrated by the rights of another. We also know that in conventional tragedy – whilst it is anachronistic to talk of rights – the claim to existence exists only to be violated. The rise of the protagonist is essentially a criminal enterprise, and the corpses that decorate his progress are the detritus of a mesmeric journey that has only one terminus – self-disgust and some form of suicide. In the Catastrophic play the invocation of Sacrifice renders the binary ethic of criminal/victim redundant. Humanist jurisprudence might argue as to whether the sexualised murder of the old king in *Gertrude – The Cry*, is murder or manslaughter, given the infatuated condition of his killers, but the play's trajectory, with its phase by phase disclosure of the origins of Claudius's passion, and Gertrude's frequently pitiful attempts to satisfy it, renders protest at injustice awesomely irrelevant. If betrayal of the Law is precisely where Claudius locates the proof of love – and it is Gertrude who identifies this for him – it is not entirely surprising that the supreme infidelity that proposes itself is the mother's betrayal of the son, and it is important to recognise the clear signs in this text of Gertrude's deep feeling for Hamlet. Hamlet is poisoned, and dies mesmerised by the spectacle of his mother's nakedness, his awareness that he is nothing less than a sacrifice to the religion of his mother's sexuality immaculately described in the controlled gesture with which – despite his agony – he replaces the glass on its foot. Hamlet reiterates out of sheer infantile provocation, 'the world is full of things I do not understand, but others understand them evidently' but at this moment he understands perfectly well the function, if not the justice, of his destiny, and accords it an exquisite affirmation.

The abolition of the Law that characterises the Catastrophic play is not followed by its restitution, and the state of anxiety created in an audience by the expected, even craved, arrival of the apology cannot be dissipated.

Wonder and Worship in the Dying Ward is a play about revelation, its irresistible compulsion, and the ambiguities surrounding the notions of the victim and the perpetrator. It is also, crucially, about the apology and its status in the Christian-Humanist tradition. Since the Church of Rome placed the confession at the very centre of its ritual, apology has been a significant personal and cultural gesture – and in recent years – astonishingly, a political device of dubious validity. The crux of the agony of apology – for it can be nothing less – is the sense of personal loss entailed in denying actions in which one located one's faith in circumstances now altered. A culture of apology – removed from the context of Christian practice – finds a congenial new residence in the contemporary dispensation of Late Democracy and its tablet of laws, partly Christian, partly secular idealism, known as Human Rights. The intensity of the social consensus surrounding tolerance and freedom – nomenclature we cannot dispute here – raises the prospect familiar from various decayed regimes of the past that one might be persuaded to apologise for what one senses was never a wrong action in the first place, and this dilemma lies at the heart of this tragedy in which revelation on the part of one character, Ostend, is followed by a terrible act of self-maiming on the part of another, an appalling reaction to a visual shock shaped by both disgust and envy.

Revelation in this narrative – its moment and its reason – is the subject of seemingly endless speculation, rather as the bizarre selection of a circus horse in preference to a motorbike by the messenger in *A House of Correction* preoccupies almost to distraction the characters of that play – and the gnawing obsession here of an entire hospital of untended patients with the chanted slogan 'The door fell open, why?' acts as a permanent and tortuous rebuke to Ostend. Given she is neither an exhibitionist nor a sadist, her showing can only be what I have to describe as divine obligation, her glimpsing of an overwhelming manifestation of spirituality compelling her to make herself visible rather as God Himself, in His devastating solitude in the waters of the universe, required to be seen, and could not *not* be seen, and made Man precisely to be His audience. To perpetuate the affinity with Genesis, the paradox of Revelation is its unpredictable consequence, for consequences there must be, and Ostend's moment of splendour is simulta-neously the triggering of the ordeal of another, here as in *Gertrude*, her own child, who as witness, must destroy herself, but in failing to do so, haunts her mother's life, a crippled rebuke to autonomy, awesomely vengeful and whilst forever prostrate, nimble on an electric bed.

Ostend senses the orchestration of events has only one purpose – to compel her to issue the apology she has refused for twenty years, and she is, for reasons of kindness and expediency, frequently on the brink of doing so. But Ostend, like most of the protagonists of the Theatre of Catastrophe, is scrupulous in her attitude to words, knowing the residual significance of 'sorry' even in a culture which has made of 'sorry' a disingenuousness. She properly assumes that to deny her participation in her Revelatory experience will annihilate her integrity. Yet this is not the ugliest aspect of the equation. Worse still is the realisation that only the denigration of this treasured experience can ever relieve the agony of rage that describes her child.

As I have suggested, love alone might compel submission, and Ostend is close to this genuflection to contemporary ethics when the third significant character of the play, a far-from-infantile resident of the Dying Ward called Childlike, a scholar, dwarf and one-eyed hermaphrodite, proposes a higher law than the law of Shame, namely, the Law of the Sacred and its ritualised manifestation, the *Sacrifice*. Childlike insists that the Sacrifice, however pitiful, cannot be compensated, and that the broken woman on the mobile bed must remain forever unconsoled.

As in *Gertrude*, *Wonder and Worship in the Dying Ward* describes the terrible phenomenon of crime without punishment, and more terrible still, punishment without crime, for both Hamlet and the broken daughter of Ostend have sinned against nothing we recognise, nor are those responsible for their injury ever driven to crave forgiveness, seek reconciliation, nor even, by their own fall, raise a quivering finger to point in the direction of a juster world. Furthermore, somewhere in this sunless garden stands a character who, like the two identified, is equally unconsoled for a savage destiny but in a further repudiation of Humanist ethics, discovers the wherewithal to applaud the arbitrary character of it. The wrecked musical prodigy Wardrobe senses the appalling significance of *loss*, the beauty of the unfulfilled, not for himself, but for others. Is he mad?

To invoke further as-yet-unperformed plays here would be tedious, and it is sufficient to say that the ruined protagonist of *Harrowing and Uplifting Interviews* attains this state of melancholy gratification without recourse to Nihilism. Childlike's gruesome status as the worst-deformed inmate of the Dying Ward similarly entitles him to repudiate the patronage of pity and the cult of rights in his triumphant exclamation – the outcome of fastidious study of causes and effects – 'Goodbye to Why …!'

The spectacle of cruel deformity, or shattered genius, scorning the rhetoric of the Culture of Restitution inevitably makes them collusive with – or more heroically, proper consorts for – the Catastrophic protagonist with her passionate self-determination. In the ethical terms of contemporary Humanism, this is a landscape without illumination; yet in a tragic form which spurns both punishment and reward, these gestures of unaccommodating autonomy, brilliant and not necessarily brief, give testimony to a human genius that declines to be coerced by the prejudices of Christ or Reason.

21

Howard Barker
in dialogue with David Ian Rabey,
City University, New York,
10 May 2010

DIR: It might be appropriate to start with a discussion of history. History was a subject you studied at university, and a theme which recurs in your work: but not in the obvious way, of something that needs or purports to be historically accurate. Your work perhaps inhabits a mythic history. You've remarked to me once in conversation, that soldiers in battle interest you, but when they are losing rather than when they are winning. It's something of a familiar phrase to say that history is written by the victors; nevertheless in your play *Golgo* the protagonist insists 'There are those who are recorded, and those who fail to be recorded, obviously there is **Other testament**'.[1] Your work often seems to address and express a testimony other than the dominant (and therefore ostensibly non-negotiable) testimony.

HB: Yes, I was educated as a historian – though in a very narrow field, actually, by choice: mainly French nineteenth-century history. But I was not a good academic, and my degree reflected that. The subtitle of my play *The Power of the Dog* – 'Moments in History and Anti-History' – reflects my sense that there is an official history, but also an unofficial history, and my interest in somehow proposing alternative readings of critical events in history: in *Victory*, for example, the punishment of Republican rebels by the Royalist regime of 1660. In that play I dramatise the (entirely imaginary and unresearched) recovery of the body of a loved one, which has been distributed over a city, by a widow, who, in the course of that act of piety, loses interest in the very object she is trying to recover. I suppose my attitude to history is that it frees you from certain obligations that apply to contemporary plays: when an audience comes into a theatre, and the situation, that is proposed by the actors and the dramatist, is not familiar to them. It removes a certain critical disposition that the audience always entertains regarding the action on the stage. The moment we have costume, the moment we have period, we enter an area of speculation, where freedom is an entitlement, on our part. If you write plays on issues of your day, or at least directly on issues of your day, every member of the audience is as great an authority as you are. But in this world of the imagined circumstance, which still claims a certain reality of course, it's a freed-up space.

DIR: And the historical (and anti-historical) events that you dramatise, invent or reinvent, very often have cultural parallels, which are there for the audience to draw, if they wish –

HB: That's true, though I must say I don't intend any of those.

DIR: Staying with the audience, and your sense of the audience: I recently read Dennis Kennedy's recent book *The Spectator and the Spectacle*, in which he recalls some of the attitudes of your namesake from an earlier period, Harley Granville Barker, who said 'I do believe my present loathing for the theatre is loathing for the audience: I have never loved them'.[2] I was also reading, on the plane over to New York, David Mamet's recent book, *Theatre*; and Mamet, at the other extreme, has a great idealistic faith in the audience being those who will recognise and confer intrinsic value.[3] It strikes me that neither of those positions accord with yours: either that despairing of an audience, or that of complete confidence in the immediate reflexes of a contemporary audience. So how would you describe your relationship with an audience during the performance of a production?

HB: That's a crucial point: during the performance rather than during the creation of the text. To start with the creation of a text: I never contemplate the existence of the audience at all, it has no bearing on the way I approach the work, so the questions 'Will anyone understand what this particular moment is about? Am I being clear enough?' never cross my mind. In any case I enjoy ambiguity and contradictions, so it would be absurd to be worried about what a public might be discovering from the stage action. Neither do I think, as a director of productions, that the audience validates the work: the applause of the audience to me has no bearing on the value or quality of the work that is onstage, because – I'm sorry to say this to an audience now, but – it's very easy to manipulate an audience. One of my great doubts about comedy as an art form is my awareness of how easy it is to induce laughter, and unanimity; and in the political text it is similarly very easy to achieve unanimity. For me the greater achievement is to disrupt the audience into sections, to atomise the audience, so that its attitude to the spectacle on the stage is divided. I've always said, for me the most satisfying moment of having produced a work with actors is the silence at the end of a play: if there is silence when the audience leave. Naturally I think they should applaud the actors for their sacrifice, but when the audience leaves the theatre and enters the foyer, there should not be that buzz of pleasure to which so many people who work in the theatre aspire.

DIR: So, instead of that cluck of satisfaction that might conventionally attend the duration and particularly the end of a performance, you seek the sense of energy that is generated by an audience that actively perceives an internal disagreement; and that is something on which your work, and the performers (if they are of a mind to do so), can thrive.

HB: Yes, but in fairness to my friends the actors, they require an audience, and they have an innate desire to contact the audience, and to some extent to please them. So when I say 'I have no interest in the effect a work has on an audience' I am speaking for myself as the dramatist, not as an actor would experience it, of course.

DIR: Might I venture that you are seeking a very deep engagement with the audience, on the part of the performers, but of an unusual yet very compelling kind: perhaps all the more compelling because it is unusual, and doesn't follow their habitual responses.

HB: Yes. The work is never intended by me as being for the audience to grasp. One of the things about creative writing classes, of which I am deeply suspicious, is the idea of clarity, that the dramatist has an intention, and that this intention is communicated. If you don't have an intention at the outset the whole engagement between the public and the stage is quite altered. I'm also somewhat afraid of the audience, I must admit that, I'm sometimes apprehensive about the presence of an audience. Some of my profoundest pleasures in the theatre have occurred when we've played to four or five people – not uncommon in the history of The Wrestling School.

DIR: Can I ask you to identify what you would regard as some of the most significant turning points in your career as a dramatist and director?

HB: I think one of the very first I can identify was very soon after I became a professional dramatist. The Royal Court theatre was, and to some extent still is, a very significant English theatre institution with Brechtian objectives, strong political commitment which entailed social realism as an almost doctrinaire position; and in order for my work to be presented by that theatre, as a young man I wrote a play about my own background, which was South London working-class, and I tried to essay and describe what that sort of life was like. No sooner had that play been mounted by the director William Gaskill, who was at that stage Artistic Director of the Royal Court and a very distinguished Marxist director, than I recoiled from, and was quite nauseated by, social realism: I found it decayed, which it very well may have been by 1970, even though it is yet more active today. That was a turning point, which drove me out of social realism, but not exactly out of a political theatre: I became very desperate to find another form, and I wandered, rather desperately, into satire. Terence says 'It is very hard **not** to write satire', at some stage of your life. So that was a critical moment, in turning from the received wisdom of English theatre of the time, which happened very swiftly. Thereafter, I think the writing of *The Europeans* was a very significant moment in my life; for some years I was a writer at the Royal Shakespeare Company, and they made the open commission of a play from me, and I responded with a play in which I embrace the idea of the unforgiving. In this play, a young woman is raped and maimed, during the Turkish occupation of Europe in the seventeenth century. She persistently refuses to reconcile herself with her pain, or to forgive; and of course in a humanist theatre, the moment of forgiveness is the fulcrum of the whole project. In declining to forgive, this violent-tempered young woman discovers herself; but she discovers a self which is socially undesirable. I found that a moment of profound alteration: I knew I wanted to write about people who did the wrong thing. It's easy to write a play about such people on the condition that they then discover what the right thing is; but if you want to write a play about someone who does the wrong thing persistently, and actually is created and individualised by her failure to be socialised, you will then get yourself into a lot of trouble.

DIR: The initiative of the transgressive character who becomes committed to a life of wrong action follows through in your re-visioning of Chekhov's *Uncle Vanya*, in which Vanya successfully shoots Serebryakov, and thereafter attempts to live with the consequences of that successful murder with Helena, in a process that pulls the two of them into a different relationship to the apologetic and mournful way of life that we see in Chekhov's original play.

HB: Yes. I had an attitude to Chekhov, which was not what the London critics thought, when they were enraged by and despised my *(Uncle) Vanya*. They thought I was attacking Chekhov, when I was attacking the use to which Chekhov is put, at least in England, where the Chekhovian text is more celebrated than Shakespeare's, and Chekhov is in effect the national dramatist. The inertia – and, what is worse, the charm which is attached to inertia, making impotence charming – was I thought a sign of national decay. I could not resist taking that moment you describe: where, in Chekhov, Vanya proves incapable even of shooting his worst enemy, and instead have the bullet strike home, so that from that moment Vanya is driven from one decision to another. That is what that moment is about, and yes it was a crucial moment in my exile from the theatre of my own country.

DIR: However, in 1988, instead of relying on productions by other companies, you were at the epicentre of a theatre company, The Wrestling School, formed specifically to stage your works, which were initially directed by Kenny Ireland, and then you took over the reins of directing the company's work yourself. Presumably this was another turning point.

HB: Yes, I became a director, which I had not been previously. Kenny Ireland, who set up the company, was a good actor with the Royal Court and the RSC, who had worked with me a number of times. He had a bee in his bonnet that my work was not being presented properly, and he thought that if we got together, we could do it. He perhaps rather idealistically thought my work was potentially popular, if only we could find the key to this potential popularity, and indeed some of his shows were very successful. But he went back to Scotland to take over the Lyceum Theatre in Edinburgh, which left a hole in the middle of the company obviously. He suggested on parting that The Wrestling School invite people in to direct, but these would often be precisely the people who we had originally argued could not produce the work. So under those circumstances I moved in to the vacant place and developed what I now think of as the style of the company, a very particular and now quite well-known aesthetic.

DIR: That leads us onto the point of style, and the importance of style. This has always been a term and a quality which you have venerated, but at this point found an opportunity to demonstrate practically, in the invention and refinement of a style and aesthetic through your direction of the productions: through the whole *mise-en-scène* and scenography of The Wrestling School.

HB: I think the greatest achievement of any artist in any form is to acquire style. For some reasons, in some English critical circles, style is regarded as a trick, as something dishonest; but style is arrived at through enormous pain and sacrifice, and it takes a very long time to acquire. You're not born with style; it comes through practice, and pain, I think. It means there is a voice, there is a colour, which belongs to that artist in particular; and therefore it carries a certain authority with it; which is, after all, what one works hard to achieve in theatre – especially if you're dealing with subject matter which is unattractive in itself. Also, style is seductive. I think if you have a relationship with a public which is not based on shared values, which is not critical realism, which does not at the outset assume we all share the same values – which is the case in my work – style is the instrument of seduction. Not all the actors in the world can play with this style; especially those who were born into naturalism. The Wrestling School is a pool of actors, it's not really an ensemble, unless a very loose ensemble, but all those actors are very particularly gifted. What they do, with their voice, is instrumental; that is to say, their voices are instruments, and this furthermore affects the ways they move. For me, when I direct, the simultaneous occurrences of movement and voice are very important. I won't go into details about my methods as a director, except to say that style must be embodied: and the actors are a select group of people, to whom I am eternally grateful, for being able to manipulate my language in the ways they can.

DIR: We were conversing earlier on the importance of time. Do you think that style, for you, is a way of re-presenting time? Making the audience have a different sense of time?

HB: Anything that breaks down naturalism assists in that process. It's quite true that the plays I write now have no time in them at all. They're not even divided into scenes. And sometimes in rehearsal, an actor will ask 'Where are we now?', 'Is this ten years later, or not'? In the end it doesn't matter. And somehow the audience knows it doesn't matter either.

DIR: It strikes me that one of the hallmarks of your work is that sometimes there seems to be a temporal compression, and at other times a temporal elongation. Pregnancies, for example, can occur and conclude in the space of a few scenes or speeches as the narrative accelerates; on the other hand, we're very often presented with a sense of characters who wait, who are in a fundamentally erotic relationship of waiting for something, some word or sign from the lover, and, as we all know, time stretches almost unendurably in these situations ...

HB: Yes, the greatest achievement would be to remove time completely as a concept from the evening, in a production, to take time out, out of the equation. Connected with that, of course, precisely is my concern about narrative. Linear narrative seems to me now to be an infantile method of staging. Somehow we should overcome the idea of the narrative, and replace it with something else. In *Found in the Ground*, I tried to do this by working with the idea of accumulation: so the audience doesn't ask what happens next, where did he go when he had said that, or she did that; so that we don't acquire the emotional value of what we're watching from the narrative, but simply from the accumulation of emotions and scenes, which may be unrelated to each other. And I suppose I began that very early with plays like *The Possibilities*, which were broken up into fragments, but had a cumulative effect. So the engagement for the audience is moment by moment, to make the audience cease to ask questions, about where it is or about what I'm trying to say, that is a real freedom for all of us. I've always detested the idea of 'what the author's saying', you hear it in the foyer sometimes, 'What is he saying?' they say to each other, as if we had an obligation to say something to you, or as if I felt entitled to say something to you. I think it's very specious in artists to think that they can tell things. They've only one command on your conscience: which is imagination; that the artist imagines, not that the artist knows something politically that I don't. One of the great pleasures of the theatre is that it's not actually susceptible to the education process: it's a confusing place, which you leave with more problems than you arrive with. So many writers want to offer therapy, they 'want people to know' something; this seems to me a fruitless, narcissistic ambition, and a diminishing of theatre's specific powers. Theatre is chaotic: it is chaotic within a certain order, or the actors could not play it; but it should remain chaotic.

DIR: I'll refer back to Mamet's book once more, because he makes a further observation which has perhaps a little more affinity with your own work: he suggests that the dramatist instils a sense of the hunt. That happens in a more easily recognisable way in your earlier work, such as *Downchild*: in which a suspenseful issue is raised, something is to be sought out, with a mystery to be solved. Nevertheless, as your work progresses, that sense of a curiosity is activated (as in the highly tense and suspenseful *Ursula*), and in that sense the spirit of the hunt is still there for the audience, but it is not answered in the conventionally simple, or simplistic terms …

HB: If what I think you're describing connects with the sense of the secret, I understand that …

DIR: And the search, perhaps …

HB: I think the audience who come to see the plays such as I write, and the theatre I'm involved in, would come in the expectation of being privileged to enter a secret: that the very darkness of the theatrical space is a metaphor for secrecy. And if the theatre is at all political, in my view, it is political in that what occurs within that sacred space, of darkness that is not connected with the street, and is about the secret: what is the secret that is occurring within this?

DIR: You spoke, concerning the performances of actors, of the sacrifice that actors make in performing your work. Indeed, sacrifice seems a theme in the matter and the manner of your work.

HB: It has become more so, in recent years.

DIR: Or more explicitly so, in your recent work; the question often resonates, even in your earlier work: 'what is the cost?' – in emotional, political, spiritual terms, beyond the merely fiscal. Is the theme of sacrifice something that has fascinated you, more consciously?

HB: It has, and it caused me to meditate on the very violent collisions that arise from the tragic form, where the definition and manifestation of self is arrived at through the destruction of others. Tragedy has no comprehension of rights, human or otherwise, but it is supremely conscious of pain. We all know that conventional sacrifice has been narrowed down to one or two areas – the military and the parental. But the tragic form insists that sacrifice is nearly random. What is more dangerous still to contemplate is this – whether the arrival of the protagonist in the epiphany of, let us say, her erotic condition, is impossible **without** the sacrifice of others, that is to say, these victims are not merely **in the way** but the very substance of this apotheosis, as light can only be made from the burning of a material, leaving only ash. This also invites consideration of the apology, a modern obsession and a political racket. In a recent work, *Wonder and Worship in the Dying Ward*, the protagonist knows to apologise for a cruel act will annihilate her sense of self, and resolutely declines to do it. Her own child has been sacrificed for the mother's claim to absolute selfhood.

DIR: Are there any other turning points in your career which you think might appropriately be identified?

HB: I suppose the way I came to think that theatrical discourse **ought** to be poetical, must be identified at some point; quite where that occurs, I'm not sure … It comes with my movement into tragedy, because I can't conceive of tragedy without poetry, the two things for me are intimately linked. There came a point obviously where I decided to risk – and again it cost me more support in the official theatre – creating a discourse between the characters which was, strictly speaking, poetical. I suppose that must have occurred before *Gertrude – The Cry* but I can't quite place it, you might recognise that point.

DIR: I can't think of a single juncture at which it occurs, but again there is a refinement and development in your work with *The Bite of the Night* [written 1986, staged 1988], the full reach and arc of that work, not only temporally but in the various shifting forms of reality in that work, that characters pass through and break into, the successive regimes that we see: there is a whole terrain there, and method of dramatic association from one point to the next which strikes me as a point where things become quite different in your theatre. There are metaphorical associative links by which that play proceeds, as well as the succession of regimes…

RICHARD ROMAGNOLI: Has your directing informed your writing at all?

HB: I haven't a clear answer to that. You would think it would, because as a director … well, what does a director do, a director solves problems, about staging, basically. So you'd think that when I create a scene that I'd be worried about whether I could direct it, subsequently. But I don't. When I'm a writer, I think as a writer; and when I come to staging it, those problems have to be solved. I don't think any stage writer should hesitate ever about describing or staging any event imaginable; because it can always be solved.

DIR: Your stage directions have changed over the course of your writing…

HB: Yes, they have.

DIR: There's a good precedent for that, in '*Exit pursued by a bear*', which we have in Shakespeare's *A Winter's Tale*: here's the cue for an ambitious effect, but let's work out later how we stage it, or maybe the varying ways in which we stage that, that vary from one production to another. That's another of the delights of your plays, in my opinion, the way you offer challenges to the imaginations of the people who work on them, without a prescription about the means of achieving a particular *coup de théâtre*.

HB: Yes, I suppose that in the earlier work such as *Victory* there is hardly a sentence of stage direction, except to say '*A field in Winter*' or '*A king enters a room*'; but in later work, yes, I tend to define reactions –

DIR: In your later more poetic work, a pictorial dimension within your theatre opens up in more specifically visual and scenic terms: a heightened sense of figures in a landscape, or traversing, or floating in a landscape, tends to emerge (I am thinking of *The Ecstatic Bible*, *Found in the Ground*, *The Swing at Night*): your more painterly vision claims a space on the stage.

HB: Yes, that's true: because I design these productions too. I suppose also working closely with actors alters you in some way – I don't quite know how, but … There's a general suspicion of writers who direct, is there not?

DIR: Probably mainly amongst directors.

HB: Probably. But because writers do work in solitude it is quite difficult suddenly to go into a room with about fifteen people and start organising them. Writers don't talk much; but you do have to talk to actors; they can't intuit everything. So that maybe has an effect.

AUDIENCE MEMBER: Do you think that when you started working with actors, as a director, did it shape characters for you differently? Or was it just frustrating, working with actors?

HB: Oh no, I like working with actors. I like actors – very unusual for a director to say that; my experience is that most directors do not; rather, most directors manipulate actors. If they can't get the actor to do what they want, they will manipulate the actor by all sorts of tricks, which I despise. I'm not a massively democratic person by instinct, particularly on stage; I will instruct the actors as to what I want from them, and they won't work with me unless they accept those rules; but you can't trick an actor into doing an action, you really have to explain it to them, whether or not they withhold consent.

AUDIENCE MEMBER: Can you speak more about how you direct?

HB: I don't have a particular method. All I can say, as a broad description of it, is that the actors must put themselves in my hands. I employ actors who have huge gifts of training and skill, and all I want them to achieve is the correct emotional level of the scene. We never talk about the overall purpose or ideological content of a scene, which I may not know myself.

AUDIENCE MEMBER: I'm curious about the origins of your involvements in theatre, at university, or how else as a poet you were drawn to such a performative medium.

HB: I was not involved in theatre as a student at all; though as a student I wrote poetry and novels, unpublished quite rightly, but someone said to me that I wrote good dialogue, and I essayed writing a dialogue piece for radio: so I came to the theatre via radio. The BBC was a very generous patron, in the 1970s and 80s, to young writers – to all writers. This is no longer the case, unfortunately. But once I got into radio of course I wanted to visualise it as well, so it was inevitable I would move to the stage.

AUDIENCE MEMBER: Could you say some more about the importance of the audience's silence in your work? And the relationship between pain and style, especially as style changes, and so may one's relationship to pain, over the course of time?

HB: The reason silence is desirable for me is that it suggests that the emotional experience of the performance has produced some breakdown of the conventional reaction of the individual audience member to the action on the stage: such as the ambiguity of laughter at the moment of awful pain, such as we often find at performances of *King Lear*: moments occur which Shakespeare knows are funny and he allows this little aperture of comedy to enter. When you create a situation in which the audience is not trained to be **one**, and there is a moment of shock or pain, some people have the courage to laugh at these moments, other people think the laugh is offensive and will almost attack them for the laughter. This breakdown of consensus is an achievement, not easily done, requiring precise action, but above all a sense of contradiction. It seems to me the silence there becomes a testament to a mood in the house which is creative. The manipulation of an audience, by a writer, by a director, is sordid: 'Now you will all laugh', 'Now you all get the message, don't you'; I wouldn't want to be part of that. A silence is a beautiful confusion. Regarding pain: I suppose one of the reasons I was attracted towards tragedy was the nausea induced in me by most of the general theatrical products which were available at the time, but also a sense that people, in a perfectly voyeuristic sense – and I don't find anything particularly obnoxious about voyeurism in the theatre, that is precisely what happens – people wish to witness the pain of others, we long to know how other people suffer – and that our own pain will yield us something: I'm not trying to talk about therapy, I don't believe in theatre therapy, but in the tragedy there is a moment of a pain which is a creative pain. The ordeal of the character is what buys him, or her, the right to be heard: Katrin in *The Europeans* is a good example of this. The whole organisation of democratic society is about the maximalisation of pleasure, and the diminishing of pain. It seems to me that is in some ways a fatuous exercise, even if it's necessary. We have to come to terms with pain, and I'm certain that tragedy enables that. Therefore we're talking about death, tragedy is how you arrive at death, how you make your death; of course death is often inflicted on you, but as the undertakers in *Hurts Given and Received* say to the protagonist, 'You must earn your grave', which puzzles this protagonist for a long time, until he perceives it at the end. That is the transaction in the tragic theatre: that we all come to think about, to contemplate, death, in a society that doesn't like death and won't acknowledge death. *Gertrude – The Cry* was the first play in which I realised my project was to write further about death: I never know what a play is about when I begin it, but it took off from the idea of what I thought was the legitimate passion of Gertrude and Claudius, and how Claudius's love of Gertrude which in this play continually forces her into one amoral position after another, is in fact his own groping after death, rather than, as he continues to think of it, a consistently erotic adventure; and a particularly beautiful moment in the play is when Gertrude helps him to die: her gift to him is to tell him something so terrible that she knows it will kill him. And at that moment, Gertrude's cry in sexual love, which is to him so erotically important, he hears not from her but from the landscape: the landscape itself becomes a stage.

AUDIENCE MEMBER: Can you identify any other forms of linguistic energy, beyond the heightened language of high culture, Shakespeare and tragedy, which have been important to you? As an audience member and reader of your work, the low culture versions of heightened language, such as that of the carnival barker, that don't usually get to be considered as legitimate theatre, seem at least as present in your work.

HB: I think the particular voice I've had as a writer consists of two elements: one, as you say, of high culture, of familiarity with literature; the other element, particularly in the rhythm rather than the vocabulary itself, I owe to my mother and my background in the working class of South London. My family, who were self-styled characters in some ways, had a mode of very passionate expression, usually abusive, which I knew had the rhythms and the linguistic energy of previous centuries. There are many reasons not to admire my background, but I love that aspect of it, I applaud and love the way language, metaphor, abuse, local slang, was carried down from generation to generation, in a way that has now ended because of the penetration of mass media. My pleasure in the use of that slang relates me to a writer for whom I have huge admiration, Louis-Ferdinand Céline, whose own voice originates in a background very similar to mine, but in the rhythms of nineteenth-century Paris. And it's true of Shakespeare also, who has moments of high discourse but also moments of very base discourse, the voice of the people of his day. And no matter how remote I am from naturalism, nevertheless it comes through, the more distinct from its rarity.

DIR: Your characters are very often working to undercut each other, or indeed are undercutting themselves in a moment of crisis, reformulating their own perceptions of that crisis, and these different rhythmic linguistic energies jostle, but also a more measured statement can also provide a more silencing moment which slows that repartee of undercutting –

HB: Yes, all sometimes within one speech. All my characters are trying to seduce each other, I don't mean sexually, but in the Latin sense of the word *seduco*, to lead you from yourself; the reason they are so energetic and so vocal is that they are trying to seduce one another into their world by the power of their discourse; and to achieve their ends they will use any language which comes to hand; or, conversely, use complexity of speech to mesmerise.

Note: this is not, and does not purport to be, a verbatim transcript of the dialogue. Both Barker and Rabey have editorially refined and where necessary amended their statements, to eliminate some minor conversational redundancies and repetitions, and render their observations more precise. Rabey has further selectively edited and condensed the audience's questions and formulations in the service of succinctness, in this context, to permit their dissemination to a wider audience.

This dialogue was the closing event in Howard Barker at the Segal Center, a day-long symposium on Barker's work held on 10 May 2010, co-presented by theatre minima and the CUNY Graduate Center's Martin E. Segal Theater Center.

Notes

1 H. Barker, *Seven Lears and Golgo* (London: John Calder, 1990), p. 71.
2 G. Barker, quoted in D. Kennedy, *The Spectator and the Spectacle* (Cambridge: Cambridge University Press, 2009), p. 175.
3 D. Mamet, *Theatre* (London: Faber, 2010), p. 124.

Howard Barker:
chronology and further reading

Dates are of first stagings, broadcasts or publications (not subsequent productions in the same medium). All places of publication London, unless otherwise noted. 'JC' = John Calder; 'OB' = Oberon Books.

All first stagings occur in Britain, and include performances in London, except where noted; 'HB' = production directed by Barker; 'TWS' = The Wrestling School production; # indicates a non-professional university or student production.

*Indicates that this unpublished text is summarised and considered in Rabey (1989, 2009).

~ Indicates that this unpublished text is summarised and considered in Rabey (2008).

1970: *One Afternoon on the 63rd level of the North Face of the Pyramid of Cheops The Great*: broadcast BBC Radio 1970; unpublished*
Cheek: staged 1970; published in New Short Plays: 3 (Eyre Methuen Playscripts 1972, volume credited to Barker, Grillo, Haworth and Simmons)
No One Was Saved: staged 1970; unpublished*

1971: *Henry V in Two Parts*: broadcast BBC Radio 1971; unpublished*

1972: *Herman, with Millie and Mick*: broadcast BBC Radio 1972; unpublished*
Edward – The Final Days: staged 1972; unpublished*
Alpha Alpha: staged 1972; unpublished*
Faceache: staged 1972; unpublished

1973: *Skipper*: staged 1973; unpublished*

My Sister and I: staged 1973; unpublished★
Rule Britannia: staged 1973; unpublished
Bang: staged 1973; unpublished

1975:   *Claw*: staged 1975; *Stripwell*: staged 1975; published together (JC, 1977)

1976:   *Wax*: staged 1976; unpublished★
       Heroes of Labour: unproduced television play; published in *Gambit* 29
           (JC, 1976)

1977:   *Fair Slaughter*: staged and published (JC)
       That Good Between Us: staged; published 1980 with *Credentials of a
           Sympathiser*, unproduced television play (JC)

1978:   *The Love of a Good Man*: staged; published 1980 with *All Bleeding*,
           unproduced television play (JC)
       The Hang of the Gaol: staged; published 1982 with *Heaven*, unproduced
           television play (JC)

1980:   *The Loud Boy's Life*: staged; published 1982 in *Two Plays for the Right* (JC)
       Birth on a Hard Shoulder: staged (Stockholm, Sweden); published 1982 in
           Two Plays for the Right (JC)

1981:   *No End of Blame*: staged and published (JC)
       The Poor Man's Friend: staged★

1983:   *Victory*: staged (dir: Danny Boyle) and published (JC)
       A Passion in Six Days: staged; published 1985 with *Downchild* (JC)
       Crimes in Hot Countries: staged (Essex University, dir: Charles Lamb #;
           published 1984 (JC)

1984:   *Pity in History*: published in *Gambit* 41 (JC); staged (Dublin and Galway,
           dir: John O'Brien and David Ian Rabey#)
       The Power of the Dog: staged and published (JC)
       'Art Matters' (sketch) staged (published in *The Big One*, eds Bill Bachle
           and Susannah York, Methuen, 1984)
       Don't Exaggerate (performance poem): staged, published with other poems
           1985 (JC)

1985:   *The Castle*: staged and published with *Scenes from an Execution* (JC);
           Downchild and *Crimes in Hot Countries* also staged in repertoire (RSC
           Barker at the Pit season, Barbican Theatre)
       Scenes from an Execution: broadcast by BBC Radio
       Pity in History: broadcast BBCTV
       The Blow (unproduced filmscript): written★

1986:   *Women Beware Women*: staged (dir: Bill Gaskill) and published (JC)

The Breath of the Crowd (performance poem): staged and published with other poems (JC)

1987:   *Gary the Thief/Gary Upright* (performance poems): published with other poems (JC)

1988:   *The Possibilities*: staged (dir: Ian McDiarmid) and published (JC)
   The Last Supper: staged (TWS, dir: Kenny Ireland) and published (JC)
   The Bite of the Night: (written 1985) staged (dir: Danny Boyle) and published (JC)
   Lullabies for the Impatient: poems, published (JC)
   The Smile: published in *New Plays: 2*, ed. Peter Terson (Oxford University Press)

1989:   *Seven Lears*: staged (TWS, dir: Kenny Ireland) and *Golgo*: staged (TWS, dir: Nicholas LePrevost) and published together (JC)
   The Europeans: (written 1987) staged (Toronto, Canada) and published with *Judith* (JC)
   Arguments for a Theatre (essays): first edition (JC)

1990:   *Scenes from an Execution*: stage production (dir: Ian McDiarmid)
   The Early Hours of a Reviled Man: broadcast by BBC Radio; staged (Aberystwyth, dir: Roger Owen#)
   Collected Plays Vol. 1 (*Claw, No End of Blame, Victory, The Castle, Scenes from an Execution*): published (JC)

1991:   *The Europeans*: staged (Aberystwyth, dir: John O'Brien and David Ian Rabey#)
   Victory: staged (TWS, dir: Kenny Ireland)
   The Ascent of Monte Grappa (poems): published (JC)

1992:   *A Hard Heart*: staged (dir: Ian McDiarmid), broadcast by BBC Radio, and published with *The Early Hours of a Reviled Man* (JC)
   Ego in Arcadia: staged (Sienna, Italy)(TWS, HB)
   Terrible Mouth (opera libretto): staged and published (Universal Edition)

1993:   *The Europeans*: staged (TWS, dir: Kenny Ireland)
   Collected Plays Vol. 2 (*The Love of a Good Man, The Possibilities, Brutopia, Rome, (Uncle) Vanya, Ten Dilemmas*): published (JC)
   Arguments for a Theatre (essays): second edition, Manchester University Press
   All He Fears (marionette play): staged and published (JC)

1994:   *Hated Nightfall*: staged (TWS, HB) and published with *Wounds to the Face* (JC)
   Minna: staged (Vienna, Austria) and published (Alumnus, Leeds)

1995:   *The Castle:* staged (TWS, dir: Kenny Ireland)

Judith: staged (TWS, HB)
(Uncle) Vanya: (written 1992) staged (Aberystwyth, dir: Andy Cornforth
and David Ian Rabey#)

1996: *(Uncle) Vanya*: staged (TWS, HB)
*Collected Plays Vol. 3 (The Power of the Dog, The Europeans, Women
Beware Women, Minna, Judith, Ego in Arcadia)*: published (JC)
The Tortmann Diaries (poems): published (JC)
Defilo (Failed Greeks) ~ written

1997: *Arguments for a Theatre* (essays): third edition, Manchester University Press
Wounds to the Face: staged (TWS, dir: Stephen Wrentmore)
An Eloquence (film) ~ written
The Blood of a Wife (film) ~ written
The Seduction of Almighty God: written

1998: *Ursula*: staged (TWS, HB)
*Collected Plays Vol. 4 (The Bite of the Night, Seven Lears, The Gaoler's Ache,
He Stumbled, A House of Correction)*: published (JC)
Ten Dilemmas: staged#

1999: *Und*: staged (TWS, HB)
Scenes from an Execution: staged (TWS, HB)
A House of Correction: broadcast, BBC Radio
Albertina ~ broadcast, BBC Radio
The Swing at Night (marionette play): written
A Rich Woman's Poetry ~ written

2000: *The Ecstatic Bible*: staged (Adelaide, Australia)(TWS, HB)
He Stumbled: staged (TWS, HB)
Animals in Paradise: staged (Malmo, Sweden)
The Twelfth Battle of Isonzo: staged (Saint-Brieuc, France, in French)
The Swing at Night (marionette play): staged and published (JC)
Stalingrad (opera libretto) ~ written

2001: *The Twelfth Battle of Isonzo*: staged (Dublin, Ireland, in English)(HB)
A House of Correction: staged (TWS, HB)
*Collected Plays Vol. 5 (Ursula, The Brilliance of the Servant, 12 Encounters with
a Prodigy, Und, The Twelfth Battle of Isonzo, Found in the Ground)*:
published (JC)
Two Skulls ~ written

2002: *Gertrude*: staged (TWS, HB); *Knowledge and a Girl*: broadcast (HB), BBC
Radio; published together (JC)
The Twelfth Battle of Isonzo: staged (Cork, Cardiff, Newtown,
Aberystwyth)(HB)
Stalingrad (opera libretto): staged (Denmark)

Brutopia: staged (Besançon, France, in French)
N/A (Sad Kissing) ~ written
Five Names ~ written

2003: *13 Objects*: staged (TWS, HB)
The Fence in its Thousandth Year: written
The Moving and the Still ~ written

2004: *Dead Hands*: staged (TWS, HB) and published (OB)
N/A (Sad Kissing): staged (Vienna, Austria)
The Moving and the Still: broadcast, BBC Radio
Christ's Dog: written
The Dying of Today: written
Acts Chapter 1 ~ written

2005: *Death, The One and The Art of Theatre* (essays): published (Routledge)
Animals in Paradise: staged (Rouen, France, in French)(TWS, HB)
The Ecstatic Bible: published (OB)
The Fence in its Thousandth Year: staged (TWS, HB) and published (OB)
Christ's Dog: staged (Vienna, Austria)
Two Skulls: broadcast (Danish Radio)
Dead, Dead and Very Dead (libretto) ~ written
Heroica (film) ~ written
Adorations Chapter 1 (film) ~ written
Let Me: written
Howard Barker/Eduardo Houth: *A Style and its Origins*: written

2006: *The Seduction of Almighty God*: staged (TWS, dir: Guillaume Dujardin) and
published (OB)
The Road, The House, The Road: broadcast, BBC Radio
Let Me: broadcast, BBC Radio
A Wounded Knife (formerly titled *A Living Dog*) ~ staged (Odense,
Denmark)
Plays: One (*Victory, Scenes from an Execution, The Possibilities, The Europeans*)
published (OB)
Plays: Two (*The Castle, Gertrude – The Cry, 13 Objects, Animals in Paradise*)
published (OB)
The Forty (Few Words): written
I Saw Myself: written

2007: *Lot and his God*: written
Howard Barker/Eduardo Houth: *A Style and its Origins*: published (OB)
The Dying of Today: staged (Caen, France)
Actress With an Unloved Child: written
Deep Wives, Shallow Animals: written
Learning Kneeling: written

2008: *I Saw Myself*: staged (TWS, HB)

       Twelve Encounters with a Prodigy: staged (Odense, Denmark, dir: Karl Hoffmeyer)

       Lot and his God: staged (Paris, France; dir: Agathe Alexis)

       Plays: Three (*Claw, Ursula, He Stumbled, The Love of a Good Man*) published (OB)

       Plays: Four (*I Saw Myself, Found in the Ground, The Dying of Today, The Road, The House, The Road*) published (OB)

       Hurts Given and Received: written

       Aceldama: written

       The Dying of Today: staged (TWS, dir: Gerrard McArthur)

       Sheer Detachment: published (Salt Publications)

2009: *Found in the Ground*: staged (TWS, HB)

       21 for 21: international initiative of performances of Barker plays

       Deep Wives, Shallow Animals: staged (Paris, France, dir: Guillaume Dujardin)

       A Wounded Knife: staged (Aberystwyth, dir: David Ian Rabey)

       Plays: Five (*The Last Supper, Seven Lears, Hated Nightfall, Wounds to the Face*): published (OB)

       Wonder and Worship in the Dying Ward: written

       Harrowing and Uplifting Interviews with Randomly Selected Victims of the Imperial Will: written

2010: *Hurts Given and Received*: staged (TWS, dir: Gerrard McArthur), alongside *Slowly* (TWS, dir: Hanna Berrigan), published together (OB) and a rehearsed reading of *Wonder and Worship in the Dying Ward* (TWS, HB)

       Smack Me: staged (TWS, HB)

       Plays: Six (*(Uncle) Vanya, A House of Correction, Let Me, Judith, Lot and his God*) published (OB)

       Deep Wives, Shallow Animals: staged (Portugal, dir: Rogério de Carvalho)

       A Dead Man's Blessing (filmscript): written

       Smell Language: written

       One Yes One: written

2011: *Blok/Eko*: staged (TWS, HB, Exeter) and published (OB)

       The Moving and the Still: staged (Strasbourg, France, dir: Fanny Mentré)

       Five Names: staged (Aberystwyth, dir: Phoebe Patey-Ferguson and William Pritchard#) alongside *Slowly*

       The Forty: staged (Aberystwyth, dir: David Ian Rabey#)

       Killing and Killing: written

       Dress: written

       Dying in the Street (Contralulu): written

       Concentration: written

2012: *Charles V*: written, workshopped (Exeter) and published (*Studies in Theatre and Performance*)
  Distance: written
  Scenes from an Execution: staged (Royal National Theatre, London, dir: Tom Cairns)

A selection of further critical reading on Barker

In English

Full-length studies

Brown, Mark (ed.), *Howard Barker Interviews, 1980–2010: Conversations in Catastrophe* (Bristol: Intellect Books, 2011).

Lamb, Charles, *Howard Barker's Theatre of Seduction* (London: Harwood Academic Press/Routledge, 1997).

——, *The Theatre of Howard Barker* (Oxford: Routledge, 2005).

Gritzner, Karoline, and Rabey, David Ian (eds), *Theatre of Catastrophe: New Essays on Howard Barker* (London: Oberon, 2006).

Rabey, David Ian, *Howard Barker: Politics and Desire: An Expository Study of his Drama and Poetry, 1969–1987,* second edition (London: Macmillan, 1989, 2009).

Rabey, David Ian, *Howard Barker: Ecstasy and Death: An Expository Study of his Drama, Theory and Production Work, 1988–2008* (Basingstoke and New York: Palgrave Macmillan, 2009).

Special dedicated issues of journals

Gambit 41 (London: John Calder, 1984) (contains text of *Pity in History*, interview with Barker by Tony Dunn, and articles by Eric Mottram, Tony Dunn, Ian McDiarmid and Ruth Shade).

Studies in Theatre and Performance, 32.3 (Intellect: Bristol, Winter 2012, ISSN 1468-2761).

Articles, essays and book chapters centring on Barker

Barnett, David, 'Howard Barker: Polemic Theatre and Dramatic Practice, Nietzsche, Metatheatre and the play The Europeans', *Modern Drama* 44.4 (Winter 2001), 458–75.

Barker, Howard, 'On Naturalism and its Pretensions', *Studies in Theatre and Performance* 27: 3 (2007), 289–93, doi: 10.1386/stap.27.3.289/3.

——, 'Afterword: The Corpse and its Sexuality', in Karoline Gritzner (ed.), *Eroticism and Death in Theatre and Performance* (Hatfield: University of Hertfordshire Press, 2010), pp. 242–5.

Bas, Georges, 'The Cunts, the Knobs and the Corpse: Obscenity and Horror in Howard Barker's Victory', *Contemporary Theatre Review* 5 (1996), 33–50.

Carney, Sean, 'Howard Barker: Will and Desire', in *The Politics and Poetics of Contemporary English Tragedy* (Toronto: University of Toronto Press, 2012).

Cornforth, Andy and Rabey, David Ian, 'Kissing Holes for the Bullets: Consciousness in Directing and Playing Barker's (Uncle) Vanya', *Performance and Consciousness* 1.4 (1999), 25–45.

Fathy, Saafa, 'The Thing that Bites in Howard Barker's Night: A Reading of "Gertrude – The Cry" from the Angle of Spectrality' in *Oxford Literary Review* 25.1 (2003), 103–21.

Freeland, Thomas, 'The End of Rhetoric and the Residuum of Pain: Bodying the Language in the Theatre of Howard Barker', *Modern Drama* 54.1 (2011), 78–98.

Gallant, Desmond, ' Brechtian Sexual Politics in the Plays of Howard Barker', *Modern Drama* 40 (1997), 403–13.

Goldingay, Sarah, 'Challenging Plural Histories: Returning to Howard Barker's "Victory: Choices in Reaction", "The Castle" and "The Last Supper"', in J. Milling (ed.), *Modern British Playwriting: The 1980s: Voices, Documents, New Interpretations* (London: Methuen, 2012).

Gritzner, Karoline, 'Catastrophic Sexualities in Howard Barker's Theatre of Transgression', in M. Sönser Breen and F. Peters F. (eds), *Genealogies of Identity: Interdisciplinary Readings on Sex and Sexuality* (Amsterdam and New York: Rodopi, 2006).

——, 'Adorno on Tragedy: Reading Catastrophe in Late Capitalist Culture', *Critical Engagements* 1.2 (Autumn/Winter 2007), 25–52.

——, '(Post)Modern subjectivity and the New Expressionism: Howard Barker, Sarah Kane, and Forced Entertainment', *Contemporary Theatre Review* 18, 3 (2008), 328–40.

Hammond, Brean, 'Is Everything History? Churchill, Barker and the Modern History Play', *Comparative Drama* 41.1 (Winter 2007), 1–23.

Kilpatrick, David, 'The Myth's the Thing: Barker's Revision of Elsinore in *Gertrude – The Cry*', *Text and Presentation* 24 (New York: McFarland, 2003).

Klotz, Günther, 'Howard Barker: Paradigm of Postmodernism', *New Theatre Quarterly* 7. 25 (Feb 1991), 20–6.

Megson, Chris, 'Howard Barker and the Theatre of Catastrophe', in Mary Luckhurst (ed.), *A Companion to Modern British and Irish Drama* (Oxford: Blackwells, 2006).

——, 'Howard Barker', 1996 interview with the author, *Modern British Playwriting: The 1970s* (London: Methuen, 2012), pp. 207–11.

Neubert, Isolde, 'The Doorman of the Century is a Transient Phenomenon: The Symbolism of Dancer in Howard Barker's *Hated Nightfall*', in Bernhard Reitz (ed.), *Drama and Reality. Contemporary Drama in English 3* (Trier: Wissenschaftlicher Verlag Trier, 1996), pp. 145–53.

Rabey, David Ian, 'For the Absent Truth Erect: Impotence and Potency in

Howard Barker's Recent Drama', *Essays in Theatre/Études théâtrales* 10 (1991), 31–7.

——, 'What Do You See ?' Howard Barker's The Europeans', *Studies in Theatre Production* 6 (December 1992), 23–34.

——, 'Howard Barker', in W.W. Demastes (ed.), *British Playwrights, 1956–1995: A Research and Production Sourcebook* (London: Greenwood Press, 1996), pp. 28–38.

——, 'Barker: Appalling Enhancements', in *English Drama Since 1940* (London: Longman Literature in English series, Pearson Education, 2003) pp. 182–90.

——, 'Two Against Nature: Rehearsing and Performing Howard Barker's Production of his play The Twelfth Battle of Isonzo', *Theatre Research International* 30, 2 (July 2005), 175–89.

——, 'Flirting with Disaster', in Karoline Gritzner (ed.), *Eroticism and Death in Theatre and Performance* (Hatfield: University of Hertfordshire Press, 2010), pp. 123–43.

Sakellaridou, Elizabeth, 'A Lover's Discourse – But Whose? Inversions of the Fascist Aesthetic in Howard Barker's Und and Other Recent English Plays', *European Journal of English Studies*, 7, 1 (April 2003), 87–108.

Saunders, Graham, 'Missing Mothers and Absent Fathers': Howard Barker's *Seven Lears* and Elaine Feinstein's *Lear's Daughters*', *Modern Drama* 42 (1999), 401–10.

——, 'Howard Barker's "monstrous assaults": Eroticism, Death and the Antique Text', in Karoline Gritzner (ed.), *Eroticism and Death in Theatre and Performance* (Hatfield: University of Hertfordshire Press, 2010), pp. 144–59.

Thomas, Alan, 'Howard Barker: Modern Allegorist', *Modern Drama* 35, 3, (1992), 433–43.

Tomlin, Liz, 'The Politics of Catastrophe', *Modern Drama* 43, 1, (2000), 66–77.

——, 'Howard Barker', in John Bull (ed.), *Dictionary of Literary Biography, Volume 233: British and Irish Dramatists Since World War II*, Second Series (New York: Buccoli Clark, 2001), pp. 9–21.

Trussler, Simon (ed.), 'The Small Discovery of Dignity' (interview) in *New Theatre Voices of the Seventies* (London: Methuen, 1980).

Wilcher, Robert, 'Honoring the Audience: The Theatre of Howard Barker', in James Acheson (ed.), *British and Irish Drama Since 1960* (Basingstoke: Macmillan, 1993), pp. 176–89.

Zimmermann, Heiner, 'Howard Barker's Appropriation of Classical Tragedy', in Savas Patsalidis and Elizabeth Sakellaridou (eds), *(Dis)Placing Classical Tragedy* (Thessaloniki: University Studio Press, 1999), pp. 359–73.

——, 'Howard Barker's Brecht or Brecht as Whipping Boy', in Berhard Reitz and Heiko Stahl (eds), *What Revels Are in Hand (Essays in Honour of Wolfgang Lippke)* (CDE-Studies 8. Trier : Wissenschaftlicher Verlag Trier, 2001), 221–6.

——, 'Howard Barker in the Nineties' in 'British Drama of the 1990s', *Anglistik & Englischunterricht* 64 (2002), 181–201.

Television documentaries

A Play for Bridport (BBC Arena, 1982)
Refuse to Dance: The Theatre of Howard Barker (Channel Four, 1986)

In French

Alternatives Théâtrales 57 (mai 1998), Numéro spécial Howard Barker, coordonné par Mike Sens.

Angel-Perez, E. (ed.), *Howard Barker et le Théâtre de la Catastrophe* (Paris: Editions Théâtrales, 2006).

———, « L'espace de la catastrophe », Éd. Geneviève Chevallier, *Cycnos* 12 (1–1995).

———, « Pour un théâtre de la barbarie: Peter Barnes et Howard Barker », Éd. É. Angel-Perez et Nicole Boireau, *Études anglaises* 52, n° 2 (avril-juin 1999), 198–210. Rééd. in *Le Théâtre anglais contemporain* (1985–2005) (Paris: Klincksieck, 2006) (à paraître).

———, Préfaces aux volumes 1–5 des *Howard Barker: Œuvres choisies* (Paris: éditions Théâtrales).

———, Notice sur Howard Barker de l'*Encyclopédie Universalis* (Paris: Encyclopædia Universalis, 2003).

———, « Howard Barker: de la catastrophe à l'épiphanie » in E. Angel-Perez. *Voyages au bout du possible. Les théâtres du traumatisme* (Paris: Klincksieck, 2006).

Boireau, Nicole, « Le paysage dramatique en Angleterre : consensus et transgression », *Alternatives Théâtrales* 61 (1999), 8–10.

———, « Dystopies » in N. Boireau, *Théâtre et société en Angleterre des années 1950 à nos jours* (Paris: PUPS, 2000).

Hirschmuller, Sarah, « Howard Barker ou la déconsécration du sens. À propos de Maudit crépuscule », Éd. Jean-Marc Lantéri, *Écritures contemporaines* 5 (2002), 25–42.

Morel, Michel, « La "catastrophe" selon Barker », Éd. Geneviève Chevallier, *Cycnos* 18, n°1 (2001), 65–76.

We thank Elisabeth Angel-Perez for assistance in compiling the French section of this bibliography.

Index